Rhythmic Activities and Dance

SECOND EDITION

John Price Bennett, EdD
University of North Carolina Wilmington

Pamela Coughenour Riemer, MA
Scotland County School System
Laurinburg, NC

HUMAN KINETICS

Library of Congress Cataloging-in-Publication Data

Bennett, John Price, 1947-
  Rhythmic activities and dance / John Price Bennett, Pamela Coughenour Riemer. — 2nd ed.
    p. cm.
  Includes bibliographical references.
  ISBN 0-7360-5148-1 (soft cover)
  1. Movement education. 2. Rhythm — Study and teaching. 3. Dance for children — Study and teaching. 4. Physical education for children — Study and teaching. I. Riemer, Pamela Coughenour, 1947- II. Title.
  GV452.B45 2006
  372.86'8 — dc22
                                  2005033373

  ISBN-10: 0-7360-5148-1
  ISBN-13: 978-0-7360-5148-4

The Web addresses cited in this text were current as of November 16, 2005, unless otherwise noted.

Acquisitions Editor: Judy Patterson Wright, PhD; **Developmental Editor:** Ragen E. Sanner; **Assistant Editor:** Carmel Sielicki; **Copyeditor:** Andrew Smith; **Proofreader:** Anne Rogers; **Permission Manager:** Dalene Reeder; **Graphic Designer:** Nancy Rasmus; **Graphic Artist:** Denise Lowry; **Photo Manager:** Sarah Ritz; **Cover Designer:** Keith Blomberg; **Photographer (cover):** David Storniolo; **Photographer (interior):** David Storniolo, unless otherwise noted; Photo on page 21 courtesy of Pamela Coughenour Riemer; **Art Manager:** Kelly Hendren; **Illustrator:** Tim Offenstein; **Printer:** Sheridan Books

Printed in the United States of America   10   9   8   7   6   5   4   3   2   1

Human Kinetics
Web site: www.HumanKinetics.com

United States: Human Kinetics, P.O. Box 5076, Champaign, IL 61825-5076
800-747-4457
e-mail: humank@hkusa.com

Canada: Human Kinetics, 475 Devonshire Road Unit 100, Windsor, ON N8Y 2L5
800-465-7301 (in Canada only)
e-mail: orders@hkcanada.com

Europe: Human Kinetics, 107 Bradford Road, Stanningley, Leeds LS28 6AT, United Kingdom
+44 (0) 113 255 5665
e-mail: hk@hkeurope.com

Australia: Human Kinetics, 57A Price Avenue, Lower Mitcham, South Australia 5062
08 8277 1555
e-mail: liaw@hkaustralia.com

New Zealand: Human Kinetics, Division of Sports Distributors NZ Ltd.,
P.O. Box 300 226 Albany, North Shore City, Auckland
0064 9 448 1207
e-mail: info@humankinetics.co.nz

John Price Bennett dedicates this book to

Lenoah Long Bennett, my wonderful mother and first dance partner;

Claudia Adams Bennett, my wife, my best friend, and lifelong dance partner;

Zachariah Price Bennett and Rebecca Adams Bennett, our two wonderful dancing children;

Norma Redmon Richmond, my cousin and "soul mate" supporter;

Betty and Gary Spitzer, our lifelong friends;

Gladys Andrews Fleming, my mentor and life-changing dance teacher; and

Louise and Steve Coggins and their families, our sisters and brothers in Christ!

Pamela Coughenour Riemer dedicates this book to

Carri Riemer Faircloth, my wonderful daughter, who gave me the inspiration to enhance the lives of all children;

Ryan Heath Faircloth, my son-in-law, who dances with my daughter;

Bailey Ryan Faircloth, my first grandchild, who joyfully danced into our lives and will benefit from the fruits of my efforts;

Nellie Briles Coughenour and Charlie Pearson Coughenour, my parents, who encouraged me and allowed me to be me;

Sallie Coughenour Crossley and Sandra Coughenour Chandler, my sisters, who truly believed my dreams could come true;

Charlie ("Peary") Pearson Coughenour, Jr., my brother, who understands my drive and creativity;

William A. Riemer, my husband, who wants me to be me most of the time;

Eric Brooks DeGroat, my colossal mentor;

Dr. Tommie Thompson, department chair at the University of North Carolina at Pembroke, and my other graduate professors; and

All of my students who were in my physical education classes and the Sycamore Lane Dance Company.

Thanks to God for the divine wisdom and strength to carry us through our lives. Our prayer is that the contents of this book will help others reach a multitude of people as much as they have helped us reach the people that we have been blessed to touch.

Second Timothy 2:3 and Second Timothy 1:7

CONTENTS

Rhythmic Activity Finder   vii

CD Track List   xiii

Key to Diagrams   xv

Preface   xviii

Acknowledgments   xx

CHAPTER 1 Starting a Rhythmic Activities and Dance Program   1

Planning Your Program 1 • Program Considerations 4 • Unit Planning 7 • Lesson Planning 11 • Rhythmic Terms 14 • Music in Rhythmic Activities and Dance 14 • Evaluation 16 • Summary 18

CHAPTER 2 Icebreaker Activities   21

Easing Students Into Rhythmic Activities and Dance 22 • Summary 36

CHAPTER 3 Rhythmic Games and Activities   37

From Old to New 38 • Music Selection 38 • Large-Group Activities 39 • Small-Group Activities 54 • Circuits 58 • Games 66 • Culmination 68 • Summary 69

CHAPTER 4 Aerobic Dances and Fitness Routines   73

Strategies for Quality Aerobics 74 • Warm-Up and Cool-Down Exercises 77 • Exercise Components for Aerobics and Dance Routines 80 • Sample Aerobic Workouts 82 • How to Create Rhythmic Routines and Dances 88 • Prechoreographed Routines 89 • Summary 95

CHAPTER 5 Line Dances   99

Line Dance Activities 100 • Line Dance Unit Planning 103 • Summary 124

CHAPTER 6 Folk Dances   127

Description of Folk Dancing 127 • African 129 •
American—North 130 • American—South 144 • Asian 145 •
European—Eastern 148 • European—Western 150 •
Summary 160

CHAPTER 7 Mixers   163

History of Mixers 164 • Teaching Social Mixers With the
Round-Robin Wave 164 • Single Circle Facing Center With a
Partner 165 • Double Circle Facing Line of Direction 169 •
Double Circle Partners Facing 173 • Free or Open 177 •
Summary 178

CHAPTER 8 Square Dances and Clogging   181

History of American Square Dance 182 • Basics of Teaching
Square Dance 182 • Appalachian Big Set 187 • Big-Circle
Figures 189 • Small-Circle Figures 195 • Square Figures 201 •
Clogging 211 • Summary 213

CHAPTER 9 Social Dances   215

Smooth American-Style Dances 217 • Latin-Style Dances
227 • Swing 236 • Summary 238

Glossary   241
Suggested Resources   245
About the Authors   251

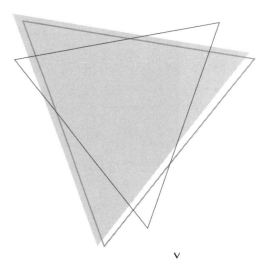

RHYTHMIC ACTIVITY FINDER

Title	Page number	Track number	Music tempo
Chapter 2: Icebreaker Activities			
Seat-to-Feet	22	Generic CD options:	
Mirror Buddies	23	Track 1—Slow	
Circle of Tricks	25	Track 2—Medium	
Have a Ball!	25	Track 3—Fast	
Roping Them In	27	Track 4—Faster	
Create-a-Dance Cards: The CDC System	31		
Step Stations	33		
Connect and Disconnect	34		
Connections	35		
Chapter 3: Rhythmic Games and Activities			
Agility Runs	39	Generic CD options:	
Big Circle	40	Track 1—Slow	
Down the Room in Waves	40	Track 2—Medium	
Eight, Four, Two	41	Track 3—Fast	
Fitness Around the World	42	Track 4—Faster	
Follow the Leader	44		
Four Wall	45		
Friday Roll Call Jog and Dance	47		
Grids	47		
Object Manipulation	48		
One Move After	49		
Open Movement	50		
Parts of Speech	51		
Run, Stop, Pivot	52		
Talking Drum	53		
Wall Work	54		
Group Creation	54		
Lines and Leaders	55		
Partner Over and Under	56		
Small Circles	56		
Tractor Treads	57		
Circuit 1 (Stations 1-8)	58		
Circuit 2 (Stations 1-8)	60		

(continued)

Title	Page number	💿 Track number	Music tempo
Countdown	61		
Four-Corner Rhythms	63		
Obstacle Courses	64		
Rhythms Circuit	65		
Happy Heart	66		
Veins and Arteries	67		
Retro	68		
Chapter 4: Aerobic Dances and Fitness Routines			
Low-Impact Sample Workout	80	Generic CD options:	
High-Impact Sample Workout	81	💿 Track 1—Slow	
Warm-Up Activity: Rhythmic Fitness Circle	82	💿 Track 2—Medium	
Aerobic Exercise Routine 1: Combo Fun	84	💿 Track 3—Fast	
Aerobic Exercise Routine 2: Freedom Hop	85	💿 Track 4—Faster	
Aerobic Exercise Routine 3: Hopscotch Fun	86		
Aerobic Exercise Routine 4: Kicking Fun	86		
Aerobic Exercise Routine 5: Rocking Horse	87		
Aerobic Exercise Routine 6: Get Away	87		
Cool-Down and Stretch Routine	88		
Sunshine Day	89		
Beach Rock	89		
Best Friends	90		
Charleston	91		
Crazy Cha-Cha	92		
German Circle Dance	92		
Jitterbug Jive	92		
Forward, Reverse Fun	94		
Mirror Dance	94		
Simplicity Shag	95		
Chapter 5: Line Dances			
Rhythmic Lead-Up 1: Line Start	100	Generic CD options:	
Rhythmic Lead-Up 2: Entry Level by Skill Level	101	💿 Track 5—Slow	
Eight Count	103	💿 Track 6—Medium	
Grapevine or Vine	104	💿 Track 7—Fast	
The Hard Way	105		
I Got a Girl	105		
Sixteen Count	106		
Alley Cat	107		
Hustle	108		
The Scoot	109		
Jessie Polka	109		
Scuffin'	110		

Title	Page number	Track number	Music tempo
Old Flame	111		
Margie Dance	111		
Popcorn	112		
Reggae Cowboy	113		
Hallelujah	114		
New York, New York	114		
Simple 32	115		
Little Black Book	116		
Continental	117		
The Stroll	117		
Have You Seen Her	118		
Bus Stop	119		
The Freeze	120		
Sport Dance	120		
Struttin'	121		
Rise	122		
Celebration Time	124		
Chapter 6: Folk Dances			
Fanga	129	8	Slow
La Bastringue	130		
The Hokey Pokey	131	10	Slow
Amos Moses (Hully Gully)	132	11	Slow
Jump Jim Jo	133	12	Slow
Bunny Hop	134	13	Medium
Ten Pretty Girls	134	14	Medium
Skip to My Lou	135	15	Medium
Red River Valley	136	16	Medium
La Raspa	137	9	Medium
Salty Dog Rag	138	17	Medium
Solomon Levi	139	18	Medium
Virginia Reel	140	19	Medium
Winston-Salem Partner Dance	141	20	Slow
Miserlou	142	21	Medium
Cotton-Eyed Joe	143	22	Fast
Carnavalito	144	23	Slow
Ciranda	145	24	Slow
Hora (Hava Nagila)	145	25	Fast
Tinikling Dance Variation	146		
Tanko Bushi	147	26	Slow

(continued)

Title	Page number	Track number	Music tempo
Savela Se Bela Loza	148	28	Faster
Biserka	149	29	Slow
Troika	149	27	Meduim
Danish Dance of Greeting	150	30	Slow
German Wedding Dance	151	31	Fast
Chimes of Dunkirk	152	32	Medium
Kinderpolka	153	33	Slow
La Candeliere	153	34	Fast
Carousel	154	35	Slow
Shoemaker's Dance	154	36	Slow
Seven Jumps	156	37	Medium
Bleking	157	38	Slow
Gustaf's Skoal	158	39	Fast
Bummel Schottische	158	40	Medium
Scandinavian Polka	159	31	Fast
Farmer's Jig	160	41	Medium
Chapter 7: Mixers			
Round-Robin Wave	164		
Circassian Circle	165	42	Medium
Lucky Seven	166	43	Fast
Bingo	167	44	Medium
Oh, Johnny	168	45	Fast
Nine Pin	168	46	Fast
Teton Mountain Stomp	169	47	Medium
Riga Jig	169	48	Fast
Angus Reel	170	49	Medium
Five-Foot Two	171	50	Medium
Sweet Georgia Brown	171	51	Medium
CJ Mixer	172	52	Medium
Sicilian Circle	173	53	Fast
Bouquet of Flowers and Scarf	173	54	Medium
Fun Mixer	174	55	Medium
Paul Jones	175	31	Fast
Jiffy Mixer	175	56	Fast
Patty-Cake Polka	176	57	Medium
Barn Dance	176	58	Fast
Broom Dance	177	59	Slow
Clap and Stamp Three Times	178	60	Fast

Title	Page number	Track number	Music tempo
Chapter 8: Square Dances and Clogging			
Circle Left and Right	189		
Forward and Back	189		
Do-Si-Do	190		
Swing	191		
Couple Promenade	191		
Single-File Promenade	191		
Single File, Girl in the Lead	192		
Ladies Turn Back or Queen's Highway, Gents Turn Back or King's Highway	193		
Girls to the Center, Boys to the Center, Everybody to the Center	193		
Wind Up the Ball of Yarn	193		
Open Tunnel and London Bridge	194		
Birdie in the Cage	195		
Swing at the Wall	195		
Take a Little Peek	196		
Mountaineer Loop	196		
Swing When You Meet	197		
Couple Couples Swing	197		
Girl Around the Girl	198		
Georgia Rang Tang	198		
Allemande Left and Right	199		
Arm Turns, Left and Right	199		
Grand Right and Left	199		
Weave the Ring	200		
Star Right and Left	200		
Star Promenade	201		
Pass Through	201		
Split the Outside Couple and Split the Ring	202		
Rollaway Half-Sashay	203		
U-Turn Back	203		
Separate and Divide	204		
Wrong Way Grand	204		
Courtesy Turn	204		
Two or Four Ladies Chain	205		
Do Paso	206		
Lead Right	206		
Right and Left Through	206		
Star Through	207		
Circle to a Line	208		
Bend the Line	208		

Generic CD options:

Track 61—Slow

Track 62—Medium

Track 63—Fast

(continued)

(continued)

Title	Page number	Track number	Music tempo
All Around the Left-Hand Lady	209		
See-Saw (Your Taw)	209		
See-Saw is a Left-Shoulder Do-Si-Do	209		
Grand Square	210		
Square Through	210		
Chapter 9: Social Dances			
Basic Box Waltz	218	64	Slow
Waltzing Underarm Turn	218	64	Slow
Waltz Hesitations	219	64	Slow
Waltzing Left Box Turn	219	64	Slow
Running Waltz	219	64	Slow
Forward Basic Foxtrot	221	65	Medium
Foxtrot Promenade	221	65	Medium
Foxtrot Promenade With an Underarm Turn	222	65	Medium
Foxtrot Ad Lib, Pivot Turn, or Left Rock Turn	222	65	Medium
Foxtrot Swing Step	223	65	Medium
Foxtrot Quarter-Turns	223	65	Medium
Basic Tango	224	66	Medium
Promenade Basic Tango	225	66	Medium
Tango Corte	225	66	Medium
Tango Promenade to Fan	226	66	Medium
Merengue Chassé to Left and Right	227	67	Fast
Merengue Forward and Backward Walk	228	67	Fast
Merengue Back-Breaks	228	67	Fast
Merengue Underarm Turns	229	67	Fast
Salsa or Mambo Basic	230	68	Fast
Salsa or Mambo Side Basic	231	68	Fast
Salsa or Mambo Back- and Front-Breaks	231	68	Fast
Salsa or Mambo Underarm Turns	231	68	Fast
Rumba Basic Box	233	69	Slow
Rumba Underarm Turns	234	69	Slow
Rumba Back-Breaks	234	69	Slow
Rumba Walk	234	69	Slow
Rumba Rocks	235	69	Slow
Basic Swing	236	70	Fast
Swing Underarm Turns	237	70	Fast

CD TRACK LIST

Track number	Song title	Length (seconds)	Tempo	Lesson recommendation
1	Space Jive	61	Slow	General use
2	Big City	64	Medium	General use
3	Full Blitz	62	Fast	General use
4	Wild Brain	64	Faster	General use
5	Down to the Wire	131	Slow	General line dancing
6	Mood Ring	123	Medium	General line dancing
7	Rock Hop	117	Fast	General line dancing
8	Fanga	61	Slow	Chapter 6, Fanga
9	La Raspa	61	Medium	Chapter 6, La Raspa
10	Hokey Pokey	132	Slow	Chapter 6, The Hokey Pokey
11	Web Walker	36	Slow	Chapter 6, Amos Moses (Hully Gully)
12	Jump Jim Jo	62	Slow	Chapter 6, Jump Jim Jo
13	Bunny Hop	46	Medium	Chapter 6, Bunny Hop
14	Ten Pretty Girls	53	Medium	Chapter 6, Ten Pretty Girls
15	Skip To My Lou	65	Medium	Chapter 6, Skip to My Lou
16	Red River Valley	60	Medium	Chapter 6, Red River Valley
17	Salty Dog Rag	60	Medium	Chapter 6, Salty Dog Rag
18	Solomon Levi	62	Medium	Chapter 6, Solomon Levi
19	Virginia Reel	62	Medium	Chapter 6, Virginia Reel
20	Spring Love	58	Slow	Chapter 6, Winston-Salem Partner Dance
21	Miserlou	51	Medium	Chapter 6, Miserlou
22	Blue Grass Country	60	Fast	Chapter 6, Cotton-Eyed Joe
23	Carnavalito	60	Slow	Chapter 6, Carnavalito
24	Ciranda	63	Slow	Chapter 6, Ciranda
25	Hora	35	Fast	Chapter 6, Hora (Hava Nagila)
26	Tanko Bushi	60	Slow	Chapter 6, Tanko Bushi
27	Troika	50	Medium	Chapter 6, Troika
28	Savela Se Bela Loza	56	Faster	Chapter 6, Savela Se Bela Loza
29	Biserka	41	Slow	Chapter 6, Biserka
30	Danish Dance of Greeting	30	Slow	Chapter 6, Danish Dance of Greeting
31	The Clarinet Polka	33	Fast	Chapter 6, German Wedding Dance Chapter 6, Scandinavian Polka Chapter 7, Paul Jones
32	Chimes of Dunkirk	39	Medium	Chapter 6, Chimes of Dunkirk
33	Kinder Polka	30	Slow	Chapter 6, Kinderpolka

(continued)

Track number	Song title	Length (seconds)	Tempo	Lesson recommendation
34	La Candeliere	66	Fast	Chapter 6, La Candeliere
35	Carousel	67	Slow	Chapter 6, Carousel
36	Shoemaker's Dance	40	Slow	Chapter 6, Shoemaker's Dance
37	Seven Jumps	173	Medium	Chapter 6, Seven Jumps
38	Bleking	34	Slow	Chapter 6, Bleking
39	Gustaf's Skoal	39	Fast	Chapter 6, Gustaf's Skoal
40	Bummel Schottische	36	Medium	Chapter 6, Bummel Schottische
41	Farmer's Jig	67	Medium	Chapter 6, Farmer's Jig
42	Circassian Circle	75	Medium	Chapter 7, Circassian Circle
43	Lucky Seven	67	Fast	Chapter 7, Lucky Seven
44	Bingo Waltz	49	Medium	Chapter 7, Bingo
45	Oh, Johnny	73	Fast	Chapter 7, Oh, Johnny
46	Rockabilly the Kid	49	Fast	Chapter 7, Nine Pin
47	The Old Swimming Hole	35	Medium	Chapter 7, Teton Mountain Stomp
48	Greased Pigs	53	Fast	Chapter 7, Riga Jig
49	Friday Bop	41	Medium	Chapter 7, Angus Reel
50	Five-Foot Two	38	Medium	Chapter 7, Five-Foot Two
51	Sweet Georgia Brown	38	Medium	Chapter 7, Sweet Georgia Brown
52	Vodi Odi O Do	55	Medium	Chapter 7, CJ Mixer
53	Harbour Road	61	Fast	Chapter 7, Sicilian Circle
54	Firelight Dance	63	Medium	Chapter 7, Bouquet of Flowers and Scarf
55	Homestead	55	Medium	Chapter 7, Fun Mixers
56	Jiffy Mixer	40	Fast	Chapter 7, Jiffy Mixer
57	Patty-Cake Polka	55	Medium	Chapter 7, Patty-Cake Polka
58	Making Merry	62	Fast	Chapter 7, Barn Dance
59	Old York Waltz	65	Slow	Chapter 7, Broom Dance
60	Picnic Pickin'	42	Fast	Chapter 7, Clap and Stamp Three Times
61	Family Dinner	74	Slow	General square dance and clogging
62	Taters and Onions	62	Medium	General square dance and clogging
63	Shoo Fly Shoe	65	Fast	General square dance and clogging
64	Waltz With Me	65	Slow	Chapter 9, Waltz
65	See the Fox Trot	65	Medium	Chapter 9, Foxtrot
66	Time to Tango	63	Medium	Chapter 9, Tango
67	Lemon Merengue	71	Fast	Chapter 9, Merengue
68	Casa Latina	65	Fast	Chapter 9, Salsa or Mambo
69	Rumba and Rhythm	62	Slow	Chapter 9, Rumba
70	Swing and Sway	62	Fast	Chapter 9, Swing

KEY TO DIAGRAMS

Since so many dances have unique formations, diagrams of the basic formations—as well as a key to the diagrams—are included here to clarify meanings.

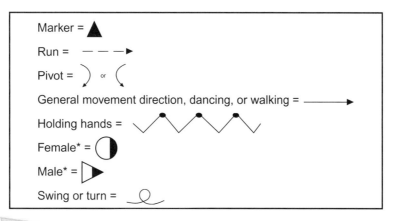

Key.1   *Dark side indicates which direction the person faces.

Key.2   Double circle, facing the line of direction.

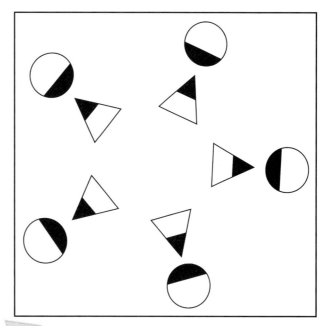

Key.3   Double circle, boys facing out.

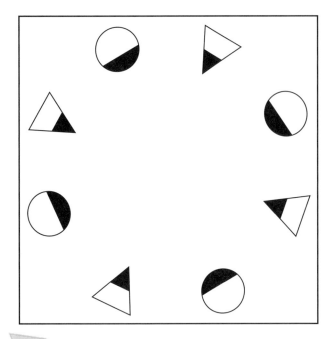

Key.4   Single circle, facing center.

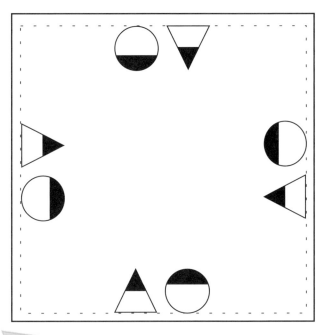

Key.5   Square.

Key.6   Sets of three, facing line of direction.

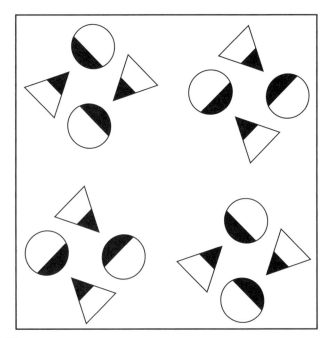

Key.7   Double circle with two couples, facing each other. This circle must be in multiples of four in order to have two couples facing the circle.

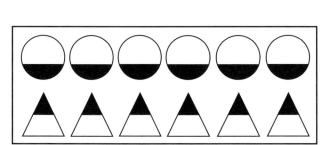

Key.8 Longways set.

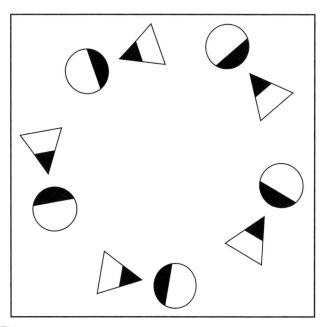

Key.9 Single circle, partners facing.

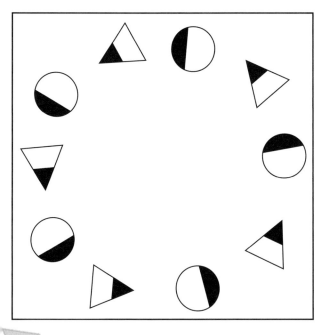

Key.10 Single circle, facing line of direction.

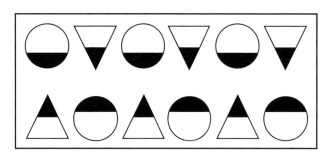

Key.11 Duple improper contra set.

PREFACE

Welcome to the latest edition of *Rhythmic Activities and Dance*. Just as life and the world change rapidly, so too has this text. Yes, Snoopy is still right: "To dance is to live and to live is to dance!" But like everyone else, we strive to continue to be on the cutting edge of our profession. For this reason, much of the content has been updated to reflect and include as much of what is now cutting edge as possible without changing the original focus of the book.

The content standards of the National Dance Association, the National Association for Sport and Physical Education, and the North Carolina Standard Course of Study continue to be the central focus for the content of the book. This has led to a much stronger experience-based approach by organizing the rhythmic activities and dances within each chapter in a progressive order, from those aimed at beginners to those for advanced students. We are now much more directed toward developing lifelong, skillful, fit, joyful movers and learners. In addition, the book is now much more user-friendly for readers of all ages. Indeed, it is our intent that everyone be able to dance their way through life.

We are trying to focus more on inclusion through the medium of dance and thereby to move more toward the internationalization of communities through dance. With this goal in mind, a new chapter on social dances has been added to further expand the partner dance forms in the book. Also new to this edition are sections at the ends of several of the chapters containing assessments that you can use with your students. With these sections you and your students can create your own dances, use rubrics to help assess growth, answer review questions to affirm acquired learning, and complete observation checklists to carefully analyze performance.

We have also increased the total number of dance and fitness activities in an effort to expand the content for the users of the book. Chapter 7, which covers mixers, has been restructured to focus on social development in a nonthreatening environment directed towards inclusion. The Suggested Resources section has been completely updated with current information and annotations to assist users in determining exactly where to go to get the best assistance.

The biggest change is the addition of a CD for use with the book. It contains the music necessary for using the activities in the book to their highest levels. This will bring the book up to speed for use in today's world. Watch for this CD icon.

Rest assured, though, that the elements, activities, and dances that worked so well in the first edition remain—they are not lost! The new and updated elements, activities, and dances have been thoroughly integrated to enhance your ability to teach rhythmic activities and dance.

- **Chapter 1, Starting a Rhythmic Activities and Dance Program,** provides an introduction to dance and rhythmic activities with updated terms, definitions, and formation drawings.

- **Chapter 2, Icebreaker Activities,** is a new chapter that provides activities to loosen up the mood of students and get them moving so that they willingly and enthusiastically participate in the rhythmic activities and dances included in the book.

- **Chapter 3, Rhythmic Games and Activities,** provides a description of starter activities that have been expanded to bring the total up to 30. There are almost enough activities to be able to have a separate one for every week in any given school year. The primary focus is on large-muscle repetitive activities that will warm up and raise fitness levels of all the students in a class.

- **Chapter 4, Aerobic Dances and Fitness Routines,** gets a new title to match its new focus! This chapter now is much more focused on developing fitness in the dance classroom and is loaded with new ways to do it. This chapter adds immensely to the creative side of dance.

- **Chapter 5, Line Dances,** begins the dance chapters and has undergone some major adjustments for the better. We start with this sort of dance because it is for all individuals and allows for "entry level by skill level." Entry level by skill level means that no matter where an individual is developmentally, she or he will be included in the activity due to the way it is structured or organized. This chapter has been updated with some newer dances, but the best change is the addition of teaching cues and tips for each dance. At the end of the chapter there are helpful assessments that provide lots of cognitive stimulation for the dancers.

- **Chapter 6, Folk Dances,** has been reorganized so as to categorize dances according to the region of the globe from which they come. Some old dances were dropped and some great ones were added. Just about every continent is represented in the new organization, which makes the text useful in other areas of the curriculum, such as history and government. This chapter also serves to support the latest international focus on preserving cultural heritage.

- **Chapter 7, Mixers,** includes newly described dances that really enhance its value to the user. This chapter contains 20 proven mixers for your classroom that are guaranteed to liven up instruction. The dances are reorganized under "starting formations" for each dance. This is much easier to follow and allows the user to pick and choose dances based on the different formations. Moreover, all of the dances have been reworked. Directions for each dance are much clearer and more concise. It is very significant to notice the name change. This is intended to make evident that the chapter focuses specifically on the social realm of fitness, an area of personal development that many of us across this country are sadly lacking.

- **Chapter 8, Square Dances and Clogging,** is still a cornerstone for this book. The history and progressions in this chapter are very logical and easy to follow. To assist the novice caller, we have added numerous sample calls and teaching tips. We have also implemented a new nomenclature. This chapter is organized progressively from least to most difficult dances, allowing you to gauge what your students are ready to perform.

- **Chapter 9, Social Dances,** is a new chapter and one that really expands the repertoire of dance material for the classroom. It is a beginner-level chapter on ballroom and Latin couples dance and is designed for all participants to be successful in order to motivate them to go on to higher levels of dance later on in their lives. This chapter is a welcome edition and one whose inclusion is long overdue.

This second edition of *Rhythmic Activities and Dance* is much more user-friendly. It includes a glossary in the back of the book to help you with the terminology. Words in **bold** have been included in the glossary. It will certainly fulfill the needs of primary- and secondary-school educators as well as those in more advanced educational environments. The addition of numerous activities and dances from around the world has really enhanced the usage and application of this book. It will be a terrific addition to virtually any program at any level. It will help to energize, educate, and raise the level of interest in dance of all readers—no matter what their background happens to be.

ACKNOWLEDGMENTS

Thanks to the students from Murrayville Elementary School in Wilmington, North Carolina for posing as models in so many of our pictures.

Thanks also to David Storniolo, Dr. Bennett's photographer, for his helpful contributions during the photo shoots.

Thanks to Dr. Tommy Thompson, professor and chairman of health, physical education, and recreation at the University of North Carolina at Pembroke, for his practical research insights.

▷ CHAPTER 1

Starting a Rhythmic Activities and Dance Program

Everything you need for starting your rhythmic activities and dance program is included in the following topics in this chapter:

- Planning your program
- Program considerations
- Unit planning
- Lesson planning

- Rhythmic terms
- Music in rythmic activities and dance
- Evaluation

▷ PLANNING YOUR PROGRAM

Perhaps one of the most critical areas of program development is planning. To repeat a popular adage, failing to plan is planning to fail. High-quality programs begin with excellent preparation both in the planning stage and later when the program is being implemented. The plan that you develop must be workable and user-friendly in order to be effective. The contents for this book have been put together to reflect the standards and requirements of the National Dance Association (www.aahperd.org/nda), the National Association for Sport and Physical Education (www.aahperd.org/naspe/template.cfm), and the North Carolina Standard Course of Study (www.dpi.state.nc.us/curriculum). This provides a very up-to-date focus and one that is applicable for programs targeted at students of any age. Students of all abilities can use the content, which is strictly skill-based in its focus. Because of the nature of dance itself, the content ranges from simple to slightly more complex so that there is literally entry level by skill level for all people. This means that no matter at what skill level people enter a new dance or rhythmic activity, they will be able to participate fully. The outcomes of this kind of planning can lead to lifelong, skillful, fit, joyful movers and learners. The content lends itself to intergenerational activities, which more closely resemble the way that we all live—or perhaps all should be trying to live in this hectic world. The CD enclosed in the book will bring to life the selections that you make as you plan your program.

Many teachers of rhythm and dance have had little preparation for teaching dance. Keeping this in mind, we focus the planning section on three basic concerns: program considerations, desired program outcomes, and organizational concepts. Activities should be appropriate both to the age and capabilities of students. The chapters are organized to progress from simpler to slightly more complex. This order is simply a suggestion, and you certainly can choose your starting point relative to the ability of your group. You may discover that some of your students, regardless of age, are ready for different challenges. You can exercise judgment about moving to more difficult (or easier, depending on the situation) activities in the book to ensure that what you offer your students is, indeed, developmentally appropriate. The program should teach mastery of the basics of rhythm. Mastering the basics will lead you and your students to success, skill development, and satisfaction.

Regardless of the ability of your students, certain cognitive, affective, and psychomotor characteristics can be addressed through rhythmic activities and dance.

Cognitive Characteristics

- Recognize that practice is the way to develop skills.
- Recognize that physical activity is important for personal well-being.
- Recognize that movement concepts are similar in a variety of skills.
- Identify appropriate behaviors in physical activities for participating with others.
- State reasons why safe and controlled movements are necessary.
- Develop patterns and movement combinations into repeatable sequences.
- Identify how movement concepts can be used to refine movement skills.
- Describe elements of mature movement patterns.
- Describe healthful benefits of regular and appropriate participation in physical activity.
- Recognize that time and effort are prerequisites for skill improvement and fitness benefits.
- Recognize the cultural role of dance in understanding others.
- Detect, analyze, and correct errors in personal movement patterns.
- Identify opportunities for regular physical activity.
- Identify training and conditioning principles.
- Identify the proper warm-up, conditioning, and cool-down skills and their purposes.
- Identify benefits of participating in various physical activities.
- Describe techniques using body and movement activities to communicate ideas and feelings.

- List long-term physiological, psychological, and cultural benefits of regular participation in physical activities.
- Describe training and conditioning principles for specific dances and physical activities.
- Describe appropriate personal and group conduct, including ethical and unethical behavior.
- Analyze and categorize activities according to the possible fitness benefits.

Affective Characteristics

- Identify feelings that result from participating in physical activities.
- Identify activities that contribute to feelings of joy.
- Identify participation factors that contribute to enjoyment and self-expression.
- Design dance sequences that are personally interesting.
- Enjoy participation alone and with others.
- Look forward to physical activity lessons.
- Appreciate the benefits that accompany cooperation and sharing.
- Accept the feelings from challenges, successes, and failures in physical activity.
- Show consideration toward others in the physical activity setting.
- Appreciate differences and similarities in others' physical activity.
- Respect persons from different backgrounds and the cultural significance of the dances and rhythmic activities.
- Enjoy feelings from involvement in physical activity.
- Celebrate your own and others' successes and achievements.
- Identify, respect, and participate with persons of various skill levels.
- Exercise at home for enjoyment and benefits.
- Feel satisfaction from engaging in physical activities.
- Enjoy the aesthetic and creative aspects of performance.
- Respect your own physical and performance limitations as well as those of others.
- Develop a desire to improve physical ability and performance.
- Enjoy meeting and cooperating with others during physical activity.

Psychomotor Characteristics

- Travel in different ways in a large group without bumping into others or falling.
- Travel forward and sideways and change direction quickly while responding to a signal.
- Demonstrate distinct contrasts between slow and fast speeds while traveling.
- Distinguish among straight, curved, and zigzag pathways while traveling in various ways.
- Combine various traveling patterns in time to the music.
- Skip, hop, gallop, and slide using mature motor patterns.
- Demonstrate safety while participating in any physical activity.
- Leap, leading with either foot.
- Develop movement patterns into repeatable sequences.
- Maintain aerobic activity for a specified time.

- Maintain appropriate body alignment during activity.
- Participate regularly in physical activity to improve skillful performance and physical fitness.
- Create and perform dances that combine traveling, balancing, and weight transfer with smooth sequences and intentional changes in direction, speed, and flow.
- Participate vigorously for a sustained time while safely maintaining the proper target heart rate.
- Monitor heart rate before, during, and after activity.
- Recover from vigorous physical activity in an appropriate time.
- Correctly demonstrate activities to improve and maintain muscular strength and endurance, flexibility, and cardiorespiratory functioning.
- Participate in dance, both in and out of school, based on individual interest and capabilities.
- Perform simple folk, country, and creative dances.
- Sustain aerobic activity, maintaining a safe target heart rate to achieve cardiovascular benefits.
- Improve and maintain appropriate body composition.
- Participate in an individualized fitness program.
- Perform dances with fluency and rhythm.
- Participate in dance activities representing various cultural backgrounds.

Remember to put a CAP (cognitive, affective, psychomotor) on every lesson! In other words, a single lesson should address each of these issues. Don't expect students to simply perform activities without having some thoughts or feelings about what they have learned. You should be prepared to address these thoughts and feelings, just as you do the more physical aspects of the lesson.

▷ PROGRAM CONSIDERATIONS

When planning your program, you need to consider several matters: overall program goals, music selection, teaching environment, equipment needs, desired program outcomes, teaching strategies, and standards for social interaction.

Overall Program Goals

While preparing for your classes, keep the following points of effective teaching in mind.

Preclass
- Believe that all students can learn.
- Be a good time manager.
- Use a variety of instructional approaches, such as whole-group, small-group, direct teaching, discovery, guided practice, and cooperative learning.
- Have high expectations.

Review
- Reinforce the concepts of previous lessons to support the newly learned activity.
- Praise the students.

Practice

- Keep students on task.
- Diagnose the skill and ability you expect and prescribe solutions that students can use to improve.
- Interact directly with students.
- Be a skillful teacher who reveals deep knowledge, good preparation, and high motivation.
- Provide clear feedback to individuals and to the group.
- Develop a climate conducive to learning (empathy, objectivity, and individuality).

Evaluation

- Acknowledge correct responses and teach to eliminate incorrect responses.
- Provide situations that promote self-assessment opportunities.
- Hold students accountable for their actions.

Music Selection

Music selection is a major issue and will require preparation time. In the beginning, select music that relates to your students' interests. Once they are hooked, vary the music you select in order to develop a variety of rhythmic dance skills. This will promote improvement in their overall movement. In choosing music, consider the lyrics and any negative connotations they might suggest.

Teaching Environment

You might have to deliver your program from a stage, in a cafeteria or gymnasium, on blacktop, in a classroom or hallway, or in any other space available in the school. Any of these facilities can work. Certainly, we'd all like our own multipurpose room, dance studio, or personal gymnasium, but we must adjust to what is available. Remember, whatever teaching location you are given, it need not be a deterrent to delivering a quality rhythm and dance program at your school.

Equipment Needs

Everyone deserves a good sound system for his or her program. There is still a need to be able to play records and tapes, but this is diminishing rapidly. A CD player has become a necessity. A microphone is critical, and a portable microphone is even better. A variable-speed cassette player or a CD player (variable pitch) would allow you to slow the music down to make teaching with the music very useful.

Desired Program Outcomes

When planning and conducting your rhythm and dance activities, include aspects that will help you to facilitate effective classes. Compare what you are planning to the following list of attributes. These elements of a high-quality program are all present in effectively planned classes.

- Basic skills—Focus on the basics of rhythmic movement and a high level of mastery.
- Student-centered activity—The student is the focus of the lesson. Teach the student, not the lesson.

- Creativity—Students have the opportunity to create and are encouraged to go to higher levels of creativity.
- Fun—Everyone has a high level of enjoyment throughout the class. For success in your rhythm and dance class, create such an atmosphere.
- Safety—Safety is one of the most critical elements in an effective lesson. Avoiding an injury or unpleasant situation is necessary for successful lessons.
- Self-esteem—Success builds more success and raises self-esteem. Students grow in a positive direction as their self-esteem grows.
- Self-evaluation—Lessons allow students to evaluate their own progress through a unit.
- Success—Every participant is successful on a regular basis throughout the lesson.
- Supplies—To maximize learning, supplies must be available for all students.
- Total involvement—Everyone is participating; no one is sitting out or waiting for a turn to be involved. Even numbers or an even split in sexes is not essential.

Keep these outcomes in mind when you develop your unit and lesson plans.

Teaching Strategies

These teaching strategies can be found in places throughout the text. They are designed to be helpful hints that serve as a constant reminder of principles to consider when planning and delivering lessons or units of the dance program.

- Use activities that intentionally have students using both the right and left sides of their bodies for total-body development.
- Teach without partners and without accompaniment at first.
- Change spatial awareness.
- Vary the time, intensity, space, and flow of dances.
- Always keep it simple; teach only what dancers have to know at that particular time.
- Instruct with patience, understanding, and compassion.
- Use clear, concise, and correct explanations.
- Use a show-and-tell format.
- Include practice and repetition.
- Remain flexible and be ready to take advantage of the "teachable moment."
- Repeat basics from various positions.
- Give lots of encouragement to dancers.
- Teach slowly.

Social Interaction

While social interaction comes last on this list of things to be considered in a dance program, this is by no means an indication that it is the least important. In fact, positive social interaction may be the most significant outcome of a good dance program. The social aspect of development in dance is perhaps the strongest contribution of all areas of dance and sport.

▷ UNIT PLANNING

Unit planning is a component of the curriculum development process. However, a yearly plan should be developed before the development of a unit plan. Decide how many lessons you will devote to games, gymnastics, and rhythm and dance activities during the year; then make your unit plans for each of these areas. Tables 1.1-1.7 are sample unit plans for starting a rythmic activities and dance program.

Unit size and length may be predetermined where you are teaching. Units are usually three to nine weeks long. If a physical education program is integrated with dance concepts, dance may appear throughout the school year. Since integration enhances learning, you should make every effort to deliver your program this way. However, most dance programs are in blocks of three to nine weeks, or 15 to 45 lessons. If a school district doesn't typically include dance, this book can be used as a guide to put together a dance program integrated with the typical physical education program. All units should include periodic evaluation throughout the program. Evaluation is addressed later in this chapter.

Since lesson plans are developed from unit plans, they contain many of the same ingredients. The following tables are suggested formats for unit planning. Starter unit plans are offered for each topic covered in this book: rhythmic games and activities, aerobic dances and fitness routines, line dances, folk dances, mixers, square dances and clogging, and social dances. Remember that plans are only guidelines. It is useful to redo this unit plan before you use it again since it is likely to change as you actually teach the course. A plan is critical for guiding your course of action. Without one, you will go nowhere. The suggested activities and lesson plans in this chapter are described fully in the appropriate chapters.

When starting a rhythmic activity and dance program, focus the units on reviewing and mastering the nonlocomotor, locomotor, and combination movement patterns. As students become more comfortable and able, you can begin to introduce selected dance steps, working until they have mastered the steps and combinations.

▷ Table 1.1 Starter Unit Plan for Rhythmic Games and Activities

Lesson 1	Lesson 2	Lesson 3	Lesson 4	Lesson 5
Opening: Agility Runs Middle: Wall Work Closing: Retro	Opening: Big Circle Middle: Group Creation Closing: Retro	Opening: Down the Room in Waves Middle: Lines and Leaders Closing: Retro	Opening: Eight, Four, Two Middle: Partner Over and Under Closing: Retro	Opening: Fitness in America Middle: Small Circles Closing: Retro
Lesson 6	**Lesson 7**	**Lesson 8**	**Lesson 9**	**Lesson 10**
Opening: Follow the Leader Middle: Circuit 1 Closing: Retro	Opening: Four Wall Middle: Circuit 2 Closing: Retro	Opening: Friday Roll Call Jog and Dance Middle: Countdown Closing: Retro	Opening: Grids Middle: Four Corner Rhythms Closing: Retro	Opening: Object Manipulation Middle: Obstacle Courses Closing: Retro
Lesson 11	**Lesson 12**	**Lesson 13**	**Lesson 14**	**Lesson 15**
Opening: One Move After Middle: Rhythms Circuit Closing: Retro	Opening: Open Movement Middle: Happy Heart Closing: Retro	Opening: Parts of Speech Middle: Veins and Arteries Closing: Retro	Opening: Run, Stop, Pivot Middle: Tractor Treads Closing: Retro	Opening: Talking Drum Middle: Retro Closing: Retro

Table 1.2 Starter Unit Plan for Aerobic Dances and Fitness Routines

Lesson 1	Lesson 2	Lesson 3	Lesson 4	Lesson 5
Opening: Agility Runs Middle: Sunshine Day Closing: Cool-down and stretch	Opening: Big Circle Middle: Beach Rock Closing: Cool-down and stretch	Opening: Down the Room in Waves Middle: Best Friends Closing: Cool-down and stretch	Opening: Eight, Four, Two Middle: Charleston Closing: Cool-down and stretch	Opening: Fitness in America Middle: Crazy Cha-Cha Closing: Cool-down and stretch
Lesson 6	**Lesson 7**	**Lesson 8**	**Lesson 9**	**Lesson 10**
Opening: Follow the Leader Middle: Circuit 1 Closing: Cool-down and stretch	Opening: Four Wall Middle: Circuit 2 Closing: Cool-down and stretch	Opening: Friday Roll Call Jog and Dance Middle: Countdown Closing: Cool-down and stretch	Opening: Grids Middle: Four Corner Rhythms Closing: Cool-down and stretch	Opening: Object Manipulation Middle: Obstacle Courses Closing: Cool-down and stretch
Lesson 11	**Lesson 12**	**Lesson 13**	**Lesson 14**	**Lesson 15**
Opening: One Move After Middle: German Circle Dance Closing: Cool-down and stretch	Opening: Open Movement Middle: Jitterbug Jive Closing: Cool-down and stretch	Opening: Parts of Speech Middle: Forward, Reverse Fun Closing: Cool-down and stretch	Opening: Run, Stop, Pivot Middle: Mirror Dance Closing: Cool-down and stretch	Opening: Talking Drum Middle: Simplicity Shag Closing: Cool-down and stretch

Table 1.3 Starter Unit Plan for Line Dances

Lesson 1	Lesson 2	Lesson 3	Lesson 4	Lesson 5
Opening: Wall Work Middle: Eight Count Closing: Grapevine	Opening: Group Creation Middle: I Got a Girl Closing: The Hard Way	Opening: Lines and Leaders Middle: Sixteen Count Closing: Alley Cat	Opening: Partner Over and Under Middle: Hustle Closing: The Scoot	Opening: Small Circles Middle: Jessie Polka Closing: Twelve Count
Lesson 6	**Lesson 7**	**Lesson 8**	**Lesson 9**	**Lesson 10**
Opening: Circuit 1 Middle: Scuffin' Closing: Old Flame	Opening: Circuit 2 Middle: Margie Dance Closing: Popcorn	Opening: Countdown Middle: Reggae Cowboy Closing: Hallelujah	Opening: Four Corner Rhythms Middle: Simple 32 Closing: Bus Stop	Opening: Obstacle Courses Middle: Double Side Step Closing: New York, New York
Lesson 11	**Lesson 12**	**Lesson 13**	**Lesson 14**	**Lesson 15**
Opening: Rhythms Circuit Middle: Struttin' Closing: Little Black Book	Opening: Happy Heart Middle: Continental Closing: The Stroll	Opening: Veins and Arteries Middle: Have You Seen Her Closing: Bus Stop	Opening: Tractor Treads Middle: The Freeze Closing: Rise	Opening: Retro Middle: Celebration Time Closing: Sport Dance

Table 1.4   Starter Unit Plan for Folk Dances

Lesson 1	Lesson 2	Lesson 3	Lesson 4	Lesson 5
Opening: Agility Runs Middle: Hokey Pokey—American Closing: Amos Moses (Hully Gully)—American	Opening: Down the Room in Waves Middle: Jump Jim Jo—American Closing: Bunny Hop—American	Opening: Eight, Four, Two Middle: Ten Pretty Girls—American Closing: Skip To My Lou—American	Opening: Four Wall Middle: Red River Valley—American Closing: Salty Dog Rag—American	Opening: Grids Middle: Solomon Levi—American Closing: Virginia Reel—American
Lesson 6	**Lesson 7**	**Lesson 8**	**Lesson 9**	**Lesson 10**
Opening: One Move After Middle: Winston-Salem Partner Dance—American Closing: Miserlou—American	Opening: Talking Drum Middle: Cotton Eyed Joe—American Closing: La Raspa—Mexican	Opening: Lines and Leaders Middle: Carnavalito—Bolivian Closing: Ciranda—Brazilian	Opening: Small Circles Middle: Danish Dance of Greeting—Danish Closing: German Wedding Dance—German	Opening: Countdown Middle: Chimes of Dunkirk—French-Belgian Closing: Kinder Polka—German
Lesson 11	**Lesson 12**	**Lesson 13**	**Lesson 14**	**Lesson 15**
Opening: Four-Corner Rhythms Middle: La Candeliere—Italian Closing: Carousel—Danish	Opening: Circuit 1 Middle: Shoemaker's Dance—Danish Closing: Seven Jumps—Danish	Opening: Rhythms Circuit Middle: Savela Se Bela Loza—Serbian Closing: Biserka—Serbian	Opening: Tractor Treads Middle: Troika—Russian Closing: Fanga—Kenya	Opening: Retro Middle: Hora—Israeli Closing: Tanko Bushi—Japan

Table 1.5   Starter Unit Plan for Mixers

Lesson 1	Lesson 2	Lesson 3	Lesson 4	Lesson 5
Opening: Agility Runs Middle: Circassian Circle Closing: Lucky Seven	Opening: Down the Room in Waves Middle: Bingo Closing: Oh, Johnny	Opening: Eight, Four, Two Middle: Nine Pin Closing: Teton Mountain Stomp (partners facing)	Opening: Four Wall Middle: Riga Jig Closing: Angus Reel	Opening: Grids Middle: Five-Foot Two Closing: Sweet Georgia Brown
Lesson 6	**Lesson 7**	**Lesson 8**	**Lesson 9**	**Lesson 10**
Opening: Grids Middle: Five-Foot Two Closing: Sweet Georgia Brown	Opening: One Move After Middle: CJ Mixer Closing: Bouquet of Flowers and Scarf	Opening: One Move After Middle: CJ Mixer Closing: Bouquet of Flowers and Scarf	Opening: Talking Drum Middle: Fun Mixers Closing: Paul Jones	Opening: Talking Drum Middle: Fun Mixers Closing: Paul Jones
Lesson 11	**Lesson 12**	**Lesson 13**	**Lesson 14**	**Lesson 15**
Opening: Lines and Leaders Middle: Jiffy Mixer Closing: Patty-Cake Polka	Opening: Lines and Leaders Middle: Jiffy Mixer Closing: Patty-Cake Polka	Opening: Rhythms Circuit Middle: Barn Dance Closing: Sicilian Circle (two couples facing)	Opening: Tractor Treads Middle: Barn Dance Closing: Sicilian Circle (two couples facing)	Opening: Countdown Middle: Broom Dance Closing: Clap and Stamp Three Times

▷ Table 1.6 Starter Unit Plan for Square Dances and Clogging

Lesson 1	Lesson 2	Lesson 3	Lesson 4	Lesson 5
Opening: Connect and Disconnect Middle: Review Closing: Understanding	Opening: Circle Left/Circle Right Middle: Do-Si-Do Closing: Swing Partner/Corner	Opening: Promenade Middle: Calling Closing: Phrasing	Opening: Honor Your Partner Middle: Allemande Closing: Right-Hand Star	Opening: Heads Pass Through Middle: Split the Couple Closing: Review
Lesson 6	**Lesson 7**	**Lesson 8**	**Lesson 9**	**Lesson 10**
Opening: Create-a-Dance Cards Middle: Split the Ring Closing: Go Back Home/ Swing Own	Opening: Roping Them In Middle: Turn It Around 'Til Your Corner Comes Up Closing: Review	Opening: Ladies Rollaway/ Half-Sashay Middle: Boys U-Turn Back Closing: Review	Opening: Head Two Girls Middle: Do Paso Closing: Left-Hand Star	Opening: Star Through Middle: Grand Right and Left Closing: Circle to a Line
Lesson 11	**Lesson 12**	**Lesson 13**	**Lesson 14**	**Lesson 15**
Opening: See-Saw Middle: Shuffle Closing: Appalachian Big Set	Opening: Big Circle Middle: Figures Closing: Review	Opening: Circle of Tricks Activity Middle: Couple Promenade Closing: Queen's Highway	Opening: King's Highway Middle: Open Tunnel Closing: London Bridge	Opening: Connections Middle: Review Closing: Assessment

▷ Table 1.7 Starter Unit Plan for Social Dances

Lesson 1	Lesson 2	Lesson 3	Lesson 4	Lesson 5
Opening: Connect and Disconnect Middle: Define Social Dance Closing: Fact Sheet	Opening: Dance Sport Middle: Mirror Buddies Closing: Review	Opening: Smooth American Style Middle: Basic Box Step Closing: Underarm Turn	Opening: Foxtrot Middle: Basic Step Closing: Foxtrot Promenade	Opening: Foxtrot Swing Step Middle: Quarter-Turns Closing: Review
Lesson 6	**Lesson 7**	**Lesson 8**	**Lesson 9**	**Lesson 10**
Opening: Swing Middle: Lindy Hop Closing: Basic Swing	Opening: Swing Underarm Turns Middle: Dishrag Turn Closing: Review	Opening: Step Stations Middle: Review Closing: Create	Opening: Salsa or Mambo Middle: Side Basic Closing: Practice	Opening: Rumba Middle: Basic Box Closing: Review
Lesson 11	**Lesson 12**	**Lesson 13**	**Lesson 14**	**Lesson 15**
Opening: Tango Middle: Basic Tango Step Closing: Promenade Basic Tango	Opening: Tango Corte Middle: Tango Promenade to Fan Closing: Review	Opening: Merengue Middle: Chassé to Left and Right Closing: Practice	Opening: Connections Middle: Discussion Closing: Review	Opening: Questions Middle: Practice Closing: Assessment

▷ LESSON PLANNING

Once you have your unit plan mapped out, you can expand on the basic information from it to create your actual lesson plan. Individual lessons are usually 30 to 40 minutes with a beginning, middle, and closing. The beginning section sets the tone for the lesson, and it should have a lively focus on familiar or simple material. This section includes the focus, review, and objectives portions of the lesson. The middle section is the time for teaching new materials. A simple delivery is the "say, say and do, and do" method for teaching new material. Connecting the verbal cues to the movements tends to accelerate learning. In this part of the lesson, instruction and guided practice usually occur. For example, when teaching a **grapevine** or **carioca** (used in this text as *vine*), step to the right, first say and do the movement, "Vine to the right by stepping right to the side, stepping left behind right, stepping right to the side, and touching left beside right." Next, have the students say and do the vine to the right while you continue to demonstrate. This time, however, only the key words, "Step, behind, step, touch," would be used. When students master this skill, they would stop saying the movements and simply do them. The closing section of the lesson is for application. Application should occur in a low-stress, high-success, fun-filled environment. This part of the lesson is devoted to independent practice and closure.

This section helps you get started with basic lesson planning. A template for an individual lesson has been included, followed by an actual starter lesson plan from the Starter Unit Plan for Social Dances (table 1.7).

Remember to Teach Children, Not Just the Lesson Plan

Teachers can get so involved with covering objectives, standard courses of study, and pacing guides—as well as with making sure they are teaching what is in their lesson plans—that they can simply forget about teaching the children for whom the plan is designed. Dance has building blocks just like math, language, and writing. Before you can teach students any fundamental concept, they must have the feeling that they are important and know that you know they can learn. The first step in having successful rhythmic activities is to build a rapport with your students so that they know they are entering a nonthreatening atmosphere when they enter your arena. This is crucial because children want to learn and be successful. They will do whatever is asked if they are gradually shown both that they can trust you and you are not going to do anything that will cause them to be embarrassed, humiliated, or picked on.

Rhythmic activities and dance are sensitive experiences because music touches the emotional being inside children: the way they feel about themselves, what others think about them, how they appear to others, what might seem dumb or stupid, and how they fear not being able to do or learn this. The steps of the dance, the sequence of the steps, and the terminology of the activities are not the first concerns when learning rhythmic activities and dance. First, we must have compassion for what students are feeling. Second, we must understand that somewhere inside they really want to do and learn what you want them to do and learn. Third, you must be willing to explore new methods of teaching strategies in order to evoke this desire from them.

Making sure students are having fun is fundamental. The activities you choose will not guarantee this. The methodology you use in presenting your objectives will help you achieve your goals. Having high expectations will show them that you know they can learn this. How you speak when trying to teach them a new concept takes much effort. You must become animated to show them your enthusiasm. You must start off very slowly to the point that they feel it is very easy. When you know they have the first step, say to them, "You are goooood! I didn't know you could learn so fast. I'd better start keeping up with you. Are you ready for the next step since you caught on to that so quickly? Here goes." Now you have their attention without having to actually instruct them to "pay attention." It is built into the approach. After you know they have the next element, say to them, "Oh, my goodness, you learn so quickly! I'd better get to something more challenging for you." Then hesitate as if you are really thinking; this gets their attention. Follow up with this: "After seeing what a grand job you did learning that step, I think you might be ready for a challenge. What do you think?" They respond in a positive manner every time. Say, "Maybe this will be too challenging for you . . . I'll go to something easier." They stop you immediately and say, "No, we can do it!" Say, "Are you sure?" Once they say yes, away you go, soaring higher than you could even imagine. They are so proud. They believe they can do it. They are getting pumped up and excited about learning something new.

This approach improves students' self-confidence, which, in turn, boosts their self-esteem. The word *dance* was never used; "quiet down so you can learn this" was never said; and there are rarely discipline problems because you jump in and get the class going with enthusiasm and excitement. The children with discipline problems also have been successful, and it feels good to them. Much of the time such children only need the teacher's attention, compassion, and understanding. They just got started on the "other" foot. Your enthusiasm can offer them an opportunity to grasp the moment, and moment by moment you can penetrate their cocoon. Then they too can soar.

Decisions at this stage should reflect awareness of classroom conditions, such as class size and students' ability, and should adhere to your unit objectives for the design and implementation of individual lessons. Thorough planning in the beginning will ensure success in your classes and high skill retention by your students.

Lesson Plan Format

This lesson plan format is simple. This template can be easily used to enhance the individual rhythmic activities and dances presented in this book.

Lesson Plan Template

GRADE AND TEACHER NAME

Students' grade and teacher

GOALS (THEME)

One to three statements about expected outcomes

OBJECTIVES (SUBTHEMES)

State them in a familiar form. There will be three categories of objectives: cognitive, affective, and psychomotor. Use no more than three objectives in each category. That way you avoid getting so busy writing objectives that you miss the intent of the lesson.

EQUIPMENT

List of needed equipment

AREA

Where the lesson is to be delivered

SAFETY

Special considerations for this lesson

OPENING

Approximately 5 to 10 minutes: Provide introduction and review to get students comfortable and interested. As part of the lesson plan, list and describe the activities with approximate times and include all special teaching cues for each activity.

MIDDLE

Approximately 10 to 20 minutes: Introduce new skills and rhythmic activities. This is the time to break down and teach the new skills, activities, dance steps, or combinations. As part of the lesson plan, list and describe the activities with approximate times and include all special teaching cues for each activity.

CLOSING

Approximately 5 to 10 minutes: This is the culmination of the lesson and the time to think about application. Students practice skills, put together routines, or practice patterned activities in a nonthreatening, fun environment.

Starter Lesson Plan (from the Starter Unit Plan for Social Dances)

GOALS (THEME)

Students will be able to execute the basic swing step.

OBJECTIVES (SUBTHEMES)

- Cognitive: Students will be able to describe the movements found in the basic swing step.
- Affective: Students will stay on task during the lesson.
- Psychomotor: Students will be able to execute the basic swing step on their own as well as while guiding a partner.

EQUIPMENT

- Sound system
- Music for a single, double, and triple Lindy

AREA

Blacktop

SAFETY

Remind students to honor the spaces occupied by their classmates and not to enter occupied spaces.

OPENING, MIDDLE, AND CLOSING FOR LESSON

Time	Task Description	Teaching Points
OPENING: APPROXIMATELY 8 MINUTES		
3 minutes	Rhythmic movement that focuses on basic locomotor patterns is put to music.	Remind students about safe use of space.
5 minutes	Four-corner rhythms	• No more than 12 people start in a corner. • Students move at their own pace.
MIDDLE: 17 MINUTES		
6 minutes	Give background on swing.	Teach and practice dance, having students walk to the music first and then "guard" one another to a drum accompaniment.
11 minutes	Discuss the different kinds of swing basics (i.e., single, double, and triple Lindy steps). Practice these basic steps individually without music and then with music.	Practice individually the single, double, and triple Lindy steps
CLOSING: 5 MINUTES		
5 minutes	Pratice the basic steps "guarding" a partner	• Remind students about safe use of space • Practice individually and then with a partner

Note: Make file cards or overheads with dance instructions if you need them for your lesson.

Organizational Concepts

Put the fun back in the fundamentals! When introducing a rhythmic activity, relate the activity to other areas of the curriculum, especially sports. Make connections for your students. Help them to see the connections. Point out previously learned steps or skills. In addition, give all the important background information that you know about a rhythmic activity to generate interest.

Several ingredients are essential for organizing an effective class. The following list is not all-inclusive, but with the other information provided in this chapter it is certainly quite helpful. As you plan your rhythmic activity classes, organize them around the following concepts:

- Cooperation and control: These characteristics are clearly on display when classes are well organized.
- Exploration: Give students an opportunity to experiment and explore.
- Individualization: Each person is able to participate as an individual.
- Problem solving: This is an excellent way to learn new information.
- Reinforcement of other areas: Reinforce other subject areas when teaching rhythmic activities. When appropriate, these activities should embody an interdisciplinary adventure.
- Self-awareness: Offer students the opportunity to expand their self-awareness in a non-threatening environment.
- Self-discovery: A characteristic of all sessions is learning through self-discovery. Allow freedom to discover!
- Teacher as a guide and facilitator: The teacher serves as a guide and facilitator and not as a dictator.

▷ RHYTHMIC TERMS

Basic terms used in the text have been included in the glossary to assist you in your teaching endeavors. The glossary has five subsections. The first subsection lists basic nonlocomotor and locomotor movements. The second subsection includes combinations of locomotor movements. The third subsection lists formations and positions such as the **open** formation where students are scattered about the room. The fourth describes the major rhythmic elements of any rhythmic, dance, or movement sequence. The fifth subsection, "Selected Dance Steps," can assist you with dance steps that occur often in K-12 programs.

These five subsections provide the terminology and building blocks for your program. Review them often to help your students become stronger and more confident dancers and rhythmic movers.

▷ MUSIC IN RHYTHMIC ACTIVITIES AND DANCE

Music makes the movement activities appealing and fun. The first step is music selection. The CD that accompanies the book will be helpful, but what is currently popular must be used as much as possible because it will motivate your students the most.

Counts

Once you have music that will appeal to your group, the next step is to listen to the music with paper and pencil in hand, making a mark on the sheet for each beat (see figure 1.1). When the music changes, draw a line under the marks to indicate the change and continue to mark the beats. Then go back and write in the margin what is happening in the music where the changes are indicated. You may add the first few words of the song to use as a cue.

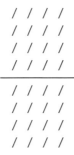

Figure 1.1 On a piece of paper, note each beat with a slash and a change in music with a line.

When you have written all the cue words, divide the song into its parts and determine the number of beats that each part gets. Here is the music for "Jingle Bells":

Counts	1	2	3	4	5	6	7	8
	/	/	/	/	/	/	/	/
	Jin	gle	bells		Jin	gle	bells	

Counts	1	2	3	4 e & a	5	6	7	8
	/	/	/	/	/	/	/	/
	Jin	gle	all	the way . . .				

These are the first 16 counts that you should use to determine what dance steps would fit to the music. Notice the "e & a" in the second line. This represents the subdivision of beats that occurs since "the" does not fall directly on the fourth beat. There are times within this book where more than one action is described for a single beat. When this happens, the subdivided counts are provided to help you know where movements line up. For example, two marches might take beats "1, 2" or they could take beats "1-and."

Here is an example of how to write out the choreography:

Introduction	8 counts
Verse A	32 counts
Verse B	32 counts
Chorus	32 counts

Now you are ready to add the steps that will create the dance.

Introduction	8 counts: Alternate right foot and left foot, then step right foot, step left foot, step right foot, step left foot.
Verse A	32 counts: Cha-cha forward and backward; repeat four times.
Verse B	32 counts: Cross cha-cha; cross right foot over left foot and reverse; repeat four times.
Chorus	32 counts: Slide right and slide left, four times.
Chorus	32 counts: Slide left and slide right, four times.

Tempo and Time Signature

Rhythmic activities and dances often require a certain degree of quickness, or an upbeat tempo, to be successful. In music, tempo is described in terms of the number of beats per minute (BPM). To determine the BPM for a piece of music, simply count the beats for a minute. To convert this to measures per minute (MPM), if it is 4/4-meter music, divide the BPM by 4. BPM is usually the most common descriptor of tempo, so this is an important concept to understand.

Another concept concerns the time signature of the music. In the music typically used by dancers, the time signature will be 2/4, 3/4, or 4/4 meter. This means, respectively, that in 2/4-meter music there are two beats per measure, in 3/4-meter music there are three beats per measure, and in 4/4-meter music there are four beats per measure.

Rhythmic Patterns

A related concept involves even and uneven rhythmic patterns. **Even rhythmic patterns** usually call for equal amounts of time being given to each movement. Walking and running are even rhythmic patterns. Contrast this to **uneven rhythmic patterns**, such as those found in skipping, galloping, and sliding. More time is given to the first motion in these combination movements than to the second motion. It is this difference in time that makes these movements fall into the category of uneven rhythmic movements. When movements are put to music, it is this element of even and uneven rhythmic patterns that can sometimes throw off the participants. Practice without accompaniment and then use very simple tunes. This is the best way to eliminate confusion when more complex accompaniments finally are added.

Quick and Slow

These terms are used frequently in dance and music descriptions. Generally, the term *quick* refers to a single beat or step in time to a piece of music, and the term *slow* refers to a step that takes two full beats of the music. Quick and slow are especially useful when teaching social dance.

▷ EVALUATION

As with all activities, especially those that are taught, evaluation is critical to future success. Evaluation of rhythmic activities appears to be more subjective than it actually is. It is possible to remove some of this subjectivity and to collect useful information.

Rhythmic activities should be evaluated regularly. Students need regular feedback, as does the teacher. Two tools follow to assist you in this effort. The first one serves as a self-evaluation of you, the teacher. It is a Likert-type scale format, and you should average 3 or better on all items throughout the year. A Likert scale evaluates skills or concepts by requiring participants to rate statements on a range from "always" to "never" with numbers from high to low. It will provide you with feedback about how you are doing in the classroom. The second tool, the Rhythmic Assessment Form on page 19, provides feedback to your students about their rhythmic activity performances and gives you a more definitive assessment for grading. It is designed to provide an analysis of a rhythmic skill for the student. Scoring is based on a 50-point scale with a 5-point bonus for higher-quality performance. This score can be doubled for a final score of 100. The test can be used again for a second try or a second rhythmic activity.

While the second tool can be used to provide specific grades, it can also allow students the opportunity to evaluate themselves and their classmates during a unit. It also may be more useful as a pretest, midterm, or posttest.

Self-Evaluation: A Key to Effectively Teaching Rhythms

Growth comes through self-evaluation and willingness to change. The Rhythm and Dance Checklist and Rhythmic Assessment Form on pages 17 and 19 are designed to assist in this self-evaluation process and to help students perform at higher levels. They have been modified for the teaching of rhythmic and dance activities. Use it to see how you are doing in the classroom.

Rhythm and Dance Checklist

Low scores on individual items on this Likert scale indicate a need for further evaluation of a particular aspect of your program. Further evaluation may eventually lead to changes in your methods of teaching.

1. I use ability grouping to meet individual needs and provide maximum learning opportunities for all in my rhythm and dance classes.
   Always 5 4 3 2 1 Never

2. I use screening tests, both formal and informal, to assess students' strengths and weaknesses in fitness and basic rhythmic skills and as a guide to planning activities to help students improve.
   Always 5 4 3 2 1 Never

3. I help organize individualized educational plans for students categorized as having special needs in learning rhythms.
   Always 5 4 3 2 1 Never

4. I maximize supplies, equipment, and facilities to keep every student engaged in activity.
   Always 5 4 3 2 1 Never

5. I use small-group activities so that students don't have to wait to be active.
   Always 5 4 3 2 1 Never

6. I have added a new activity to the curriculum for each grade to which I will teach rhythms and dance this year.
   Always 5 4 3 2 1 Never

7. I do not repeat the same rhythmic and dance activities without a change in approach or scope.
   Always 5 4 3 2 1 Never

8. I decorate my teaching area with educational bulletin boards, floor patterns, pictures, and a new vocabulary for rhythm and dance.
   Always 5 4 3 2 1 Never

9. I involve older students in assisting younger students with equipment maintenance, special events, clubs, or programs related to rhythms.
   Always 5 4 3 2 1 Never

10. I belong to my professional organization and keep abreast of new methods and materials in the rhythm and dance area.
    Always 5 4 3 2 1 Never

11. I communicate with the staff about dance education experiences and related issues.
    Always 5 4 3 2 1 Never

12. I am a resource to my staff and community regarding community activities that are intended to enhance fitness.
    Always 5 4 3 2 1 Never

From *Rhythmic Activities and Dance, 2nd ed.*, by John Bennett and Pam Riemer, 2006, Champaign, IL: Human Kinetics.

Suggested Student or Teacher Evaluation

The sample Rhythmic Assessment Form on page 19 can provide a wealth of information to both students and teachers when used in the classroom. It can be used repetitively or on a one-time basis. Teachers can do the assessment, or students can use it on themselves or other students. It can put a numerical value on student activity and assist the teacher in evaluating what is taking place relating to the cognitive, affective, and psychomotor aspects of development. However, the items to be evaluated should be designed to meet the specific needs of your classes. The strength of this instrument lies in the flexibility of selecting or developing items conducive to your program. The items can be given numbers from 1 to 10 or 1 to 5. Another suggestion would be to use either an "s" for satisfactory or a "u" for unsatisfactory when evaluating the performances of your students. Whatever you decide, implementing regular assessments will provide another opportunity for growth within your classes. Students always want to know their scores and grades. They have worked hard and are eager to know whether they were successful.

Create Your Own Dances

Create Your Own Dances is a new feature in this edition that pushes students cognitively and takes the class in a totally new direction. It promotes independent thinking at a level that fits right in with the strong focus on developing critical thinking.

Also new to this edition are rubrics that focus on the content of the chapter so that competency with it can be assessed at four different levels: exemplary (level 1), acceptable (level 2), needs improvement (level 3), and unacceptable (level 4). Each of these levels contains descriptors for meeting the particular demands of that level. The rubrics can be used by students to assess their own work or can aid teachers greatly with assessment of their students' work in creating their own dances.

Review Questions

The addition of review questions likewise has greatly enhanced each chapter. These questions reinforce the information that is contained within each chapter and allows the teacher effectively to check on student progress.

Observation Questions

Finally, the addition of Observation Questions is another great tool that has been added to assist with evaluation of what is happening within each class. Students can use these checklists and worksheets to describe what they have observed in class. They provide valuable information to the teacher to assist with his or her determination of the direction that the class should take in the future.

SUMMARY

This chapter focuses on planning for your rhythm activities program, rhythmic components, classroom management, and evaluation. In-depth guidelines on unit and lesson planning and samples are included along with specific suggestions for making teaching easier to assist you in developing your own program. Student and self-evaluations were provided to guide you, your students, and your program in the future. This evaluation process supports student assessment and participation, is nonthreatening, and helps to promote the joy of learning rhythm and dance.

Rhythmic Assessment Form

Student's name _____

Cognitive Evaluation

_____ 1. Recognizes the count being used.

_____ 2. Understands the concept and pattern used in the dance.

_____ 3. Understands the concepts of following and leading a partner.

_____ 4. Understands styling concepts.

_____ 5. Understands the concept of presenting the dance.

_____ 6. Understands the concept of rhythm.

Affective Evaluation

_____ 1. Can maintain own working space.

_____ 2. Can mirror a partner or leader without teaching.

_____ 3. Can work with a partner on the footwork.

Psychomotor Evaluation

_____ 1. Can clap to the various rhythms of the dance.

_____ 2. Can verbally count out the rhythms of the dance.

_____ 3. Can lead and follow.

_____ 4. Can display the proper footwork for the dance.

_____ 5. Can distinguish and demonstrate the styling for the dance.

_____ 6. Can demonstrate the rhythm of the dance.

_____ 7. Can present the dance.

From *Rhythmic Activities and Dance, 2nd ed.*, by John Bennett and Pam Riemer, 2006, Champaign, IL: Human Kinetics.

Adhering to the content in this chapter will ensure that your program is balanced and fulfills the developmental needs of every student by putting the "fun" in fundamentals.

The opportunities for the rhythmic and dance portion of your program to burst with energy are waiting for you in this book. Try activities from all the chapters and then return to the areas that you and your students like the most. Take notes in the margins of this book that might add to your success in teaching the activity: Change the way you presented an activity to make it work better, note music that works well and cue words that relate well to you students, and so on. The last section of the book contains a helpful resource list to answer any questions you have about your own rhythmic and dance program.

CHAPTER 2

Icebreaker Activities

Children need to know how to be social before they can dance together. Socialization comes from positive interaction in a nurturing environment with other children. Socialization occurs in several ways. Students touching each other (holding hands first) is a major obstacle (I call it a challenge).

One of the biggest barriers a teacher will face is attempting to have students work in partners. Students come to us with very little expertise in "social fitness." We as teachers can use the activities in this chapter to ease the difficulty of working together in close quarters. We must always be patient and kind. We must allow absolutely no teasing of any student. The good thing about the methods in this chapter is that they allow connections with partners to be very brief so that students realize they will not be stuck with a particular partner. This is often the reason children do not like to choose partners.

The strategies in this chapter can only work if the students understand what it takes to make the class successful. They must know what makes them feel good about themselves and what gives them confidence is the very same thing their classmates need. Students cannot learn social skills unless the time is taken to help them learn. One such skill, dancing, has caused the feelings of many children to be hurt. This, in turn, has damaged their self-esteem, stripped them of their confidence, and adversely affected their self-image.

Another barrier is that students may absolutely balk at the very idea of dancing. A child might avoid learning rhythmic activities, saying, "I can't do it because it's too hard," "I don't want to look silly in front of my friends," "I'm too embarrassed," or "That's stupid." Whatever the excuse, they all come from the same source: a lack of self-confidence and security. If you ask adults why they haven't become comfortable enough to perform rhythmic and dance activities in front of others, you will hear the same reasons.

▷ EASING STUDENTS INTO RHYTHMIC ACTIVITIES AND DANCE

You can use many strategies to ease the social and mental barriers students have to learning rhythmic activities and dance. The rhythmic activities that follow are social, interactive activities that are meant to strengthen the foundation on which dance can be built. These approaches are tried and true. They help to create an atmosphere that will nurture the desire of students to dance for fun and fitness.

Seat-to-Feet

Goal   Help students learn rhythmic activities by helping them to become comfortable enough to abandon their insecurities and feelings of not wanting to dance.

Formation   Students start by sitting on the floor in a cozy cluster to ensure security.

▷ Procedure

1. Students clap the rhythm of the activity. Next they snap their fingers to the rhythm. Students are to practice to the beat and get used to it. They will be much more successful if they first spend time learning the rhythm; they can then concentrate on the steps.

2. Once the hand-clapping session is successful, ask the students to keep time to the music with their feet. They are still sitting in a scattered formation, so the worry of appearing awkward is absent. They keep time with the music by having each foot represent a beat and by alternating which foot strikes the beat. Which foot leads, or starts, has little significance at this point. You are trying to teach a rhythm and increase self-confidence, not teach a dance step. The students should practice with the music until they feel comfortable. You will probably see a high level of success. Walk around to accustom them to having you present; help and encourage them in such a way that you do not bring attention to them or embarrass them in front of their friends. If you present this step correctly, the students will feel challenged to be truly successful, and they will try even harder.

3. The next phase begins to approach the standing-up portion of the process. Students come up to their knees, clap to the music, and then snap their fingers. Because they were successful with the clapping and snapping session, they will gladly come to their knees to try something new. They now have the background and self-confidence to want to try each challenge, seeing these challenges as adventures.

4. At last it is time to stand up. Rather than having the students stand up, waiting to start the rhythm, have them stand up while they are clapping. Then change the clapping to snapping; the change will not be as noticeable. As soon as all students are up, they can begin keeping time with their feet. They will be at ease at this point because it is familiar and they have been successful at it.

5. They are ready to learn any basic rhythmic dance step that you wish. Remember to begin by having students sit on the floor and from there to gradually let them come to a standing position.

▷ Teaching Tips

- Keep in mind that you teach the children, not the lesson. Help them to feel comfortable while they are sitting. They will then begin to show eagerness to move forward. This may take more time than you feel comfortable taking, but you will surely save time and accomplish more in the long run.

- Using key words, such as *slow* and *quick,* will help the students get the correct rhythm with their dance steps and also help them differentiate the various dances. For example, while teaching the cha-cha, recite, "Slow, slow, quick, quick, quick." While teaching the **waltz**, recite, "Slow, quick, quick"; for the **foxtrot**, "Slow, slow, quick, quick"; for the tango, "Slow, slow, quick, quick, slow"; for the **shag**, "Quick, quick, quick, quick, quick, quick, slow, slow."

- Have the kids move around the room doing the **rhythmic pattern** in all directions. Patterns make learning easy, since students are used to using patterns in math.

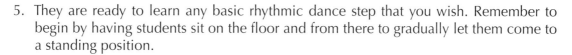

Mirror Buddies

Goal The mirroring approach is a fascinating method for getting students involved in dancing very quickly.

Formation Students are in pairs—a boy–girl combination is preferable but not necessary. (This is a good time to use the fast "connect-and-disconnect" method of partner selection that is described later in this chapter.)

▷ Procedure: Part A

1. Pairs sit down on the floor facing the front.

2. Choose a student to help you demonstrate. Choosing a very popular student, a respected leader, or an athlete is very helpful because the other students think that if it is cool for her or him, it will be cool for them too. Tell this student ahead of time that you need her or his help because this will enhance her or his willingness to do what you request. Do not tell her or him what is going to transpire; you want this to be unrehearsed (see figure 2.1).

3. The selection for the first step must be fun and possibly unusual to catch the students' interest. You are to be "on stage." Fun must leap out at them!

4. Show the step, first moving to your right.

5. The designated student is to copy the step but must move to the left; hence she or he is your mirror buddy. (Do not use words to indicate in which direction the student should move. It is not important at this point. All you want her or him to do is to follow you as if she or he is looking into a mirror and is copying everything you do.

6. Throw in some facial or body movements that will cause a fun reaction. (This laughter helps the students to let down the barrier of fear, anxiety, and sense of doom.)

7. Students can be creative at the same time they are learning the steps needed to be successful.

Figure 2.1 Asking a popular student to mirror your movements can help to get the rest of the students involved. Remember, words are not as interesting to mirror! Provide fun and silly movements that are designed to enhance the fun!

▷ Procedure: Part B

1. Use the "step together, step, touch" step.
2. The leader is to perform this step to the right.
3. The mirror buddy is to perform the same step to the left. It does not matter that the mirror buddy is learning the step to the left first because she or he will have to learn the step to the left anyway.
4. All you are trying to do is to get students comfortable with the step. It will be much easier than having them stand behind you and trying to follow what you do. Repeat the process. They must feel comfortable with each step in the dance. Feelings of comfort arise with successful repetition of the steps.
5. The student couples who were facing each other now move so that they are side by side and do the steps.

▷ Procedure: Part C

At this point, the steps have been taught in progression, the students understand the concept, and they have learned to use it to achieve success in dancing. Fun will follow.

1. When you call out, "Mirror Buddies," students will find a connection (partner).
2. The students will get into the formation for the step that you want to teach.
3. You have made a comfortable, nonthreatening environment for them.

▷ Teaching Tips

Demonstrate! This is the time for you to be an actor on stage. Making a fun lunge at them will produce laughter and relief at the same time. Then face a connection and put your hands together with her or his hands to make following easier. Students will follow your lead and not even think about touching hands.

Circle of Tricks

Goal   This activity has proven to be an adventure that will last 20 to 30 minutes with tremendous physical fitness benefits—not to mention new communication with different classmates (social interaction), new movements to experience with the cards (reading), new props (creative movement), and new music (an instant motivator). When making the cards, ensure that they are easy to read, colorful, and filled with a variety of fonts to make it interesting.

▷ Procedure: Part A

For one minute, students warm up by walking single file in a circle in the same direction. No music is used at this time.

▷ Procedure: Part B

This can be a great way to remove props so as to ease the students into choosing connections without having time to think about it; all they really want to do is be successful at the task.

1. Use music with a moderate tempo.
2. Students begin in a circle, walking in the same direction.
3. When you signal the students, have them divide into two clusters. Have one group go to the center of the room, pick two cards from a pile that you have placed there, and bring them back to another student.
4. The students with the cards select a prop and perform the skill written on the card in time with the music.
5. They return the card to the center of the room while doing the skill written on the card and using the prop they choose.
6. When the music stops or changes, students who did not choose cards the first time around get two cards and share one card with someone else.
7. Each student chooses a new prop and continues with the activity.
8. As the activity goes on, you can remove four props; this leaves four students who must pair up and choose one locomotor skill to do together.

▷ Safety Tips

- Remember to monitor the students' breathing; make sure that they don't overdo it, but give them a good workout.
- Remember to explain how to be safe while participating in the activity and that running into other students is inappropriate behavior.

▷ Teaching Tip

Students can demonstrate their routines, teach them to the class, or write their routines down so you can teach them to other classes. The sky's the limit!

Have a Ball!

Goal   Work with a partner.

Music   Choose music of various tempos that the children will readily relate to.

Formation   This activity is best performed in a gym or recreation facility.

▷ Procedure

Getting children to dance with a partner has to come about before they even realize it. How is this accomplished? When the class begins, do not announce, "You will learn how to dance today." Instead, during the warm-up, have the students get a ball of their choice from a selection of balls that bounce: volleyballs, basketballs, soccer balls, or playground balls. They will love that they have a ball in their hands, and they will think they are going to play with the balls from the beginning. They will be ready to do whatever you say. Now ask the children if they are ready for a challenge. In order to have organized chaos, the rules have to be enforced.

1. Explain and demonstrate certain commands that are to challenge them as they jog around the gym.
   - Bounce and catch the ball with two hands.
   - Dribble the ball with one hand.
   - Alternate the dribbling from right hand to left hand.
   - Air-dribble the ball (throwing the ball up in the air and catching it with two hands).
   - Air-dribble the ball, alternating tossing the ball with the right hand to left hand.
   - Carry the ball and shoot at possible goals located around the gym.
   - Circle the ball around the waist.
   - Change directions. Never have the students attempt these challenges while jogging backward.

2. There are patterns in this game. Ask the students to choose the order of the challenges they do with the ball. This helps them to develop a sense of ownership with regard to their activities. (You can choose the challenges you want them to choose from by just demonstrating those specific challenges.) This activity is a very good sequencing exercise. When the pattern is chosen, the students are told that when the music gets softer it will be time to start the next challenge, and so on.

3. Music is introduced while the students are moving in order to give them a rhythm to follow. The choice of music is crucial because the children must be able to relate to it without the tendency to get rowdy. This is the time to introduce them to the dance tempos you are going to teach. The music needs to be loud enough that students easily can hear the underlying beat.

4. When the music stops, all action with the balls must stop as well so that students can hear the next command. If a student does not stop the action, he will be given a stopper. Receiving a stopper means that one is forced to *stop* participating in the game. Stoppers are intended to make it possible to have a safe and successful challenge. Here are some activities that demand a stopper:
   - Not following the pattern
   - Not stopping the action of the ball
   - Allowing the ball to bounce on the floor
   - Horseplay

5. Have the students choose a connection and give the two partners one ball. As they are walking, have them do the following:
   - Toss the ball back and forth to each other and catch it.
   - Toss the ball and crisscross paths so as to change places.
   - Bounce the ball back and forth to each other.
   - Face each other and side-gallop while passing the ball back and forth.
   - Face each other and side-gallop while bounce-passing the ball back and forth.

6. Have students begin jogging while repeating the same actions. This is where the socialization process really begins.

7. Next, have them attach to one another in any manner they choose. This may take a minute because they will have to stop, communicate, and decide. Allow time for this but get them moving right away. They will choose the attachment that is comfortable for them. Once they start moving they will quickly see if their attachment works. Most of the time, they resort to holding hands. This is where they begin to subconsciously process that they can move together more easily with a partner by holding hands. Holding hands was not your idea but theirs!

▷ Teaching Tips

You will get a feeling for how much time to allow when the activity begins. You want them to have enough time to be successful but not so much time that they lose interest.

Roping Them In

Goal	Work with a partner.
Music	Choose music of various tempos that the children will readily relate to.
Formation	This activity is best performed in a gym or recreation facility. You will need a rope or some type of cord that is strong enough for students to pull without it breaking. It must be made out of a material that will not hurt their hands when holding on to it. Tie it together at the ends to form one continuous piece of material that is long enough for each student to hold with both hands, yet that still allows for there to be at least 24 inches (61 centimeters) between each child. Cotton rope from a hardware store at least one-half inch (1 centimeter) thick is very good.

▷ Procedure: Part A

1. The activity will begin when the students form a circle, alternating boys and girls, and are facing toward the center of the circle at least 24 inches (61 centimeters) apart.

2. Stoppers are to be discussed.
   - The rope is never to be put near the neck.
   - The rope is never to be wrapped around the arms or legs.
   - Your space is yours only.
   - Horseplay is unacceptable.

3. The direction in which the rope moves will give another indicator to the student which way to move while holding onto it and learning the steps.

4. Give verbal directions regarding the precise movement you want students to perform, and demonstrate it several times. Have the students model your movement.
   - Walk into the center of the circle and walk out backward.
   - Jump into the center of the circle, turn around, and hold the rope behind you with both hands as you then jump away from the center to the edge of the circle.
   - Jump again into the center of the circle.
   - Holding the rope with the right hand, release the left hand and turn to the left 90 degrees; the students will be facing clockwise.
   - Side-step four steps to the right—that is, toward the center of the circle—beginning with the right foot.

- Side-step four steps to the left—away from the center of the circle—beginning with the left foot.

- Students hold the rope with both hands, face the center of the circle, step with the left foot, and kick first the right and then the left leg four times.

- Have the students raise both hands while holding the rope and put it behind them at waist level. Note: students may need to let go with one hand. They have their back touching the rope and both hands are holding the rope. The main thing to remember is that students are concentrating on following your directions for the activity rather than on the idea of dancing. Marching music is a good choice for this first run-through because it has a very definite tempo.

5. Have the students stand around the circle, alternating boy–girl. Any dance step can be taught while holding on to the rope. I stress again, however, that you should not call these dance steps; they are patterns for running formations. Tell the students that there are patterns in math, sentence structure, and even ballgames. Use terminology that they know, and demonstrate the step-step-step-hop, step-step-step-hop, and step/hop-step/hop-step/hop-step/hop pattern that makes up the **schottische** step. Indicate that the step-step-step-hop is the same pattern used for a lay-up in basketball. Ask the students if they can think of other places where patterns are used.

6. Once the students have been exposed to the various patterns and had time to practice, they will be ready to put the steps to appropriate music. You can use Schottische music. Watch the reaction of the students.

▷ Procedure: Part B

1. The girls turn to the left, facing clockwise and holding the rope with their right hand. The boys turn to the right, facing counterclockwise and holding the rope with their left hand. (See figure 2.2.)

2. As this occurs the students will automatically be facing a partner of the opposite sex. Holding the rope will also act as a safety net, especially for those students who are timid and very unsure of how to do the formations. The students' confidence and success will be elevated to a level that will cause them to try even harder and want to learn more.

Figure 2.2   This formation is great for teaching any "same-same" or "opp-opp" dance step.

3. A same-same example would be the cha-cha. An opp-opp example would be a backward rock-step.

4. Some dance patterns will require partners who are facing each other to go in the same direction, meaning that when the girl is going backward the boy will be going forward at the same time. I simply call out, "Same-same," and they learn what to do with this command. This is the pattern of movement used, for example, in the cha-cha and the waltz.

5. Dance patterns can also require partners to face each other while moving in the opposite direction, meaning that the girl steps backward and the boy steps backward at the same time. I call out "opp-opp" in this situation. This is the pattern used in the jitterbug and the shag.

6. Play the selected music for the dance and have them indicate which one of them will be going in which direction. This will take a few minutes because they will have to take turns being the leader until both realize who the real leader is. The dominant dance partner will emerge through communication and trial and error. The students will be able to work together because the ground rules for how they are to proceed are already set.

▷ Procedure: Part C

1. It is now time to give students guided practice. Call out the steps and have the students follow your instructions and demonstration. Have the students practice for about two minutes on their own with their partner.

2. The music should be ready to go because the students will learn quickly. Start the music and call out, "Ready, set, jump in." This will make them start together and work to keep up.

3. There must be an orderly method of rotation so that they experience a new connection. I will say, for example, "Boys, rotate forward two places." All the boys will step to the right and pass two girls. The next girl will be the boys' new connection. The next time you can call for the girls to rotate. It is best when students do not know who rotates and to which position they are to move.

4. You can also have each student remember each connection by number order. They will have to communicate and remember who their first connection is, who their second connection is, and so on. Do not maintain the same connection for more than two or three minutes. The students should have as many connections as there are couples.

5. This rotation method becomes comfortable to them. They realize that they are not with the same connection for very long. They come to understand that they can last through a rotation without suffering embarrassment or "getting cooties." Most important, students' feelings will not be hurt. This is the time to discuss the importance of being courteous and complimentary, which is yet another socialization skill that is so crucial to learn.

▷ Procedure: Part D

1. Once the students learn the rotation routine, they will be ready for the fun to start. (There must be stoppers for this activity.) The teacher can call out, "Boys, connection 4." All the boys will step to the outside of the circle and jog around the circle in the direction they are facing until they get to the fourth girl they encounter. At the same time the girls are standing in their place holding the rope and waiting for their connection to arrive. Some of the students will try to pass other students; this is acceptable as long as they do not touch the other student or get into his or her space. This is a stopper. This rotation method will offer a fun fitness activity as well.

2. The teacher may then say, "Girls, connection 6." All the girls will step to the outside of the circle and follow the same rules of rotation as described in the last point. All children's numbers must be called. Take an index card and write the rotation down; that way there is no hesitation regarding what comes next. The children will be more excited with the organized dance game.

3. As the students become comfortable with this format, you will be able to teach them any dance. Eventually the day comes that you can forget the rope. You can have the students get in a circle, alternating boy–girl, and ask them to hold an imaginary rope. They will try to do the familiar. Before they realize it they will be holding hands in order to do what you ask successfully.

4. After you see this happen, stop the class and talk about how much easier it is to hold on to each other. Do not say, "Hold hands." Ask the class what makes doing the movements easier. Bring to their attention how stable holding others' hands makes them, how it increases their ability to guide one another, and that it enhances their capacity to sense what direction their connection is going. That way students work as a team and talk about the importance of teamwork. The lessons can go on and on. This is the time for the teacher to add anything that will enhance the students' socialization skills; it is a teachable moment. This transition away from using the rope is very easy. Since you used a confidence-building approach, the students will not even want the security the rope once provided. You have now removed their training wheels, so to speak.

▷ Teaching Tips

- The following little lesson has had a major impact on the students who have passed through our classes. You can have the students sit down while it takes place. Ask these questions and allow the students to answer aloud: How many days are in a week? How many hours are in a day? How many minutes are in an hour? How many seconds are in a minute? How many minutes are in a day? Answer for the students if they struggle. Next, ask this question: How long does a song last? An acceptable answer is generally between two and four minutes. Then say this with a very serious tone: "If you have all these minutes in your day, and you only have to dance with a connection for 30 to 60 seconds, is it worth hurting someone's feelings and making them feel of little worth because you refused to dance with them, made a face, or said something that hurt their feelings? I know I will see some major changes made and some great dance connections from now on because I believe you just hadn't taken the time to really think about this." This lesson truly does reap great benefits.

- Once the students have had exposure to the circle rope, it will be easy for the class to get into the correct formation, alternating boy–girl and lining up face to face. The person each student is facing is her or his first connection. While the rope is still being used, the boy releases his right hand, reaches over to the part of the rope that is in front of his connection, and takes it in his hand. The girl does the same with her left hand. They keep the remaining hand on the rope. This is the perfect setup for teaching any opp-opp dance. Teach the dance step and watch the students thrive. When it is time to rotate, the students simply release the rope, rotate to the next connection, and connect as before. When the students get really familiar with this rotation pattern, mix up the connection numbers and watch them work together to get back to the connection you called. The students end up having their hands right beside each other. Eventually they will find that it is easier to just simply hold hands because you have them moving and dancing and moving and dancing. They get so involved that they don't even think about that stuff.

Create-a-Dance Cards: The CDC System

Goal   Create-a-Dance Cards provide another way to make the creation of rhythmic aerobic routines and dance very simple. They are extremely workable.

Music   Any music composed of 4, 8, or 16 counts will be suitable for this activity. Students can understand these counts quite easily. By using music with a definite beat, the students can concentrate on the movement and not really have to focus on the counting.

Formation   Prepare dance cards. On one side of each card, the dance step will be written. The other side will contain the description of the step and an explanation of how to do the movement. There is a list of dance movements and steps in the glossary that will make it easy for you to create your cards that fit with your students' reading and comprehension level. Once ready for the classroom, divide the class into small clusters of four, six, or eight students. Uneven numbers are okay too.

▷ Procedure

This procedure will give you thousands of combinations that will enhance a dance or exercise class. It also will prevent boredom from taking over. You can take this idea to another level by adding props to be used in correspondence with the movement or having the students add a different variation.

This approach to creating your own dances or rhythmic movement routines has proven successful and will yield magnificent results. At the same time, you and your students are learning skills beyond just combining moves that work.

1. When the music has been selected and analyzed, as described in chapter 1, choose a card at random or ask students to pick their own cards. It is better to use easier steps at first so that students can master them before moving on.

2. Add a more challenging movement or step during the next class; continue adding and changing the routine until the students have reached the level of competence that you desire.

3. Diagrams also can be drawn to add clarity to the steps.

4. To make sure that your students are successful with the step, review the count and practice with the music (see figure 2.3). Try the step with the introduction, a particular verse, the chorus, or an instrumental segment.

Figure 2.3   Sample CDC card.

5. Once students are comfortable, have them work in groups. Each student should select a movement card. That movement will be his or her contribution to the routine. In each cluster, have the students decide how many times to do the movement, in what order to arrange the movement, the formation for the routine, and the objective of the routine.

▷ Teaching Tips

- Not only can you use dance steps in your creations, but you can use sport steps as well. For example, dribbling a basketball requires good timing and rhythm. By using music to maintain a definite tempo for every bounce, the student creates a pattern that is consistent. The unconscious success will enable the student to transfer this skill to the game. The same principle holds true for the **pivot step** in basketball, the drop kick in soccer, the punt in football, and the three-step approach and release in bowling. These and other such sport skills can be done to music. What better way could you choose to improve a student's timing and rhythm!

- Music selection is crucial because music is a primary source of motivation for students. Motivation will determine the success of the activity. As you will discover, there are as many unique routines as there are groups. The class can learn each group's routine. This activity alone could last for two weeks. The students will feel that their contributions are worthwhile, and both you and the students will experience real success. This activity can even give you, the teacher, greater confidence, which can lead you to want to teach dance even more enthusiastically.

▷ Variation

This variation adds a twist to the CDC system.

Music

Choose an instrumental selection. Seasonal music adds variety to this rhythmic activity.

Props

Students love to have props that add to their creativity. To prepare for this activity, collect all kinds of gym equipment that will be easy to use as props for the students to rhythmically create movements and patterns. Initially, the number of props should equal the number of students in your class. After each movement or pattern, take away two props so that two students end up performing the activity together.

Procedure

Make 4-inch by 6-inch (10-centimeter by 15-centimeter) cards that list basic locomotor skills, combination skills, and selected dance steps (refer to the glossary) on one side and are blank on the other. Use the cards to create a dance that uses the props you collected.

Teaching Tips

Make sure you start off with simple locomotor skills to create a successful adventure. Then add some combinations and, finally, selected dance steps. Each time reduce the number of props by two or four in order to have everyone end up with a connection. Make sure the props are used in an appropriate way to ensure safety.

Step Stations

Goal   This is a great fitness activity as well as an excellent way to learn dance steps and combination movements. This activity will allow for some creativity; boredom does not stand a chance.

Formation   Stations.

▷ Procedure

1. Put the name of the dance steps and the directions on poster-board-size cards. Also, include the mode of movement to the next station on the cards. Teaching combination moves by placing these cards on the wall enhances students' reading ability, their skill in following directions, their confidence with problem solving, and their ability to successfully perform the desired skill. Having a lesson plan that indicates which dances you will teach for the next week helps you decide which dance steps you will want to choose. By having the students learn the steps in a nonthreatening activity, the dance will come together much faster and leave very little idle time. Students who are engaged are happier students.

2. There should be eight stations, and selecting the eight groups of students who will be working together can be a math activity in itself. If there are 32 students in the class, there will be 4 students at each station working together. Their challenge is to hop to the station of their choice with the understanding that only four students can be at each station. If a student arrives at a station and there are already four students there or if there is a tie between two students going to a particular station, they have to decide who stays and who goes to another station.

3. Using music is not necessary when students are trying to learn the steps. After about six minutes, turn on medium-speed music, and they will automatically start making the steps go along with the music. You want to give the students enough time to learn the step, but you do not want to give them too much time to start playing around and losing interest.

4. When the music stops the students are to side-slide to the next step station. The order in which the steps are learned is not important; allowing students to choose their destination will give them some feeling of control. This has proven to be very effective. Getting to all eight stations in one class period may not even be possible.

5. After the students have been to all the stations, ask them if they are ready for a challenge. They will be very positive and will want to have their efforts tested. Present the dance they will be performing and give them some information about it. Use the music they practiced with since it is familiar to them, then change the music to something new. You can watch the students' success unfold. Change the music yet again. The students will realize that it will not make any difference what music you choose; they will be successful because they have learned the steps. They will be very proud.

6. To add a different dimension, have the directions on a poster-board-size card that includes the combination steps provided in this chapter. This would be an added challenge, but make sure that students have first mastered the single steps.

7. After students have learned the combination steps, have the groups create and present a dance of their own. Allow them to teach it to the others in the class, and watch their confidence level rise.

▷ Teaching Tips

Students will begin to take ownership in their creation and will want to be successful. Showing your enthusiasm and excitement about their creations will have the class cheering each other on!

Connect and Disconnect

Goal   Rhythmic activities are a wonderful vehicle for this. The following method can take the trauma out of socializing. When you ask students to get a partner and hold hands, you may have asked them to do the worst thing in the whole world. Therefore, make getting a partner a grand thing to do.

Formation Invite the students to sit on the floor in a cluster, not in any specific formation.

▷ Procedure

1. Ask them to define the word *connect*. Then ask the students to define *disconnect*.

2. Now let the students demonstrate the terms. Have one student turn to a classmate and ask him or her to connect his or her index fingers by touching only the fingertips. This person becomes the student's first connection. Ask the students to disconnect their index fingers. (Holding hands is not considered cool, especially in grades 6 through 8. You have remedied that problem by not asking them to hold hands, but you have allowed them comfortably to identify a partner.)

3. The class is now ready for the adventure of connecting with a specific person without holding hands. If there are an uneven number of students, allow one group to have a connection with three students. This way, no one is left out or embarrassed. Say aloud, "Connect with your first connection," and the students will find a partner immediately. Say aloud, "Disconnect," and the students will disconnect their index fingers. Make sure that the students remember who their first connection is.

4. Now say aloud, "Connect with a second connection," and the students will find a new partner with whom to touch index fingers. This activity can continue until you have as many connections as you have activities.

5. What will you do with these connections? Begin teaching rhythmic activities. Turn on music that your class can relate to and that is medium paced—120 BPM is good—for the first connection partners. Have them perform five or six activities, such as these:

   • First connection partners cross-clap their hands.

   • Second connection partners cross-kick their legs. Partners face each other. They touch index fingertips from both hands. They then kick with the right foot crossing in front of the left foot and then with the left foot crossing in front of the right. This way they are kicking in opposite directions and never colliding or touching each other with their kicks.

   • Third connection partners do the bump. They swing their hips and bump them together.

   • Fourth connection partners do the elbow swing. They swing with their elbows locked for four counts one way and then reverse direction.

   • Fifth connection partners do the cha-cha.

▷ Teaching Tips

- The concept of connection lets you teach many skills, using equipment (balls, hoops, scarves) as well as basic or creative movement. Since students are partners for a very short time, they can learn to be comfortable with many other students.
- The process is a grand memory exercise. Try some other music that is faster, such as 150 BPM, to practice this connect and disconnect activity and to emphasize remembering the connections. Add some combinations: boy–girl, three-person, four-person, two boy–two girl, and so on. This will involve the children in paying attention to directions and not to potential partners. They will be eager to get anyone to connect with so they can get the task right and please the teacher.

Connections

Goal	Work with a partner.
Music	The music should be fun and enjoyable for the students.
Formation	Give the students a basketball, soccer ball, volleyball, or playground ball. Have them get in a line, alternating boy–girl, while holding a ball.

▷ Procedure

1. Have boys step forward and turn to their right. The girl that is in front of each boy will be his first connection.

2. Have the students hold their ball at chest level and touch their connection's ball.

3. Give the instructions for the dance. The method of rotation is to have the girls move to the right one boy. This will create the students' second connection, and so on.

4. Once everyone has been through the line and everyone has the respective connections, it is time to start mixing up the order of the connection numbers. The music should be playing. When it stops the students are asked to either rotate or shoot the ball into a goal that you have set up. Each connection has two chances to make the goal. If the partners in the connection make one or both of the shots, they are still in the game. If they miss both, they have to put the ball in a ball barrel and go to the next connection called. Once the partners have to turn in their ball, they will be asked to hold hands. Having the balls as the median makes this dance a game, and the balls will start to phase out.

5. Keep the music going and watch the fun. The line disappears and a dance appears. The students are all over the area having fun—dancing. Stop the dance and start the game again. They will love this and eagerly participate. This activity will probably take two classes to get the structure you need, but it is well worth it.

▷ Variations

1. This activity easily can be matched with many of the dances that you will want to teach. It is also very good to use to teach various dance steps, especially line dances. Just follow the same format by having each connection do the step you want to be done. Put students in the proper order. When the dance steps are put together the dance is already familiar and the rest is history.

2. To change the median, use tennis balls. The students have to concentrate to keep the tennis balls together. Place a target very high on the area wall. It can be a piece of paper, an actual bull's-eye target, or anything the students can try to hit with the tennis ball. The same concept applies and the rules remain the same, but they have to get the ball

back to be able to throw again. They will try to throw really hard. That is why the target is very high. You may have to have the custodian use a ladder to place the target. Have them almost as high as the rafters. When they miss, the ball goes away.

3. Place five-gallon buckets around the outside of the basketball court against the wall. The number of buckets is based on the number of students. Using a tennis ball as the median, the same concept can be used again. This time if they lose contact with their connection, they have to try to toss the ball in the bucket. If they miss, they must go find another place on the floor to move. Both have to get the tennis ball in the bucket. All the time the music is being changed; if the students guess the dance and can do the steps in a connection, they get their tennis ball back and are permitted to start over. They love this. This is a real challenge and should be used only after the students have a good grasp of the dance steps. You will find that the students help each other to succeed. You will experience communication and socializing at its best.

4. Tennis shoes worn by young children have very little wear and tear because they are worn for such a short time. I have been collecting them by having my students bring them in from home. There should be a pair of shoes for every two students. In other words, if you have 20 students, you will need 10 pairs of shoes. Create cards with one dance step and its description. Have the cards on the bottom bleacher (if you are in a gym) or on the floor turned face down. The students take one lap around the gym. As each student jogs by, she or he picks up a card, reads it, and studies it while jogging. The teacher puts all the shoes in a pile on the gym floor while the students are jogging and selecting their cards. When the music stops, each student is to walk to the pile and pick a shoe. When the music starts again, the students must jog around until they find the person with the matching shoe. Whoever has the match becomes the student's 1 connection for the next rhythmic activity. (There is one serious stopper that must be emphasized for this activity. The students must *walk* to the pile of shoes.) The students with the matching pair of shoes find a place where they want to practice. While they are going to find their workplace, they are to place the pair of shoes in a designated spot. The music is turned on again and they are to teach others their step. While the students are working with their connection, the teacher takes half the pairs of shoes and places them in the middle of the gym floor. When the music stops, one person from the team *walks* to the center of the gym and gets one shoe. When the music starts, the teams must find the match to its shoe. When the team of two students finds its match, a team of four students is formed; they combine their dance steps to form a dance or an aerobic routine. Make sure the students understand what is in a routine. Choose music with a moderate tempo for this activity. The students do well with this activity and there is very little down time. You have to be very organized.

▷ SUMMARY

It's not so difficult to get students to the point that they are willing to loosen up, dance a little, and actually touch each other. Your challenge is to be the excited actor on stage and to show enthusiasm for their accomplishments. The teacher is responsible for their success as social candidates to their peers. What kid doesn't want to be popular? Being popular could very well be the driving force for their achievement. Remember, the goal is not to make students into perfect dancers by the end of your class; it is to have a wonderful journey along the way!

CHAPTER 3

Rhythmic Games and Activities

This chapter of rhythmic activities is designed for you, the teacher of rhythmic activity and dance. It is intended to introduce rhythms and dance movements to students of all abilities in a no-fault, nonthreatening atmosphere. This chapter contains enough warm-up activities to take any program through years of success.

Many opportunities are provided to reinforce and improve the basic skills needed for rhythmic activities and dance. The activities will assist your dance program, while stimulating students to develop at their own pace. Dance skills can be enhanced when students do not recognize that they are working on dance skills. The activities in this chapter will motivate your students to work on dance skills without any risk of embarrassment.

As you begin using these activities, you will notice opportunities to integrate subjects like math, social studies, science, and language arts with your physical education classes. Take advantage of these connections and help your students see them as well.

Counting, adding, and subtracting occur in Eight, Four, Two; in the circuits; and in Countdown. Games like Happy Heart and Veins and Arteries provide teachers with an opening to examine some basics of the physiology of exercise with their students. Fitness in America could lead to a lesson in social studies. Parts of Speech and Partner Over and Under allow language arts to be integrated with our teaching in the physical education classroom. These activities are the obvious places to integrate material. The only limitations for integration are those we place on ourselves.

You will recognize familiar activities as well as a variety of new ones to expand your students' dance skills. All are designed to promote the development of dance skills and fitness. The familiar activities have been reshaped into dance-related fitness activities. This new look to old activities makes them appealing for all age groups. Give your students an opportunity to add new ways to integrate. The feeling of ownership makes students feel important.

▷ FROM OLD TO NEW

Although you will recognize many of these activities immediately, look closely because they may not be what you think they are. Each one has been modified with a focus on the elements of dance. Each one reinforces dance skills and fitness simultaneously. Whether the changes appear small or large, you will be able to focus on new directions through some old organizational patterns.

This chapter is arranged into four categories of activities: large-group, small-group, circuits, and games. Large-group activities may lead to high-quality movement, as do the small-group activities, depending on how they are used. The circuits provide opportunities to practice dance skills in nonthreatening environments, and the games move to a higher level application of a rhythmic dance activity.

Within these four categories are many activities that will be appropriate for your program. You can enliven your classes by applying basic dance skills and using new and challenging conditions. Use these activities and modify them to your needs. With slight changes, you could move one to a different category.

The activities are listed in their respective groups. Individual descriptions follow. Try them as openings and closings to your lessons. They may fit as the middle of your lessons, depending on your focus. When you are working with students who are just starting out, the focus will be on the locomotor basics of walking, running, leaping, jumping, and hopping in a rhythmic manner. When these have been mastered, you will move to combination moves like skipping, sliding, galloping, doing the **polka**, and so on. When you are teaching students with intermediate abilities, your focus will be first on the combination movements, then shift to the selected dance steps suggested in chapter 1. With advanced students, the focus shifts to mastery of the selected dance steps found in the first chapter. As you select activities from this chapter for your program, be aware of this progression.

▷ MUSIC SELECTION

Selecting music is a critical element in all the following activities. Each activity is designed to improve the students' rhythm and dance development. The intent is to increase overall coordination, agility, stamina, and power to maximize and ensure total physical development. It is the combination of rhythmic movement with fitness activities that raises motivation and frees movement more than many other fitness activities. Different tempos and types of music will promote and provide different levels of development.

To get students hooked on the activity, select music in the beginning that students will like. Later you can vary the music to enhance the overall quality of your students' movements. Getting the participants hooked on an activity is the critical element. Always remember this analogy when selecting music: When you go fishing, do you bait the hook with what you want or what the fish wants? Selecting music is similar. Once you've hooked the audience, you can play it any way you like. You can take everyone on a journey to being a better, more balanced, and more confident rhythmic mover.

As you introduce these activities into your program, be sure to select rhythmic movements that are developmentally appropriate for your group of students. Basics are basics. (Refer to the section on rhythmic terms in chapter 1 for a refresher.) Begin with locomotor movements, progress to combination movements, and then select dance steps to use in your lessons. Following this progression will ensure that all students progress to higher levels of mastery.

As your students improve, vary directions, extensions, props, and partnering. This will enhance your students' growth in rhythmic dance skills.

▷ LARGE-GROUP ACTIVITIES

The selection of large-group activities covered here should fill the needs of your classes. We have chosen these activities and modified them primarily to provide your students with activities to help develop total fitness and learn or reinforce a variety of dance skills.

Agility Runs

Goal   Students match their movements in and out of markers or between lines to the rhythms, using many different dance steps.

Formation   This is determined by the way the activity is designed.

▷ Procedure

This activity is done in and out of markers or between lines, with different dance movements being performed (see figure 3.1). It is a low-cost activity with a high return. By using some locomotor, combination, and dance steps from the rhythmic terms section in chapter 1, students will that find Agility Runs become more challenging. They can greatly increase growth and learning over the long term.

▷ Teaching Tips

Provide rhythmic accompaniment for the movements, particularly music that students really like. It should have rhythms to which they can match their movements.

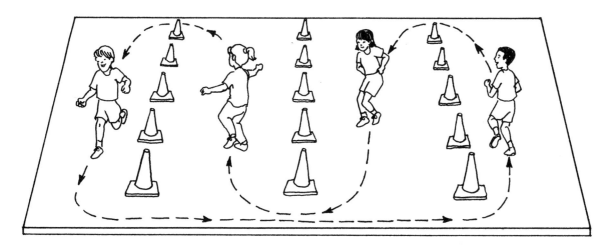

Figure 3.1   Students performing Agility Runs.

Big Circle

Goal   Students experience large-group participation and develop a variety of dance skills.

Formation   Students form a big circle holding hands and move as directed (see figure 3.2).

Figure 3.2   The Big Circle here moves clockwise.

▷ Procedure

Give cues for movements that build around the rhythmic terms. Also, as in the previous activity, add music that will elicit different types of movements from your students.

▷ Teaching Tips

Direct students to circle left and right, move in and out, and change tempos as you choose for each situation.

Down the Room in Waves

Goal   Students improve locomotor and combination movements with and without equipment while combining sport skills with dance movements.

Formation   Students line up along one side of a room.

▷ Procedure

Move the length of the room in large waves (see figure 3.3). Practice locomotor, combination, and other dance steps over the length of the room. Include equipment, such as balls and ropes. Encourage students to make up variations on the basics. Don't forget to combine sports skill movements with dance movements.

▷ Teaching Tips

Focus on basic locomotor movements with beginning students, combinations with intermediate-level students, and selected dance steps for advanced students.

Figure 3.3   In Down the Room in Waves students can choose, among other things, to hop, slide, run, walk, or gallop.

Eight, Four, Two

Goal   Students experience large-group participation and develop a variety of dance skills.

Formation   Students are spread out in the room with everyone facing front.

▷ Procedure

After a designated dance movement is performed eight times, everyone makes a quarter-turn to the right and repeats the movement eight times (see figure 3.4). Repeat with a quarter-turn right (students are now facing the back of class), and have students do it again. When the students make one more quarter-turn to face the front, repeat all movements four times, and follow the preceding sequence. Then repeat the movements two times through the entire sequence: thus the name Eight, Four, Two.

▷ Teaching Tips

- Use any number of movements—from one to several.
- Let students contribute suggestions for the activity.
- Always use music.
- Post moves for the day on the third wall that the group faces so that they can continue without stopping.

▷ Suggested Moves

Begin with basic locomotor movements, then combinations, then the selected dance steps from the first chapter. This should be the progression to follow when organizing your program.

Figure 3.4 Students start out facing front and do eight repetitions before making a quarter-turn right.

Basic Locomotor Movements

- Walk
- Run
- Leap
- Jump
- Hop

Combinations

- **Slide** and lunge
- **Gallop** and leap
- **Skip** and jump
- Polka and turn

Selected Dance Steps

- Step touches
- Vines
- Pivots
- Push-ups
- Knee lifts
- Sit-ups or curl-ups
- **Bleking** steps
- Schottische steps
- Lunges
- Cha-cha
- **Lindy** steps
- Jazz circles
- Jazz walk

Fitness Around the World

Goal   Students participate in an interdisciplinary unit that combines dance with social studies, language arts, economics, math, and science. Students can learn countries or states and their spellings, their capitals, poetry alliterations, science terms, classical music appreciation, creative imagining of terrain, as well as a variety of dance movements. The exercises are to be interpreted by the students, and they may do them under the guidance of the teacher.

Formation   Students set up stations representing their chosen countries or states. The class is presented as a circuit-training unit.

▷ Procedure

The directions for this activity are very flexible. Each student stays at the station for a specific time, from one to three minutes. Classical music with this activity is a great motivator and helps to incorporate cultural arts into the physical education program. Each student can draw a country or state, cut it out, and mount it on a piece of cardboard. She or he can draw what the place produces and label its important areas, capital, recreation facilities, and professional athletic teams. These visual aids widen the scope of the student's education by integrating physical education with other aspects of the curriculum.

▷ Teaching Tips

The following are examples of different countries and the American states and what can be done at each station (see figure 3.5). This activity allows you to introduce classical music into the physical education curriculum. The "Hooked on Classics" collection is ideal for Fitness Around the World.

Figure 3.5   Playing Fitness Around the World helps students associate movements with the states in the United States and thereby learn state names and their capitals.

▷ Suggested Moves

The names beside each state or country simply serve as a starting point. They promote problem solving by allowing the students to create the movements. The names serve only as stimulators of ideas. The students will develop the movements and later create new names as well. Maybe the students could create a motion that indicates a state product or act out the recreational activity for which the state is noted. The student could display the state's shape by walking out its outline. There are many activities that could be incorporated here. It can be used for every grade level, making the activity either simple or complex. Children will have ideas that inspire more excitement and spontaneity in their actions. Let the children create and be free.

Countries

- China Curl-Ups
- Japanese Jumping Jacks
- Italian Inverted Push-Ups
- South African Stand-Ups
- British Bunny Boops
- Germany Gym Jumps
- Austrian Animal Advances
- Switzerland Swishes
- Azerbaijan Aviator Leaps
- Angola Aerobic Airplanes
- Turkey Tiny-Tucks
- Korea Kute Kurls

States of America

- Alabama Arm Crosses
- Alaska Alley Cat Leaps
- Arizona Airplanes
- Arkansas Arm Circle
- California Cancan
- Colorado Charleston
- Connecticut Crunches
- Delaware Dips
- Florida Frog Leaps
- Georgia Gallops
- Hawaii High Kicks
- Idaho Idle Walk
- Illinois Isolated Ice Skating
- Indiana Indy Jogs
- Iowa Inverted Push-Up
- Kansas Kicks
- Kentucky Karate Kicks
- Louisiana Lunges
- Maine Motor Bikes
- Maryland Mambo
- Massachusetts Magic Step
- Michigan Muscle Man
- Minnesota Mini Kicks
- Mississippi Mash Potatoes
- Missouri Moon Walks
- Montana Mountain Climbers
- Nebraska Knee Lifts
- Nevada Knee Bends
- New Hampshire Nervous Jumps
- New Jersey Neck Stretchers
- New Mexico Nonsense Walks
- New York Nose Wiggles
- North Carolina Knuckle Bends
- North Dakota Knee Slaps
- Ohio Over and Under
- Oklahoma Over-Jumps
- Oregon Overflows
- Pennsylvania Push-Ups
- Rhode Island Rope Jumper
- South Carolina Standing Scale
- South Dakota Sit-Ups
- Tennessee Toe Touches
- Texas Tuck Jumps
- Utah Umbrella Turns
- Vermont Vertical Jumps
- Virginia V-Sits
- Washington Waltz
- West Virginia Waves
- Wisconsin Wind Mills
- Wyoming Waddles

Follow the Leader

Goal Students learn the basics, then gradually develop the more complex dance steps.

Formation One large group, small groups, or partners move around the room and change the effort qualities (time, force, space, and flow) of their dance movements according to your directions (see figure 3.6).

Figure 3.6   The teacher as facilitator in Follow the Leader.

▷ Procedure

Everyone can follow you, or several leaders can be selected. Change leaders when you feel it is appropriate.

▷ Teaching Tips

When using this activity to begin a rhythmic activity and dance program, focus on the basics. Then gradually move to more complex dance steps.

Four Wall

Goal	Students experience large-group participation and develop a variety of dance skills.
Formation	This activity is a variation on Eight, Four, Two. Students go into the room and start walking, jogging, or practicing a dance step.

▷ Procedure

On your signal to begin, students move to the center of the room and face the front wall: wall A (see figure 3.7). Begin at level A1 (as described in the following list of suggested moves) with medium-speed music, perhaps 120 BPM. On your signal, students turn to face the wall on their right: wall B, and do the activity for level B1. Continue turning right on the signal, and move down the list—C1, D1, A2, B2, and so on—until you complete all movements on it or you want to stop.

▷ Teaching Tips

Start with the basic locomotor movements, then progress through the movements as previously described.

Figure 3.7   Four Wall allows your students to explore many levels of dance and movement.

▷ Suggested Moves

Wall A

- A1: **Step-touch**
- A2: **Jazz square** going both left and right
- A3: Skipping
- A4: **Double Lindy**

Wall B

- B1: **Step-kick**
- B2: Sliding
- B3: Schottische
- B4: **Triple Lindy**

Wall C

- C1: **Side touch**
- C2: Galloping
- C3: **Two-step**
- C4: Shag step

Wall D

- D1: **Heel shuffle**
- D2: Running
- D3: **Cha-cha**
- D4: Foxtrot

Friday Roll Call Jog and Dance

Goal   Students see how many minutes of dance or how many laps they can run while waiting for class to start.

Formation   Students do a 5- to 10-minute run or dance for their warm-up (see figure 3.8).

Figure 3.8   Having students play a game instead of waiting around at the start of a class period gives them an incentive to get on task quickly.

▷ Procedure

1. Instruct students to run or dance as they enter the classroom.
2. Take roll call or other similar start-of-class activities.
3. When it is time to stop, have students respond with the number of laps or the amount of time that they ran or danced on each Friday. This will help students reinforce the importance of being active.

▷ Teaching Tips

Let students keep their own records of the number of laps they ran or the amount of time they danced.

Grids

Goal   Students maximize all components of development in the dance and games skill areas.

Formation   Grids are squares 20 to 30 feet on a side marked off with cones or lines (see figure 3.9).

Figure 3.9 Grids provide excellent boundaries for personal or group choreography.

▷ Procedure

Students move according to the task you set. Squares can be used either by individual students or shared by more than one student. The tasks follow the familiar progression from basic to more complex. With students of lower grades, start with the locomotor movements, go to the combinations, and then proceed to the selected dance steps.

▷ Teaching Tips

Review the basics at all grade and ability levels.

Object Manipulation

Goal   Students use dance moves in and through the teaching station with their choice of an object: balls, ropes, hoops, beanbags, or ribbons.

Formation   This is determined by the design of the teaching stations.

▷ Procedure

Vary the tasks you ask the students to perform. For example, first ask them to move directly through the open spaces in the teaching station while dribbling a ball; second, ask them to move indirectly through the open spaces while dribbling the ball (see figure 3.10).

▷ Teaching Tips

By varying the elements of time, force, space, and flow, the movement task can be given a new meaning.

Figure 3.10 Object Manipulation has a flexible formation, and it can be tailored to your methods of teaching.

One Move After

Goal Students at the K-2 level master the basic locomotor skills and as many of the combinations as possible; at the 3-5 level, students master the combination movements and some of the selected dance steps; at the 6-8 level, students master all the previous material and as many of the selected dance steps as possible.

Formation Open.

Figure 3.11 Students do hops while the teacher introduces skips.

▷ Procedure

Either you or a student leader repeats a dance pattern several times, then stops. The group begins performing this movement. The leader starts a second dance movement. When the leader begins a third dance movement, the group switches to the second movement. This continues for as long as you want (see figure 3.11 on page 49). The activity gets its name because the group is always doing the move after the leader has completed it. This is a great activity for introducing movements, reviewing movements, and promoting leadership in your classes.

▷ Teaching Tips

Use a variety of music to promote a wide range of rhythmic movements.

Open Movement

Goal	Students demonstrate quality movement in and through the open spaces of the teaching station.
Formation	Open.

▷ Procedure

You direct nonlocomotor, locomotor, combination, and dance movements through the entire teaching area (see figure 3.12). Insert changes in the types of movements performed and in their time, force, space, and flow. Combinations like running and jumping, as well as moving and stopping to work on specific areas of the body, also may be included. The focus is on quality dance movement within the set task range.

▷ Teaching Tips

You may set tasks like the following: Walk through the room's empty spaces in direct pathways in time with the music. Walk and turn as you move through the spaces in time with the music. Walk, turn, and lead with different body parts through the spaces. Skip through the spaces in time with the music. Add a turn to this skip as you move through the spaces. Create movement phrases in groups of four with walks and skips. Smooth this sequence with short running steps instead of walking.

Figure 3.12 Randomly galloping is an appropriate open movement for this activity.

Parts of Speech

Goal   Students experience an interdisciplinary study unit combining physical activity and language arts to enliven parts of speech.

Formation   Open.

▷ Procedure

Use adverbs, verbs, and prepositions for this activity. These words are defined as follows:

- Adverb—a word used to modify a verb, adjective, or another adverb (quickly, slowly, happily, or sadly)
- Verb—a word that expresses action (run, jump, slide, or leap)
- Preposition—a word that reveals the relationship of a noun, pronoun, verb, or modifiers in a sentence to another noun, pronoun, verb, or modifier (on, off, over, under, around, and through)

Make cards large enough so students can read them from 25 yards (23 meters) away (see figure 3.13). Make the adverb cards one color, the verb cards a different color, and the preposition cards a third color. Write the parts of speech and the words on the cards. Three students can hold up a card, and the students participating can read and follow the direction that the card indicates. For example, the adverb *happily,* the verb *run,* and the preposition *along* might be a combination that appears.

Figure 3.13   This game enables students to have fun while making a connection between physical activity and the parts of speech.

▷ Teaching Tips

- Change the cards when the students are successfully doing what they describe. This will give them a variety of actions to perform and a hilarious interpretation of some movements. Turn on the music. This is a great way to reinforce the qualities of dance.
- This activity offers a tremendous opportunity for creative movement and dance and for learning these three parts of speech.

A List of Adverbs to Help Get Started

rapidly, calmly, cheerfully, lively, happily, suddenly, teasingly, sneakily, quietly, loudly, slyly, furtively, forcefully, swiftly, slowly, quickly, foolishly, laughingly, busily, beastly, sternly, stiffly, patiently, playfully, merrily

A List of Verbs to Help Get Started

jump, sit, run, jog, hop, skip, twirl, leap, gallop, catch, crawl, stumble, pedal, roll, shake, cha-cha

A List of Prepositions to Help Get Started

about, above, across, along, among, around, behind, before, below, beneath, beside, between, beyond, down, through, from, inside, into, near, off, on, out, over, past, toward, under, up

- To motivate the students, add classical music, current music, or instrumental music with a definite beat. A natural follow-up would be for students to add nouns, pronouns, and adjectives to form sentences and to combine them to form paragraphs.

Run, Stop, Pivot

Goal   Students run, stop, and pivot through open spaces (see figure 3.14). Open spaces are simply spots where no one else is dancing.

Formation   Open.

Figure 3.14   Run, Stop, Pivot can improve students' fitness and provide them a foundation for many other dance activities.

▷ Procedure

This activity is basic to many of the dances and games we play today. As the name implies, it involves running, stopping, and pivoting through open spaces. Run, Stop, Pivot can also be done with a partner. The partners are to stay together as if they are guarding one another or dancing with each other. Using partners is also a great way to practice and improve both of these skills simultaneously.

▷ Teaching Tips

With different kinds of music, use the movements to help develop the participants' dance skills to their highest levels. As you plan, remember to progress according to your students' abilities. Move from locomotor skills, to combinations, to selected dance steps.

Talking Drum

Goal   Students move to the beat of a drum or other percussion instrument.

Formation   Open.

▷ Procedure

Students follow the talking drum, changing movements according to the speed and intensity of the beats (see figure 3.15). You can suggest movement changes in direction, level, pathways, body parts, and so on.

Figure 3.15   Moving to a drumbeat is a great way for students to learn new movements.

▷ Teaching Tips

Using equipment—such as balls, hoops, and ropes—would be a strong addition to this activity. Tell the students what movement to do, or have a student select the movement to do with your drumbeat. Practice all movements with even and uneven drumbeats.

Wall Work

Goal   Students develop strength and flexibility.

Formation   Students stand along the walls in your gyms, rooms, and buildings (see figure 3.16).

▷ Procedure

Use the walls for resistive work and stretching.

▷ Teaching Tips

Dance movements can be done between exercises to raise activity levels and to reinforce or teach dance movements. Follow the usual progression: locomotor movements, combinations, selected dance steps.

Figure 3.16   Walls offer a good surface to work on, and they allow several students to participate at the same time.

▷ SMALL-GROUP ACTIVITIES

As with the large-group activities, small-group activities assist you in meeting your fitness and dance needs. They have been modified to teach your students fitness and a variety of dance skills.

Group Creation

Goal   Students create a dance sequence using elements you suggest.

Formation   Open.

▷ Procedure

Use this as a culminating activity for the students. Groups of 2 to 10 students create a dance sequence using elements set out for them (see figure 3.17).

▷ Teaching Tips

After your students have practiced a number of the dance steps, instruct them to put these movements together in their own creative sequences.

Figure 3.17   Students hold hands and create a new shape from their first formation.

Lines and Leaders

Goal   Each student can be a leader to further develop and enhance dance skills.

Formation   Put the class in lines with about 5 feet (1.5 meters) between each person; the first person in each line faces those in his or her line and becomes its head or leader (see figure 3.18).

Figure 3.18   Jumping, sliding, and skipping are locomotor movements your students can use in Lines and Leaders.

▷ Procedure

Everyone gets to be a leader. The student at the front leads dance movements that have already been learned in class. On your signal, everyone rotates forward and the leader goes to the end of the line. The exercises continue. During rotation, everyone jogs in place until the new leader starts the next dance movement.

▷ Teaching Tips

You can determine the types of dance movements or can ask the students to select the movements they want to do. This is done with musical accompaniment. Again, follow the locomotor, combination, and selected dance step progression.

Partner Over and Under

Goal   Students develop movement skills through changing environments.

Formation   Open.

▷ Procedure

One partner moves over, under, around, and through the empty spaces formed by a bridge made by the other partner's body (see figure 3.19). A variation of this activity is to have movers go from one bridge to another.

▷ Teaching Tips

You can suggest changing how, where, and what occurs in a student's movement pattern to raise the quality of the overall movement. All movements in and through space should be dance movements.

Figure 3.19   One student crawls through another student's arched body. This activity can help students adapt their movements to other situations.

Small Circles

Goal   Students have an opportunity to develop leadership skills while improving rhythmic skills.

Formation   The students stand in circles (see figure 3.20).

Figure 3.20   Small circles allow for an intimate and confidence-building environment with less risk for the students.

▷ Procedure

Change leaders in the circles periodically to provide variety in the activity and the movements. The leader selects a dance movement to demonstrate; the students in the circle do the dance with rhythmic accompaniment.

▷ Teaching Tips

Remember to work progressively according to students' abilities. Reinforce locomotor movements, support combinations, and develop the selected dance steps along with everything else.

Tractor Treads

Goal	Students have an opportunity to develop leadership skills while improving rhythmic skills.
Formation	The students stand in oblong circles, like tractor treads, over the length of the teaching space (see figure 3.21).

▷ Procedure

Change leaders on the treads periodically to provide opportunities for all students to be in a leadership role. The leader has the opportunity to direct his or her particular group in accordance with the directions of the teacher, or the teacher can direct the leaders to change movements every time, or every other time, so that the tractor tread makes a complete cycle.

▷ Teaching Tips

Remember to work progressively according to students' abilities. Reinforce locomotor movements, support combinations, and develop the selected dance steps along with everything else. Don't forget to vary the tempo to enhance the level of learning of all the groups.

Figure 3.21 The oblong circles look like tractor treads.

▷ CIRCUITS

You might be wondering, "Circuits? In a book on rhythm and dance?" The answer is a definite yes! For instance, in every circuit that you design, there is a good reason to include a rhythms station. The travel from station to station can focus on rhythmic and dance movements. Another way to get rhythm and dance into your circuits is to come to the middle of the teaching area before switching stations and practice rhythmic dance movements. The following examples offer ideas to do what has just been discussed.

Circuit 1 (Stations 1-8)

Goal Students have an opportunity to learn activities that will help them develop and achieve total fitness as well as to learn and reinforce a variety of dance skills.

Formation Set up stations as shown in figure 3.22.

▷ Procedure

Instruct students to start walking, jogging, or practicing a dance step and then go to a station when the music changes and do the task posted there. Suggest no more than five people per station; do 1 to 10 repetitions of each exercise but no more than double the specified number. Instruct students to switch stations when you are ready. (Options: Go to the center of the room for 90 seconds of aerobic dance; practice locomotor or combination movements around the teaching area; practice selected dance steps to the next station.) Move around the room clockwise.

▷ Suggested Moves

Station 1: Abdominals

- Do curl-ups.
- Do full sit-ups.
- Perform knee-to-chest twists.

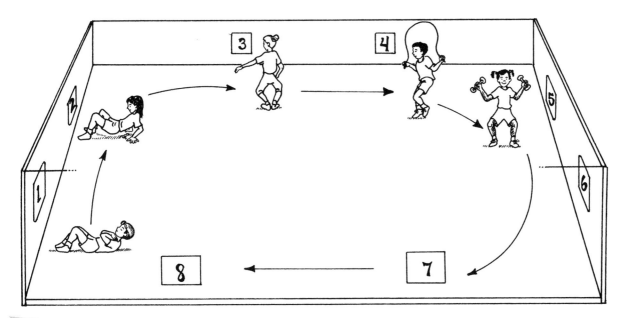

Figure 3.22 Students can do a number of movements at Circuit 1 stations, including abdominal crunches, crab push-ups, and pliés.

Station 2: Arms

- Do crab push-ups.
- Do pull-ups.

Station 3: Quadriceps

- Perform **pliés**.
- In plié position, bounce a ball off the wall up to 20 times.

Station 4: Jump Rope

- Use continuous movement forward and backward with varying patterns.
- Lay the rope in a straight line on the floor, then jump back and forth or sideways over it continuously.

Station 5: Upper Back and Rhomboids

- Standing with bent knees and legs in straddle position, do fly wings with weights up to 20 times.
- Standing with bent knees and legs in straddle position, do upright rows with weights up to 20 times.

Station 6: Chest

- Lie on a bench or the floor and do fly wings with weights up to 20 times.
- Do push-ups or modified push-ups (on knees) up to 20 times.

Station 7: Aerobic Dance Steps

- Gallop between markers.
- Slide between markers.
- Skip between markers.

Station 8: Line Touch

- Run back and forth between the lines, touching the line with the hand each time; do up to 20 repetitions.

- Variations: Use a different locomotor movement each time, use different combinations, or perform different dance steps.

▷ Teaching Tips

The rhythmic skills that can be reinforced during this activity are endless. Your choice should be based on both the grade and ability levels of your students, as discussed earlier.

Circuit 2 (Stations 1-8)

Goal Students have an opportunity to learn activities that will help them develop and achieve total fitness while also reinforcing a variety of dance skills.

Formation Set up stations as shown in figure 3.23.

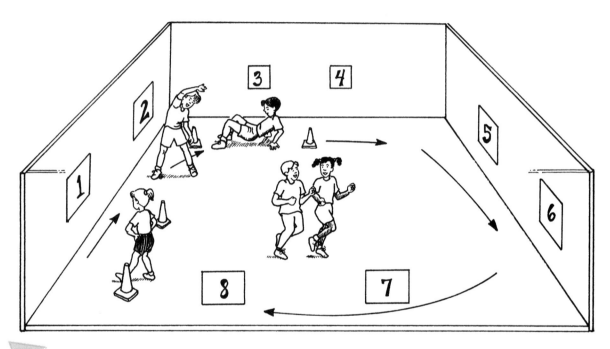

Figure 3.23 Circuit 2 stations like these give students the chance to work on flexibility, upper-body strength, and cardiovascular fitness.

▷ Procedure

Instruct students to start walking, jogging, or practicing a dance step. Then on a signal have them go to a station and do the activity. Suggest that there be no more than five people at any station. Have students switch stations on a signal or go to the center of the room for 90 seconds of aerobic dance between stations. Students should move around the room clockwise.

▷ Suggested Moves

Station 1: Shuttle Station

1. Move between the markers and touch an imaginary line between them.
2. Move forward, backward, and sideways while turning and changing patterns from, for example, the skip, to the gallop, to the Schottische, and so on. Focus on rhythmic elements at the appropriate level.

3. Repeat the sequences until a signal is given; then move to the next station. (Special note: Movement to the next station can include any of the rhythmic movements or can bring everyone to the center to practice any movements that you choose.)

Station 2: Flexibility—Hip Girdle Stretching

1. Select your own stretch.
2. Do a slow, gentle, static stretch.
3. Move to the next station on the signal.

Station 3: Crabwalk

1. Crabwalk between markers.
2. First go forward, then backward, then sideways.
3. Repeat until the next signal is given, then move to the next station.

Station 4: Jump and Reach

1. Practice jumping vertically, over and over.
2. Practice the standing long jump repeatedly, for distance.
3. Move to the next station on the signal.

Station 5: Sit-Ups

1. Use slow, continuous movement.
2. Do as many as possible; move to the next station on the signal.

Station 6: Flexibility—Shoulder Girdle Stretching

1. Select your own stretch.
2. Do a slow, gentle, static stretch.
3. Move to the next station on the signal.

Station 7: Walk on All Fours

1. Walk on all fours back and forth between the markers.
2. First go forward, then backward, then sideways.
3. Repeat until the next signal; then move to the next station.

Station 8: Rope Jumping

1. Turn the rope continuously until the next signal; use a variety of turns and jumps.
2. End the activity when the signal is given.

▷ Teaching Tips

As with the previous circuit, many opportunities exist to develop and reinforce the basic rhythmic and dance movements. Work progressively according to your students' abilities, first focusing on the locomotor skills, next emphasizing the combinations, and finally developing the selected dance steps and reviewing all that has preceded. By following this progression you will support your students' developmental needs.

Countdown

Goal   Students have an opportunity to learn activities that will help them to develop and achieve total fitness while also learning and reinforcing a variety of dance skills.

Formation Set up stations as shown in figure 3.24.

Figure 3.24 An activity set up in different stations can hold your students' attention as well as enhance their physical fitness.

▷ Procedure

Instruct students to start walking, jogging, or practicing a dance step around the outside of the room or the markers. On the signal, they work their way from a "Jog five laps" sign you have on display down to a "Walk one lap" sign. They should not do more than twice the suggested number of repetitions. Students work at their own pace.

▷ Suggested Moves

- Jog one lap or do aerobic dance for one minute.
- Jump rope forward up to 30 times.
- Jump rope backward up to 30 times.
- Jog two laps or do aerobic dance for two minutes.
- Balance on each leg for 15 seconds.
- Do mule kicks up to 15 times.
- Jog three laps or do aerobic dance for three minutes.
- Do a long sit with single-leg lifts up to 10 times for each leg.
- Sit and reach for your toes up to 10 times for each leg.
- Jog four laps or do aerobic dance for four minutes.
- Do up to 10 push-ups.
- Do up to 10 crab push-ups.
- Jog five laps or do aerobic dance for five minutes.
- Do up to 10 crunches.
- Do knee-to-chest twists up to 10 times on each side.

▷ Teaching Tips

Since this activity calls for the students to jog in between stations, this is an opportunity for them to practice locomotor skills, combinations, or selected dance steps according to where they are developmentally. The grade and ability levels of your students determine the appropriate rhythmic and dance elements to include at each station.

Four-Corner Rhythms

Goal   Students have an opportunity to learn activities that will help them develop and achieve total fitness while also learning and reinforcing a variety of dance skills.

Formation   Set up stations with one poster or sign in each corner of the designated exercise space.

▷ Procedure

In each corner of the teaching area is a task card giving directions for how to proceed to the next corner (see figure 3.25). Use music to stress the rhythmic performance of the movements. On your signal, the students go to one of the four corners of the teaching area, with no more than 10 students per corner. When the music starts, they move to the next corner one after another, traveling counterclockwise around the teaching area. They do the activities at level A the first time around (as described in what follows), level B the second time, and level C the third time. For example: Slide from corner 1 to corner 2, skip to corner 3, gallop to corner 4, and run and turn to corner 1. When you get back to your original corner, drop down to level B and move around the room while doing the activities listed for that level. Continue the activity until you decide it is time to stop.

Figure 3.25   While some students read their card for instructions, others use a sliding movement to get to the next station.

▷ Suggested Moves

Corner 1

A. Slide

B. Polka

C. Run and turn

Corner 2

A. Skip

B. Vine

C. Two-step

Corner 3

A. Gallop

B. Schottische

C. Skip and turn

Corner 4

A. Run

B. Run and leap

C. Schottische and turn

▷ Teaching Tips

A variation of this activity is to have students work with a piece of equipment while moving around the room. Balls, ropes, and hoops can accompany these movements. Now invent your own rythmic courses.

Obstacle Courses

Goal   Students have an opportunity to learn activities that will help them develop and achieve total fitness while also learning and reinforcing a variety of dance skills.

Formation Set up stations in one big circle or in a line down the center of the exercise space.

▷ Procedure

Use equipment to set up obstacle courses for students to negotiate. When setting up a course, be sure all components of fitness are being developed. The equipment arrangement should provide students with the opportunity to climb and to use both their upper and lower bodies (see figure 3.26). While traveling between obstacles, the students are to use the rhythmic dance movements described in the glossary in accordance with their ability levels.

▷ Teaching Tips

The focus on rhythmic movements between obstacles is the element that makes this obstacle course different from others.

Figure 3.26 An obstacle course can challenge students' coordination and strength as well as liven up their class period.

Rhythms Circuit

Goal   Students have an opportunity to learn activities that will help them develop and achieve total fitness while also learning and reinforcing a variety of dance skills.

Formation Set up stations as shown in figure 3.27.

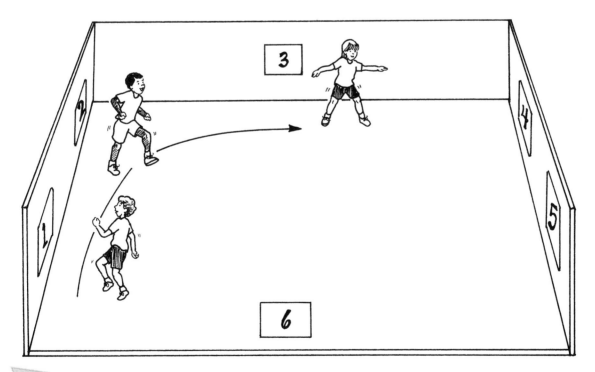

Figure 3.27 Rhythmic movements abound in the Rhythms Circuit.

▷ Procedure

Instruct students to go to the activity area of their choice and start walking, jogging, or practicing dance steps. On your cue, students go to any station and do the rhythmic movement activity on the task card at that station. Rotate to the next station every 60 to 90 seconds. Suggest that no more than five to eight students be at any one station at the same time. Switch stations on the signal. Move in a clockwise direction.

▷ Suggested Moves

1. Skipping (walk-hop)

Skip in the designated area; change directions and stay with the music. Skipping can be done forward, backward, and sideways.

2. Galloping (walk-leap)

Gallop in the designated area. Cover the entire area, and remember that galloping can be done forward and backward.

3. Sliding (walk-leap)

Slide in the designated area. Let the left foot then the right foot lead the slide sideways.

4. Polka (slide and skip or gallop and skip)

Practice the polka step in the designated area. Pretend to use or use a ball to dribble while practicing this step. Find a partner to act as a guard while dribbling and practicing the step.

5. Schottische (walk, walk, walk, hop)

Practice the Schottische step forward, backward, and sideways. Include 180-degree and 360-degree turns in the sequence. Practice the run, run, run, shoot sequence with or without a ball.

6. Running

Run through the designated area, changing directions, stopping, and pivoting with or without equipment. Find a partner to act as a guard or to begin the process of partnering in dance.

▷ Teaching Tips

Options

- Go to the center of the room and do aerobic dance for 90 seconds.
- Do this activity with equipment at the station.
- Have the student carry the equipment from station to station and perform the task.

▷ GAMES

Most of us really like to learn by using game-like situations. The games in this section are exciting yet low intensity and nonthreatening. Students can learn how to get themselves fit and can acquire dance skills at the same time.

Happy Heart

Goal   Students have an opportunity to learn activities that will help them develop and achieve total fitness while learning and reinforcing a variety of dance skills.

Formation   Open.

▷ Procedure

Give four or more players heart-shaped beanbags or some other object to pass to other players while you play music (see figure 3.28). The students with beanbags try to get rid of them by passing them to those without beanbags (the beanbag or object is a "hot potato" in this sense). Instruct the class to use a set dance movement to travel anywhere in the designated area while the music plays. When you stop the music, all students holding beanbags go to the "Happy Heart" area, and the rest play the game again. The students in the Happy Heart area practice rhythmic dance steps that you select until the next group comes. Thus, the first group returns to the game without having been inactive. This activity continues as long as you want to play the game.

▷ Teaching Tips

Those who are in the Happy Heart area can do flexibility exercises, strength development exercises, rhythmic and dance movements, or whatever you choose until they return to the game.

Figure 3.28   Happy Heart provides a wonderful opportunity to introduce cardiovascular fitness concepts to your students.

Veins and Arteries

Goal Students have an opportunity to learn activities that will help them develop and achieve total fitness while also learning and reinforcing a variety of dance skills.

Formation Following the lines on the floor (see figure 3.29)

▷ Procedure

This game is similar to Happy Heart with one change. Instruct players to travel only on the lines in the gym. Players cannot pass others but can turn around and head the other direction. When the music stops, the players holding the object must go to the Vitals Area. These

Figure 3.29   Students must follow the lines on the floor, but they still enjoy fun and fitness.

players return to the game when the next group enters the area. However, while in the Vitals Area, students are to jog in place. As with Happy Heart, this game offers an opportunity to discuss components of cardiovascular fitness.

▷ Teaching Tips

In Happy Heart and Veins and Arteries, have students work on rhythmic and dance movements, such as skipping, galloping, sliding, running, and doing the polka in time with music.

▷ CULMINATION

This last activity is the ultimate for relearning and emphasizing elements of movement you may want to focus on during any given lesson. Students soon learn to move to the open formation on the floor that this activity provides and wait for directions for their individual activities. The main key to this activity is to select a musical accompaniment that your students can relate to. This will increase motivation immensely when moving to this activity.

Retro

Goal   Students have an opportunity to learn activities that will help them develop and achieve total fitness while also learning and reinforcing a variety of dance skills.

Formation   Open.

▷ Procedure

Call out the activity by name. They will learn to move to an open space immediately. Right away, start students moving through spaces in straight, curved, and zig-zag pathways while also turning and sometimes traveling on body parts other than their feet. In other words, push your students to increase the variety in the types of movements they perform. Musical accompaniments at different tempos can assist in this effort. They can practice getting close to others as they move without entering into others' personal space. They also can practice guarding with a partner and holding hands as they move through space. The options are endless in this activity. It will allow you to reinforce and introduce almost any movement that you could imagine (see figure 3.30).

▷ Teaching Tips

- If you cannot remember all of the various types of movement patterns that have been learned up to this point, go back to chapter 1 and make yourself a list of things to include in Retro. Your students will love the name, the music will motivate them, and you will have fun seeing the growth of each and every student in your class.

- If you run out of directions to give for this activity, call on students for ideas. Trust me, they will have plenty by this time in your program.

Figure 3.30   Retro uses an open formation as an organization pattern.

▷ SUMMARY

Large-group activities, small-group activities, circuits, and games: what is your choice? A myriad of opportunities has been provided for your use. These rhythmic activities are for you to use, enjoy, and modify for your special needs. Provide your students with opportunities to modify them and create their own versions. Watch motivation rise.

Create Your Own Warm-Ups

This is an opportunity for students to do both individual and group work, depending on your preference and needs. Creating warm-ups—and later, dances—can also allow for development of critical thinking skills and the ever-so-important social skills needed throughout life.

Checklist for Creating a Warm-Up

- Instruct students to create their own warm-ups based on the movements and practices they have learned so far.
- Ask the students to create warm-ups that are 5 to 10 minutes in length and that contain continuous, repetitive, large-muscle, rhythmic movements at an intensity high enough to get them to begin sweating.
- Have students try this alone and with partners or small groups, changing the social dynamics and increasing the development of social skills.
- Instruct students to write up their descriptions and turn them in to you to practice language, reading, and writing skills.

Rubric

Now that you have your students into creating their own warm-ups, here is an example that could work for this particular activity or, with modifications, for others. By just changing a few words, this rubric could work with other aspects of your warm-ups.

4 Points—Exemplary	5- to 10-minute warm-up that contains continuous, repetitive, large-muscle, rhythmic movements at an intensity high enough to get students to begin sweating.
3 Points—Acceptable	5- to 10-minute warm-up that contains repetitive, large-muscle movements at an intensity high enough to get students to begin sweating.
2 Points—Needs improvement	5-minute warm-up that contains continuous, repetitive, large-muscle, and rhythmic movements.
1 Point—Unacceptable	A warm-up that does not contain continuous, repetitive, large-muscle, rhythmic movements at an intensity high enough to get students to begin sweating.

Review Questions

Have students submit questions for the class to answer, or have students answer questions similar to these that follow. In addition, these questions could be used as a homework or in-class assignment or even for class discussion.

1. What are the benefits of good warm-ups?
2. When creating warm-ups, what are the most important elements of the activity?
3. Collect and write up several warm-ups from other sources that meet the class rubric for excellence.
4. Describe the physiological benefits received from an exemplary warm-up.
5. What makes exemplary warm-ups appealing to all students?

Observation Questions

Students can write down answers during class, at home, or answer the questions individually or in groups during class. Alternatively, the entire class can discuss the observation questions. You, the teacher, can ask the students to write what they think the most important elements of the activity are. By doing this, the students are involved in critical thinking.

1. List the different locomotor movements that you observed in this activity.
2. List the combination movements that you observed in this activity.
3. How many walls did the students face during the warm-up?
4. Did the participants raise their heart rates to a level considered to be in their "work zone" for aerobic benefits?
5. Was there an opportunity for the students to develop movements in all directions?
6. Was there an opportunity for leading with different feet? Please describe the level at which this occurred.
7. Was the music selection appropriate for your class?

CHAPTER 4

Aerobic Dances and Fitness Routines

Aerobics has been and always will be a great medium to develop personal fitness. The more dances and dance steps in a person's repertoire, the more possibilities there are to add variety and excitement to the aerobic and dance program. The American College of Sports Medicine (ACSM) defines aerobic exercise as "any activity that uses large muscle groups, can be maintained continuously, and is rhythmic in nature." It is a type of exercise that overloads the heart and lungs and causes them to work hard. Aerobics calls on us to get up and get moving!

This chapter will expand and enhance your base of information immeasurably for your future programs. It includes guidelines and tips for quality aerobics with selected warm-up and cool-down exercise descriptions. These are followed by both low-impact and high-impact sample workouts as well as eight routines in a sample workout. The chapter closes with suggestions for creating your own routines and 10 sample aerobic routines for you to try, modify, and use in your classes.

Don't neglect this dimension of your dance program. Aerobics and dance movements may well be the ingredients that will open up the entire dance component in your classes.

▷ STRATEGIES FOR QUALITY AEROBICS

The following guidelines will help you provide quality programs for your students. Try to incorporate as many into your classes as you can.

- Keep the class running smoothly.
- Monitor breathing and pulse rates regularly.
- Train adequately in first aid and cardiorespiratory resuscitation (CPR).
- Advise students on appropriate footwear and clothing.
- Screen students for physical abnormalities, such as scoliosis.
- Indicate to students when high-impact and low-impact aerobics are being used.
- Tell students to slow down when they begin to breathe especially heavily or have difficulty with the activity.

Elements of Fitness

General rules for achieving fitness are best followed if certain parameters are considered:

- The ability to sustain physical activity for 10 to 45 minutes without undue breathing discomfort is a must. This improves blood circulation, strengthens the heart, and has profound positive effects on all the body's systems.
- A large percentage of the muscle mass from the waist down relies on slow-twitch muscle fibers (the ones you use in daily life). This type of exercise strengthens these fibers, contributes to good health by aiding in the regulation of weight, and enhances physical endurance.

Strategies for Achieving Fitness

A number of elements allow students to be successful in the activities. Here are some of the elements that allow students to become rhythmic movers in the pursuit of lifetime fitness.

- The activity is enjoyable for the students.
- The activity requires each student to move, support, transport, and pressure her or his own body (or parts of it) in some manner.
- The student maintains a comfortable working pace to ensure continued participation.
- The student must monitor her or his comfort zone; the moment she or he feels labored breathing, she or he must slow down. The student's pace thereby should be the fastest comfortable rate she or he can sustain—a rate at which she or he is breathing deeply and noticeably but no panting or gasping.

How to Calculate Resting Heart Rate

After you wake up in the morning, while still lying in bed, count your pulse for a full minute at either the carotid or radial arteries (that is, on the neck or the wrist). Simply place your index and middle fingers on the skin above the artery with enough pressure to feel a heartbeat and start counting for a full minute. This number is your resting heart rate.

How to Calculate Your Target Heart Rate Zone

The Karvonen formula has become a standard in the exercise industry for calculating target heart rate zones. The intensity at which you exercise can be modified to accommodate individual fitness levels depending on age. The formula is as follows:

1. 220 – age = estimated maximal heart rate
2. Maximal heart rate – resting heart rate = heart rate reserve
3. Heart rate reserve × 0.40 = _____ + resting heart rate = target heart rate
4. Target heart rate – 10 = lower end of target zone
5. Target heart rate + 10 = higher end of target zone

Teachers do not necessarily have to check heart-rate pulse because the students can be reasonably certain that they have reached their current safe heart rate when they begin to hear their own breathing. Such a pace is enough to reap cardiovascular aerobic fitness benefits without having to check pulse.

Do not make a big deal about finding the heart rate. Some students become frantic when they are asked to find their pulse; they cannot find it and become uncomfortable, feeling like they have failed. Treat finding your pulse, target heart rate, and recovery time in a very nonthreatening manner.

Borg Rating of Perceived Exertion

The Borg Rating of Perceived Exertion (RPE) scale (see figure 4.1) can be an effective tool for monitoring students' tolerance of the exercising they are doing. The idea behind this scale is that students rate their perception of exertion during the exercise. They must consider the strain and fatigue they experience in their muscles, the comfort or discomfort of breathing, and any aches and pains in their chest.

The Borg Scale is subjective, but there is a very high correlation between a person's RPE, when multiplied by 10, and the actual heart rate while exercising. For example, if a student's RPE is 15, and 15 × 10 = 150, the student's heart rate is expected to be in the region of 150 beats per minute. Understand that this is only an approximation; heart rate can vary considerably depending on the student's age and physical condition. (Source: U.S. Department of Health and Human Services, Public Health Service, Centers for Disease Control and Prevention, National Center for Chronic Disease Prevention and Health Promotion, and the Division of Nutrition and Physical Activity. 1999, *Promoting Physical Activity*. Champaign, IL: Human Kinetics, pp. 30-31.)

6	No exertion at all
7	
8	Extremely light
9	Very light
10	
11	Light
12	
13	Somewhat hard
14	
15	Hard (heavy)
16	
17	Very hard
18	
19	Extremely hard
20	Maximal exertion

Borg RPE scale
©Gunnar Borg, 1971, 1985, 1994, 1998.

Figure 4.1 The Borg Rating of Perceived Exertion Scale

Reprinted, by permission, from G. Borg, *Borg's perceived exertion and pain scales* (Champaign, IL: Human Kinetics), 47.

Four Criteria to Make Movements Aerobic

Aerobic benefits occur whenever the following four criteria are met:

1. Movement is continuous.
2. It lasts at least 10 minutes but can be as much as 60 minutes in length.

3. It is performed three to five times per week.

4. It is performed at 60 to 80 percent of the target heart rate.

Low-impact aerobics is characterized by movements (in which one foot stays in contact with the floor) that are less stressful on the joints. During high-impact aerobics, both feet will have no contact with the floor at various times. Having the option of doing high- or low-impact aerobics will allow students and teachers to decide which level is best for a particular workout.

Three Parts of an Aerobic Routine

A balanced aerobic workout has three parts.

1. Warm-up: A balanced combination of static stretching and rhythmic limbering exercises that warm the muscle core; students should warm up after walking briskly in place.

2. Aerobics: 10 to 45 minutes of rhythmic movement consisting of leg, arm, chest, and shoulder work. The goal is to raise the heart rate to improve cardiovascular respiration. Select low-impact movements and dance steps at first and gradually move to high-impact and more complex steps.

3. Cool-down: This involves a balanced combination of stretching and breathing that reduces heart rate and muscle soreness.

Exercise Guidelines

To develop sound aerobic routines, you need to consider several factors. Keep in mind the following points:

- Establish a resting pulse rate before starting the session.
- Make sure that workouts include a gradual 3- to 5-minute warm-up, a 10- to 45-minute aerobic period, and a gradual 5- to 10-minute cool-down (minimum).
- Start slowly; gradually increase the number of minutes of continuous movement.
- Encourage participants to walk for 3 to 5 minutes before the session as an initial warm-up.
- The choice of exercises and the way you do them make the workout effective, productive, and fun.
- Slow, gentle (static) stretches are much better than fast, violent movements.
- Knees and elbows should not be locked, or hyperextended, while exercising.
- Squats should not exceed 90 degrees.
- Sit-ups should be executed in a curling motion with the bent knees and the lower back flat on the floor. Curl only about 40 degrees from the floor.
- Double-leg lifts are not to be done at any time.
- Students should be reminded to pull their bellies in and buttocks under while exercising ("dining room in and sitting room under" or "suck and tuck").
- Routines should develop harmony in movements; teach fine balance, coordination, grace, and control.
- Indicate whether the routine is low or high impact.
- The cool-down should be done slowly and with adequate stretching to avoid muscle soreness.

▷ WARM-UP AND COOL-DOWN EXERCISES

Exercises for virtually every area of the body are covered in this section, with at least one exercise for each to be incorporated into your routines. Use music for these exercises to keep the beat while walking or marching and to offer a rhythmic experience by grouping movements in counts of eight.

The safety of your students depends on your monitoring and careful observation while the students are participating in these exercises. Make sure you correct the students who are not exercising properly by showing them the correct posture or movement. Students tend to follow the easiest method, the way that feels good or better than the correct way. Use a very positive approach when correcting them. Students are very sensitive. If they have one bad experience with an unfeeling teacher, it could cause them to hate movement and never care about their fitness.

Head and Neck

Head and neck exercises will improve circulation and reduce stress and tension. Use slow, soothing music.

• Neck extensions will improve flexibility and range of motion. Sit up comfortably (standing is also acceptable but may not be as comfortable). Bend the head forward gently toward the chest, straighten the back up to the vertical position, return to the starting position, and slowly rotate the head to the left. Return to the starting position and slowly rotate the head to the right. Return again to starting position. The head may also be tilted slowly and comfortably to the left and the right. Do not tilt the head backward or move the head backward and from side to side.

• Face stretches relieve muscle tension in the face. Raise the eyebrows and open the eyes as wide as possible. At the same time, open the mouth, stretch the muscles around the chin and nose, and stick the tongue out. Hold this stretch 15 to 30 seconds.

Shoulders

Shoulder exercises are designed to improve flexibility, prepare for exercises that strengthen the upper body, and relax the muscles at the base of the neck. Use slow music.

• The shoulder shrug is for the upper back; it relaxes the muscles at the base of the neck and the shoulders. Lift the shoulders up and then relax them.

• Touching shoulders is performed to increase the flexibility of the shoulders and elbows and to stretch the upper arms. It can be done in a seated position. Touch the shoulders with the hands, extend the arms straight out (without hyperextending) with the fists closed, and bring the arms back to the starting position.

• Shoulder stretch 1 is for shoulder flexibility. Interlace the fingers above the head. Now, with the palms facing upward, push the arms slightly back and up (see figure 4.2). Hold this stretch for 15 to 30 seconds. Feel the stretch on the upper arms, shoulders, and upper back. This is great for slumping shoulders. Be careful not to hyperextend or lock the arms.

• Shoulder stretch 2 is designed to stretch the triceps and the tops of the shoulders. With the arms overhead, hold the elbow of one

Figure 4.2 Shoulder stretch 1.

arm with the hand of the other arm. Gently pull the elbow behind the head, creating a stretch. Do this slowly, and hold it for 15 to 30 seconds. This can be done while walking.

• Shoulder stretch 3 is intended to stretch the shoulders and upper back. Gently pull the elbow across the chest toward the opposite shoulder. Hold this stretch for 15 to 30 seconds.

• Shoulder stretch 4 is used to stretch the arms, the sides of the body, and the shoulders. With the arms extended overhead, hold the outside of the left hand with the right hand and pull the left arm to the right side. Keep the arms as straight and comfortable as possible. Hold this for 15 to 30 seconds on each side.

• Cat stretches are performed with both hands and knees shoulder-width apart on the floor. Leaving hands and knees on the floor at all times, arch the back up as high as you can and hold for 30 seconds. Release and come back to the starting position. Do not slump the back in the middle.

Arms

Arm exercises include muscles of the upper torso, biceps, triceps, forearms, hands, and wrists. They prepare for strength exercises and improve range of motion and flexibility.

• Arm curls are designed to warm up biceps and forearms. Use a weighted object, such as a book or a can of vegetables, not more than 5 pounds (2.3 kilograms). Sit or stand erect with the arms at the sides, palms facing up, holding the weighted object. Bend the arm, raising the weight. Lower it slowly without hyperextending or locking.

• Arm extensions are used to warm up the triceps muscle on the back of the arm. Sit or stand erect with the arms at the sides, palms facing up. Holding a weighted object of less than 5 pounds (2.3 kilograms), extend the arm overhead. Slowly bend the arm until the weight is behind the head. Slowly extend the arm to its original position. The arm curl and arm extension can be done separately or together, alternating arms.

• Elbow stretch 1 is used to stretch biceps. Alternate flexion and extension of the elbow joints.

• Elbow stretch 2 is meant to stretch the chest and upper arms. Stretch the arms behind the back with fingers interlaced behind the back. Slowly turn the elbows inward while straightening the arms.

• Forearm stretches are done while standing erect. With the palms of the hands flat, the thumbs to the outside, and the fingers pointed backward, slowly lean the arm back to stretch the forearm. Be sure to keep the palms flat.

• Hand rotations are intended to maintain wrist flexibility and range of motion. Grasp the right wrist with the left hand. Keep the right palm facing down. Slowly rotate the hand five times clockwise, then counterclockwise.

Front of the Legs

Because the quadriceps represent the largest muscle group in the body, they are used constantly and therefore need to be warmed up and stretched to help prevent injury.

• Quad stretches are usually done against the wall after walking or running. Grasp the ankle with the opposite hand and pull the leg up, attempting to pull the sole of the foot toward the buttocks. Do not lean forward. Hold this for 15 to 30 seconds. Tightness should be felt in the front of the thigh. Go only to the point of tightness; do not push it. Repeat this with the other leg.

Back of the Upper Legs

Exercising the hamstrings will help the muscle balance between the front and back of the legs and help avoid knee injury.

• Trunk bending starts in a sitting position with legs slightly bent and the toes pointed. Bend forward slowly until you feel tightness in the back of the legs. Hold it for 15 to 30 seconds. Relax. Gradually work toward the toes.

• A trunk-bending variation helps reduce some of the stress if the back hurts when bending. Lie on the back with the feet flat on the floor and near the hips. Bring one leg toward the face. Grasp the lower leg and pull it toward the chest until there is tightness behind the leg. Relax.

Back of Lower Legs

Warming up and stretching the gastrocnemius will lessen chances of knee injury.

• The achilles stretch uses the stride position with one leg in front of the other and the toes near a wall. The front knee is bent, and the hands are on the wall (see figure 4.3). The back leg is straight with the heel flat on the floor; do not lock the knee. The heel must not be turned inward. Lean toward the front knee, keeping the back foot and heel flat. Hold this for 15 to 30 seconds. Relax. Repeat this with the other leg. If tightness does not occur in the calf during this exercise, the hips may not be pushed enough toward the wall, or the heel may be coming off the floor.

Figure 4.3   Achilles stretch.

• The calf raise is used to warm up and stretch the lower leg and ankle. Stand erect with the hands on the hips or on the back of a chair for balance. Spread the feet 6 to 12 inches (15 to 30 centimeters) apart. Slowly raise the body up on the toes, lifting the heels. Return to the starting position. Repeat 10 to 15 times.

Groin

The groin stretch will improve flexibility and allow the legs a larger range of motion.

• Spread groin stretch starts in a sitting position with the legs spread apart. Place the hands on the inside of the leg, eventually attempting to reach the inside of the ankles. Bend forward from the hips, keeping the knees flat but not locked. Hold this position as soon as there is tightness on the inside of the legs. Relax and repeat. Think of stretching from the head down; this allows for a total stretch, not just a waist bend.

Ankles

Ankle and foot exercises prepare the feet to support the body, especially with sudden changes in direction.

• Ankle and foot circles will improve flexibility and range of motion in the ankles. While sitting with the knees at 90°, cross the right leg over the left knee; rotate the foot slowly, making large, complete circles. Do 10 rotations to the right; then 10 to the left on each foot.

Chest and Trunk

Chest and trunk exercises are designed to stretch the chest cavity for better ventilation, develop the upper body, and maintain muscle tone.

• Knee push-ups are very good for upper-body development and maintaining muscle tone. Start on the hands and knees with the hands parallel to each other, slightly more than shoulder-width apart. The wider the hands are, the more work will be done by the pectoral muscles.

• The chain breaker begins by standing with the arms raised to shoulder level in front of the chest. The elbows should be out and the palms down, parallel to the floor. Straighten the elbows and reach back with the hands, palms facing forward. Do not allow the shoulders or the arms to drop below shoulder level.

▷ EXERCISE COMPONENTS FOR AEROBICS AND DANCE ROUTINES

In choosing the exercise selections for your warm-up and cool-down routines, select exercises that cover the major muscle groups: biceps, triceps, quadriceps, gastrocnemius, hamstrings, pectorals, deltoids, and abdominals. The use of 4/4-tempo music offers the student an opportunity for rhythmic movement efficiency and ease.

Understanding the importance of knowing the components of a low-impact aerobic routine can mean the difference in a student's good attitude about safe exercise and feelings of defeat.

Low-Impact Sample Workout

▷ Description

Low-impact aerobics is best described as at least one foot remaining in contact with the floor at all times while exercising. It originated from marches, toe taps, lift steps, and other basic moves. Low-impact aerobics includes those movements involving large muscle groups used in continuous rhythmic activity. It came into being to decrease the risk of lower-leg overuse injuries associated with high-impact classes. Very little stress is placed on the knee and ankle joints. This is a body-friendly workout because of the lack of pounding on the legs and joints. It is vital that the proper technique be used to prevent injury.

▷ Counts and Steps

1. Warm-up (3 to 5 minutes)
   • Walking or marching
   • Shoulder shrugs
   • Arm extensions
   • Quad stretches
   • Trunk bending
   • Spread groin stretches
   • Ankle and foot circles
2. Aerobic period (10 to 45 minutes at target heart rate)
   • Walk and jog around the room or designated area.

- Vine four times in each direction, right to left, then left to right.
- **Charleston** eight times, four beginning with the left foot and four beginning with the right foot.
- Heel touch in front by lifting the right heel and touching with the left hand.
- Walk in circles, four to the right (clockwise) and four to the left (counterclockwise).
- Repeat these exercises for the duration of this period, keeping it simple so the students can remember and be successful.

3. Cool-down (5 to 10 minutes)
   - Walking or jogging three to five minutes
   - Calf stretches
   - Straddle sits with one leg bent in toward the body
   - Cat stretches

High-Impact Sample Workout

▷ Description

High-impact aerobic dance occurs when the body is moved through space and both feet lose contact with the floor. High-impact aerobics uses aerobic movements, such as jumping and hopping. It provides great cardiovascular advantages along with good metabolic benefits. Doing high-impact aerobics greatly increases one's risk of injury, particularly in the lower body and the back. It may be inappropriate for students prone to injuries in the lower legs or the feet. It is vital that the proper technique be used to prevent injury.

▷ Counts and Steps

Both feet may leave the floor.

1. Warm-up (3 to 5 minutes)
   - Walking and jogging
   - Neck extensions
   - Shoulder rolls
   - Arm circles
   - Quad stretches
   - Trunk rotations
   - Achilles stretches
2. Aerobic period (10 to 45 minutes)
   - Jog around the room or designated area.
   - Step-hop while circling counterclockwise four times and clockwise four times.
   - Jump forward and backward.
   - Perform slides, four to the right and four to the left.
   - Polka-step for 16 counts.
3. Cool-down (10 to 15 minutes)
   - Walking for 5 to 10 minutes
   - Straddle sits with one leg pulled in toward the body
   - Cat stretches with the back arched

▷ SAMPLE AEROBIC WORKOUTS

Get a resting pulse rate before starting the session. Encourage participants to walk for three to five minutes before the session as an initial warm-up. Modify movements to be low or high impact as necessary to best fit students' endurance levels or personal requirements.

Warm-Up Activity: Rhythmic Fitness Circle

▷ Part A

Music

None at this time.

Counts and Steps

1 minute—Students walk single-file in a circle around the gym or room, all going in the same direction.

▷ Part B

Music

Slow-paced classical music (watch the change in the students' gaits).

Counts and Steps

- 1 minute—Give a signal for students to find a connection by scrambling around.
- 1 minute—Have students get back into the circle formation and continue to move around with their connection.

▷ Part C

Music

Change to a faster-paced instrumental selection.

Counts and Steps

6 minutes—Continue to move with that connection.

▷ Part D

Music

Change to a more popular selection that is moderate in tempo.

Counts and Steps

- 1 minute—Give a signal for the connected students to connect with another connection (two students) making a cluster of four students.
- 3 minutes—Students then encourage each other to jog to the music or to maintain a comfortable pace in their cluster of four.

▷ Part E

Music

The music changes into a polka selection.

Counts and Steps

- 1 minute—Give a signal for the connected students to get into a formation of their choice in which they can still move around the circle without colliding or interfering with another cluster.
- 3 minutes—Direct the students to move around the gym by skipping to the music in their cluster and trying to stay together.

Safety Tips

Remember to monitor the students' breathing. Keep them moving at a comfortable pace so as not to tire them, but still be sure to give them a good workout. Remember to explain how to move safely and that running into other students is inappropriate behavior.

▷ Part F

Music

Square dance selection.

Counts and Steps

Give a signal for the students to begin walking for one minute, and direct them to combine with another cluster of four so as to form a cluster of eight.

Give the students further directions to do in time with the music:

1-8 The group joins hands and circles to the left.

1-8 Circle to the right.

1-4 Students should join right elbows with someone in the circle and swing around in one direction.

5-8 Connect left elbows with the same student and swing around in the other direction.

1-8 All group members join hands, walk to the middle of the circle, and shout, "Hooray!"

1-8 Everyone walks backward out of the center of the circle.

Repeat this exercise four times, changing connections within the circle of students.

▷ Part G

Music

A popular and familiar selection.

Counts and Steps

1-16 All students leave their small circles and make a large circle.

Repeat Part F with the large circle.

▷ Teaching Tips

Changing music and tempo can add variety. You will have a better chance of pleasing more students with different music while also allowing them to rest by having different tempos. Students will see that you are really trying to please them and make it more their program. Enthusiasm and encouragement will take you far as a caring teacher. Allowing students to choose music from your collection shows that you want them to enjoy the activity.

Aerobic Exercise Routine 1: Combo Fun

Music   Any music with a moderate tempo, perhaps 120 BPM, will work with this exercise routine.

▷ Counts and Steps

Strive to reach the target heart rate zone during this aerobic routine. The next four routines can be either low or high impact depending on your needs. Any of the routines may be modified from high impact to low impact or vice versa. Simply remember what designates a high- and low-impact activity.

Part A

1-16 Walk or jog in place, lifting knees high and moving arms.

1-8 Lunge forward, dip (hands go down toward the floor) then dive (stretch to touch the floor) and lunge, two times with each foot in front.

1-8 Plié four times.

Part B

1-8 Lunge to both sides and then dip (hands go down toward the floor) and dive (stretch to touch the floor) two times to each side.

1-16 Push and pull, push and pull, push and pull, push and pull (forward for eight counts and backward eight counts) two sets with the arms.

1-8 Skip to the right four times, then to left four times.

Part C

1-16 Walk to the right while facing front and bend four times each to the right and left sides.

1-8 Make arm circles while walking in place, four times forward and backward; always have the arms slightly bent.

Part D

1-16 Perform step-kicks or knee lifts.

Part E

1-32 Gallop to the right, gallop to the left, and then to center four times.

Part F

1-16 Twist to the right, then make a full turn to the left; do this four times.

1-16 Plié four times.

Part G

1-8 Alternate arm circles while walking in place, four times forward and four times backward; the arms should be bent slightly.

1-8 Perform breaststroke arm movements while walking in place, eight times.

Part H

1-16 Walk to the right, back to the left, and then to the center with the arms moving and knees up high; alternate right and left, two times.

1-16 Perform a standing straddle stretch, reaching to the floor four times; maintain a flat back and bend the knees slightly.

▷ **Teaching Tips**

This routine has a variety of high-impact movements and steps. Give all your students time to learn the routines and the variations before going to the next activity. This is a great activity and well worth your time to teach it correctly for safety and fun.

Aerobic Exercise Routine 2: Freedom Hop

Music   Wham! "Freedom," *Wham! Make It Big*, Sony.

Formation   Form the students into lines.

▷ **Counts and Steps**

Part A

1-32 Step right, step left, step right, and kick left forward; step left, step right, step left, and kick right backward. Repeat this eight times with a quarter turn after each set.

Part B

1-16 **Chassé** step; step right foot, left foot, right foot, place left foot behind right foot to rock back, and rock weight forward onto the right foot (counted 1-and-2, 3, 4); step left foot, right foot, left foot, place right foot behind left foot to rock back, and rock weight forward onto the left foot (counted 5-and-6, 7, 8). Repeat this entire set one more time.

1-16 Step-hop back step; step back on right foot and hop on right foot; step back on left foot and hop on left foot. Repeat this four times.

Part C

1-16 Do four complete cha-cha steps, counting 1, 2, 3-and-4; 5, 6, 7-and-8.

1-16 Repeat the steps for the second part of counts in part B.

Part D

1-32 Repeat part A.

Part E

1-16 Repeat the steps for the first set of counts in part B.

1-16 Repeat the steps for the first set of counts in part C.

Part F

  1-8 March four steps forward and four steps backward.

 9-16 Turn right a quarter turn and march four steps forward and four steps backward.

17-24 Repeat 1-8.

25-32 Turn left a quarter turn and march four steps forward and four steps backward.

▷ **Teaching Tips**

This is a very fluid and fun routine to do. The transitions flow very easily and make one feel good while doing it.

Aerobic Exercise Routine 3: Hopscotch Fun

Music   Billy Joel, "Tell Her About It," *An Innocent Man,* Columbia Records CBS.

Formation   Have the students form lines.

▷ Counts and Steps

Have students work their way through the steps once and then repeat the dance. After the dance is done, have the students check their heart rates.

Part A

1-16   Perform the hopscotch step four times; jump with both feet on the floor, then jump with right knee bent and foot back. Alternate legs, twice each.

1-16   Vine to the right four steps, then to the left four steps.

Part B

1-16   Slide right as in the gallop, then to the left.

1-16   Perform pull-downs. Lift the arms above the head and pull them down as the knees are lifted; begin with the right and alternate right and left eight times.

Aerobic Exercise Routine 4: Kicking Fun

Music   Mike Post, "The A-Team Theme," *It's Post Time: Encore Collection,* BMG Special Prod.; Mike Post, "Footloose," *It's Post Time: Encore Collection,* BMG Special Prod.

Formation   Have the students form into lines; when successful, try a circle.

▷ Counts and Steps

Have students work their way through the steps then repeat the dance.

Part A

1-8   Step-kick, beginning on the right foot and then moving to left foot; alternate four times.

1-8   Perform jumping jacks four times.

Part B

1-8   Step left foot behind right foot step-kick, step-kick, step-kick.

1-8   Repeat stepping right foot behind left foot step-kick, step-kick, step-kick.

1-8   Rocking horse side to side, right-left, right-left, right-left, right-left for eight counts.

1-8   Jump and turn 180 degrees and repeat the rocking horse step.

▷ Teaching Tips

The routine has a different twist to it with the three consecutive kicks. Help your students to master this and they will reap the rewards of success.

Aerobic Exercise Routine 5: Rocking Horse

Music   Elvis Presley, "Good Luck Charm," *Greatest Hits,* volume 2, RCA International.

Formation   Have the students form into lines.

▷ Counts and Steps

Have students work their way through the steps and then repeat the dance.

Part A

1-16 Perform the rocking horse; rock forward on the right leg and back on the left leg, or forward on the left leg and back on the right leg, eight times.

1-16 Step, turn around, step together to the right, then to the left, four times.

Part B

1-16 Pivot step to the right, making a quarter-turn on each pivot; return to the front. Then pivot step to the left, making a quarter-turn on each pivot; return to the front.

1-8   Click the heels together four times over the eight counts.

▷ Teaching Tips

Students will find this routine fun, especially with the Elvis music. Any similar Elvis music can be used. Suggest to the students that they may act out how they think Elvis would do this routine. Watch the fun!

Aerobic Exercise Routine 6: Get Away

Music   Bobby Brown, "Get Away," *Bobby Brown—Greatest Hits*, MCA.

Formation   Have the students form into lines.

▷ Counts and Steps

Part A

1-16 Step-close-step over two counts moving side to side; do this eight times.

1-16 Perform step-hops while circling; do this eight times.

Part B

1-16 Vine right and left two times.

1-16 Perform ankle rotations (make circles with the foot while the leg is outstretched) eight times with each foot.

Part C

1-16 Rock forward and backward, four times each way.

1-16 Perform arm circles in front of the body, bending low and reaching high with the arms bent, four times each way.

Part D

1-16 Lunge forward, make big arm circles, and pull with the arms bent; do this eight times with each foot in front.

1-16 Perform a modified hurdle stretch four times, first with the right foot and leg bent in toward the left leg and then with the left foot and leg bent in toward the right.

Part E

1-16 Perform curls at your own pace over the 16 counts; make sure the knees are bent and the arms crossed.

1-16 Perform push-ups at your own pace over the counts.

▷ Teaching Tips

Remind the students not to lock their knees when they are reaching.

Cool-Down and Stretch Routine

Music   It should be slow in tempo and 4/4 time.

Formation   Have the students form into lines for easy observation.

▷ Counts and Steps

1-8 Perform a kneeling press and stretch; a slow lunge forward with the right foot while stretching the left foot behind slightly without locking the knee. Extend the arms forward on the lunge and flex the arms when returning to a neutral position. Do twice each left and right.

1-8 Perform a knee-to-chest pull, four times for each side, while lying on back.

1-8 While still lying on back, perform a both-knees-to-chest pull four times.

1-8 Do a total-body stretch one or two times with a static stretch; don't bounce.

1-32 Stand and breathe. Do a push-pull, or inhale and exhale, for eight counts at a time. Stress relaxing the body and maintaining good posture.

Check the heart rate. Walk for rest of the song (or longer, if the heart rate is still high).

▷ Teaching Tips

Make sure that the students take advantage of the cool-down and stretch to relieve any chance of being very sore the next few days.

▷ HOW TO CREATE RHYTHMIC ROUTINES AND DANCES

This section can provide every class the opportunity to develop creativity and to put on a performance as a culminating activity for the program. Creating a dance fulfills a desire for something new. This can decrease boredom and improve the quality of movement.

When teaching youth, teachers must stay up to date by keeping the music youthful and vital. Invite students to contribute, and they will feel important if you use their music, suggestions, or ideas. Please note that you must screen the music before using it in a class. Do not be caught in a situation where previewing could have saved your credibility.

▷ PRECHOREOGRAPHED ROUTINES

The following dances were created using this format and method. The selections are varied with low- and high-impact routines. As you practice the dances, review the process to further develop them. You will see how easy it is to create them, and you will become more proficient at developing them yourself.

Sunshine Day

Music   Any 4-count music with a medium tempo will do.

Formation   Have the students make a circle or form a line; the directions are the same for boys and girls.

Part A Counts and Steps

1-4   Perform the sunshine up and down; move the hands and arms up and down in a spread-open fashion to imitate the sun's rays.

5-8   Extend the left heel and then the right one per beat; left, right, left, right.

1-8   Perform the **hustle** to the right, beginning with the feet together. Step to the side on the right foot, step behind the right foot with the left foot, step to the side on the right foot, and kick with the left foot. Turn around and hustle left. Turn around again.

1-8   Perform knee lifts four times; lift right knee, step right. Repeat, alternating legs.

1-8   Step-kick four times.

Part B

1-8   Turn around in a complete circle, making four steps.

1-8   Hustle right and turn; hustle left and turn.

1-8   Do eight knee lifts.

1-8   Step left and lunge left; punch diagonally right and left, alternating until the music ends.

▷ Teaching Tips

The students will enjoy the feeling of freedom in this dance routine. Allow the students to choose the way they want to express the Sunshines. Step back and watch the different variations. There is no way to write down all of them!

Beach Rock

Music   Any 4- or 8-count music with a medium tempo will work.

Formation   Have students form a line.

▷ Counts and Steps

Have students work their way through the steps and then repeat the dance.

Part A

1-16   Hustle eight steps forward and eight steps back.

1-16   Vine right eight steps and left eight steps.

Part B

1-16 Repeat the steps for the first set of counts in part A.

1-16 Perform six step-kicks; begin on the right foot.

Part C

1-8   Do two rock-steps, forward and backward.

1-16 Do four step-pulls to the right and four to left.

Part D

1-16 Repeat the steps for the second set of counts in part B.

1-16 Do four rock-steps, forward and backward.

▷ Teaching Tips

The steps have the students kicking and rocking. Emphasize the importance of safety while kicking and rocking.

Best Friends

This piece is choreographed by Carri Riemer, 11; Kelly Meshaw, 13; Evan Overton, 11; and Charlie Smithwick, 13.

Music   Bill Medley and Jennifer Warnes, "I've Had the Time of My Life," on *Dirty Dancing,* MCA.

Formation   Form the students into lines facing front.

▷ Counts and Steps

This dance is appropriate for any cha-cha. Use new music to keep the students interested and challenged; this recommendation was made by the creators. Have students work their way through the steps once and then repeat the dance.

Part A

1-8   Boys and girls hold hands forming a line and chassé together. Begin with the feet together; step right foot, left foot, right foot, place the left foot behind the right foot, and rock back onto the left foot. (Count 1-and-2, 3, 4.) Step left foot, right foot, left foot, place right foot behind left foot, and rock back onto right foot. Boys and girls release hands and turn to their right on count 8. (Count 5-and-6, 7, 8.)

1-16 Do the shag step; boys begin on the left foot, right foot, left foot, right foot, left foot, right foot, rock back on left foot and forward on right foot. Girls begin on their right foot.

1-8   Repeat the steps for first set of eight counts.

Part B

1-16 Repeat the steps for counts 1 to 16 in the second part (shag step) of part A.

▷ Variation

This can be a great partner dance in the contra formation.

▷ Formation

Partners' directions are for the boys, and the girls do the opposite. Each boy faces a girl and holds hands. The boy rolls the girl into his arms, then rolls her out.

▷ Counts and Steps

The girl will do opposite feet. Have students work their way through the steps and then repeat the dance.

Part A

1-4   The boy faces the girl and holds hands. Chassé together facing each other. Begin with the feet together, step right foot, left foot, right foot, place the left foot behind the right foot, and rock back.

5-8   Step left foot, right foot, left foot, place right foot behind left foot, and rock back. The boy turns the girl to his right and under his arm on count 8.

1-16   Do the shag step; begin on the left foot, right foot, left foot, right foot, left foot, right foot, and rock back on the left foot and forward on the right foot.

1-4   Repeat the steps for the first four counts of the first set.

5-8   Repeat the steps for the last four counts of the first set.

Part B

1-16   Repeat the steps for counts 1 to 16 in the third part of part A (with the shag step).

▷ Teaching Tips

The students who created this routine were advanced dancers, and you may want to hold off on this one until the students have more experience.

Charleston

The authors were assisted by Donna Cannon and Linda Horne in preparing this piece.

Music   Louis Armstrong, "12th Street Rag," *Hot Five and Hot Seven 1927*, Epm Musique.

Formation   Form the students into lines.

▷ Counts and Steps

Have students work their way through the steps once and then repeat the dance.

Part A

1-16   Do four Charleston steps; begin on the left foot.

1-16   Jog around an imaginary circle for eight counts to the right and eight counts to the left.

Part B

1-16   Do four side lunges, right, left, right, left.

1-16   Perform eight arm circles from the elbow with both arms.

▷ Teaching Tips

The students will have fun with the Charleston, but make sure you teach them slowly and allow for adequate practice time. They will really get into this routine because they will love the music.

Crazy Cha-Cha

Music   Any cha-cha music will be appropriate. This dance is very easy to adapt to any music with the count of 1, 2, 3-and-4 (or 1, 2, cha-cha-cha).

Formation   Partners face each other; directions are for the boys, and the girls do the opposite.

▷ Counts and Steps

Have students work their way through the steps once and then repeat the dance.

Part A

1-16 Do four cha-cha steps forward and backward; begin on the left foot.

1-16 Do four cross-cha-cha steps; cross the left foot over the right. Begin on the left foot.

Part B

1-16 Do four cha-cha steps forward and backward; begin on the left foot.

 1-4   Perform four cha-cha chassé steps; begin on the left foot and instead of rocking backward, rock forward as you would in a cha-cha.

▷ Teaching Tips

Review the cha-cha steps and allow for practice before attempting this routine. The students will think it is very easy after that. Build that confidence!

German Circle Dance

Music   Any polka music will be good.

Formation   Make a circle with no partners; stand in a circle facing the center, feet together.

▷ Counts and Steps

1-4   Step with the right foot to the right side and back together. Step with the left foot to the left side and back together.

5-8   Step with the right heel forward and back together. Step with the left heel forward and back together.

1-8   Turn counterclockwise to the right and step right foot, left foot, right foot, together; then step left foot, right foot, left foot, together.

1-8   Do one-half of a vine step; step right and put weight on the right foot, step left behind right and put weight on the left foot. Step right and put weight on the right foot, and turn a full circle clockwise until facing the center of circle.

Repeat the dance.

▷ Teaching Tips

Allow time to practice the vine step. Call it out loud while the students walk through it.

Jitterbug Jive

The authors were assisted by Carri Riemer, 12, who told us that this would be an easy way to teach the jitterbug.

Music   Any good jitterbug music will do.

Formation   This dance incorporates the double Lindy step, the three-step turn, the jitterbug jump, and the sugar-foot turn and can be done with or without partners before students learn the actual jitterbug. This dance made teaching the jitterbug very simple. Students face the front with boys and girls alternating in a straight line and hands joined.

▷ Counts and Steps

1-8   Begin with the feet together. Step left foot, turn right foot to the right and step left foot all the way around making a full turn, and step right foot. Girls start on the opposite foot.

1-4   Do the double Lindy step; left toe heel (toe dig, heel plant), right toe heel, and left rock-step backward. Girls start on the opposite foot.

5-8   Jitterbug jump; jump on both feet to the left, and jump on both feet to the right. Each jump is made diagonally.

1-8   Repeat the steps for second set of counts.

1-8   Do a Suzie-Q turn clockwise. Place weight on balls of the feet and twist the feet, alternating left foot and right foot. At the same time twist the upper body, hips, and torso. Pull against each other with one hand while turning clockwise and shake the other hand in the air as if you are waving. On the completion of the turn, face the front again.

Repeat the dance.

▷ Variation

This dance incorporates the double Lindy step, the three-step turn, the jitterbug jump, and the sugar-foot turn with partners before students learn the actual jitterbug. This dance made teaching the jitterbug very simple. Boys and girls face each other, boy on the inside of a circle and the girl on the outside, both hands joined. These directions are for the boys; girls do the opposite.

▷ Counts and Steps

1-8   Begin with the feet together. Step left foot, right foot behind left foot; step right foot, touch right foot to left foot; step right, making a complete turn. Step right foot, left foot, right foot.

1-4   Do the double Lindy step; left toe heel, right toe heel, left rock-step backward.

5-8   Do the jitterbug jump; jump on both feet to the left and then jump on both feet to the right. Each jump is made diagonally with the boy and girl jumping in opposite directions, holding hands.

1-8   Repeat the steps for second set of counts.

1-8   Do a Suzie-Q turn; join right hands at shoulder level and turn clockwise using the Suzie-Q turn. Place your weight on the balls of the feet and twist the feet, alternating left foot and right foot. At the same time, twist the upper body, hips, and torso. Pull against each other while turning clockwise and shake the other hand in the air as if you are waving. On the completion of the turn, move to the right to face a new partner.

Repeat the dance.

▷ Teaching Tips

This dance was created by my daughter because she saw how much trouble some students were having learning the jitterbug. She saw that if the students were busy trying to learn a dance with the jitterbug in it, they would be so focused on learning the routine that the jitterbug would be comparatively easy and the stress and anxiety would go away. The focus was taken from learning to jitterbug (a small component of the whole) to concentrating on where to put the jitterbug and in what order. It has been very successful.

Forward, Reverse Fun

The authors were assisted by Carri Riemer, 12, in putting together this piece.

Music   It should be for 8-count movements and have a moderate tempo.

Formation Form a double circle with couples side by side holding inside hands and facing clockwise. Boys are on the inside and girls on the outside of the circle. Instructions are for the boys; girls do the opposite.

▷ Counts and Steps

1-8   Walk four steps forward in the line of direction. Turn around individually, releasing the hands. Rejoin hands as you walk backward four steps in the same line of direction.

1-8   Reverse directions and walk forward four steps counterclockwise. Turn around individually, releasing hands. Rejoin hands as you walk backward four steps in the same line of direction.

1-8   Step back on the left foot, right foot, left foot; and step forward on the right foot, left foot, and right foot.

1-4   The boy turns four steps to the left to meet a new partner. The girl turns around to the right, in place.

5-8   With a new partner, repeat the steps for the third set of eight counts.

Repeat the dance.

▷ Teaching Tips

Practice walking forward, turning around, and walking in the same direction. This will be awkward for students, but go slow until they see the pattern and groove to it!

Mirror Dance

The authors were assisted by Carri Riemer, 12, in putting together this piece.

Music   Any slow-tempo cha-cha music will do.

Formation Boys and girls face each other. All boys face the same direction, and all girls face the same direction.

▷ Counts and Steps

Part A

1-16 Hands are touching at shoulder level as if they are against a mirror. Perform arm circles to the side with the right hand for girls and left hand for boys.

1-8   Both hands make circles at the same time.

1-8   Both hands do bicycle arms alternating right and left.

Part B

1-16 Do four cha-cha steps; boys step forward on the left foot and girls step backward on right foot.

1-16 Do four cross-cha-cha steps; boys cross the left foot over the right foot and girls cross right over left.

Part C

1-16 Repeat the steps for first set of counts in part B.

1-16 Perform four cha-cha pivot turns; boys step across the left foot with the right foot and turn away from the girls; girls steps across the right foot with the left foot and turn away from the boys.

Part D

1-16 Do four cha-cha chassé turns; boys turn forward on the left foot first and girls turn forward when on the right foot.

1-16 Cha-cha until the end of the music.

▷ Teaching Tips

Review the cha-cha step and practice until the students feel comfortable with it. Suggestion: Use the "Step Station" activity on page 33 to teach the steps. Success will follow.

Simplicity Shag

Music   Any beach music with four or eight counts and a moderate tempo works well.

Formation Girls are on the right side of the boys; students are holding hands and are side by side facing front.

▷ Counts and Steps

Part A

1-8 The shag step is the same as the triple Lindy step, except instead of moving side to side, the step moves forward and backward. The count is 1-and-2, 3-and-4, 5, 6, adding a quarter-turn facing the partner.

1-8 Do the shag step and make a quarter-turn facing backward; this is done with partners side by side.

1-8 Do the shag step and make a quarter-turn facing your partner.

1-8 Each partner does the shag step to turn in a circle.

Part B

1-32 Shag for 32 counts, facing your partner.

Repeat the dance.

▷ Teaching Tips

Standing side by side takes some pressure off the students because their connection cannot really see them if they "mess up."

▷ SUMMARY

Rhythmic aerobics and dance provide great ways to motivate students to reach their potential with regard to the rhythmic expectations you hold for them. They are also an excellent source students can draw on to achieve total fitness. The dances and activities are thereby wonderful avenues to venture down when a teacher wants to go beyond the standard approach to fitness. With music as an instrument and conscientious instruction as a guide, the children's development will thrive. This chapter gives you an opportunity to experience the joy of teaching using innovative methods. Take it from here and you are on your way rhythmically.

▷ Create Your Own Aerobic Dance or Fitness Routine ◁

Having given the students the tools they need to learn the steps, it is very easy to say the next logical progression is to create an aerobic dance or fitness routine using very easy beginning steps. This enhances the students' desire to want to create and be successful. It likewise gives students self-confidence, can produce immense self-esteem, aids in the development of their critical thinking skills, and improves those important social skills that they will use over the course of their lives.

Checklist for Creating an Aerobic Dance or Fitness Routine

- Instruct students to create their own aerobic dance or fitness routine based on the skills and steps that they have learned.
- Ask them to come up with a routine that is developmentally appropriate for them, progressing in stages from a 16-count aerobic dance, to an aerobic routine that is 24 counts, then 32 counts, up to 64 counts in length. The dance should incorporate at least four different steps and turns. Music should be used, and the steps should be done in time to the beat. Longer routines should display a definite pattern to the choreography.
- Allow students to do both individual and group work, depending on your preference or needs.
- Instruct them to write up their descriptions and turn them in to you to practice language, reading, and writing skills.

Rubric

Students' success can be determined quickly by their positive comments as they work on their tasks. Look for cooperation with fellow students and signs that they are taking ownership of their products. You will see not only the effective outcomes but also the positive cognitive and the psychomotor results.

4 Points—Exemplary	The student choreographed the assigned number of counts. She or he created a dance or aerobic routine using four different steps and turns or changes in direction. She or he executed the movements properly in time to the music. If assigned a longer set of counts, the dance displays a pattern.
3 Points—Acceptable	The student choreographed the assigned number of counts. She or he created a dance or aerobic routine using four different steps but without turns or changes in direction. She or he executed the movements properly in time to the music. If assigned a longer set of counts, the dance displays a pattern but could use some fine-tuning.
2 Points—Needs improvement	The student choreographed only half of the assigned counts. She or he used only two or three different steps and showed very little variety. Movements were rarely executed to the music and were without a clear pattern.
1 Point—Unacceptable	The student choreographed less than half of the assigned number of counts. She or he tried with little success in putting together the routine and used only one step for the dance.

Review Questions

Have students submit questions for the class to answer, or have students answer questions similar to these that follow. In addition, these could be used as a homework assignment, as an in-class assignment, or for class discussion.

1. What are the physical benefits of aerobic dancing?
2. What is one method to find one's target heart rate?
3. What must you remember when creating your own aerobic dance routine?
4. How would you go about finding other aerobic dance routines?
5. What would come first in creating an aerobic dance routine—the music or the steps?

Observation Questions

1. List the different locomotor movements that you observed in this activity.
2. List the combination movements that you observed in this activity.
3. How many steps were included in the students' routines?
4. Was the tempo of the music suitable for the routine?
5. Did the students capture the theme and attitude of this aerobic dance routine? Please describe your observations.
6. Did the students raise their heart rates high enough to meet their target heart rates?
7. Was there an opportunity for the students to develop movements in all directions?
8. Was there an opportunity for the students to lead with a different foot?
9. Was the aerobic dance routine developed in multiples of the following counts: 4, 8, 16, 32, and even 64?
10. Was the music selection appropriate for the aerobic dance routine? For example, if the music is spunky, did the dance represent this feeling?

▷ CHAPTER 5

Line Dances

Line dancing is one of the most enjoyable and exciting forms of dance being done today. It blends familiar dance steps into a routine that can be adapted to many pieces of music. It is an excellent opportunity for students to create. It also enhances rhythmic development and reinforces basic and combination movements. A very appealing feature of line dances is that you can use them with current popular music that children enjoy. It's all about attraction to the activity, and nothing motivates students more than when you can select music that appeals to the group you are currently working with.

Line dancing can provide a great addition to your overall fitness program as well. Keep your students moving in a developmentally appropriate progression that allows them to experience high levels of success. This raises their motivation and level of fitness. Remember to do heart-rate checks occasionally during class as this is the easiest and quickest indicator that your students are actually working during the class. Line dancing lends itself to entry-level activity by skill level, which means that no matter what developmental level a student currently maintains, he or she can be included in every activity in this chapter. It is a very inclusive form of dance.

Another great attribute of line dancing is that it lends itself quite well to interdisciplinary teaching. Math is certainly one of the easiest and most logical areas to integrate, through actions like counting, forming geometric shapes, and doing fractions (to name just a few such points of overlap). Language arts can be greatly enhanced through vocabulary development, oral communication, and choreographing routines. Moreover, all of these activities can be written up into compositions to reinforce reading and writing.

Line dancing is one of the oldest forms of dance. The earliest dances were executed in lines and circles—the latter of which simply entails bringing the two ends of the line together. Many of the early dance forms in the 1500s and 1600s were court dances in which virtually all of the dancing was executed in line formations. It was not appropriate at that point in history for the two sexes to face each other in public for any extended length of time. Facing partners in a **closed** dance position came on the world scene with the advent of the waltz, thanks in large part to the work of great classical composers like Mozart, Brahms, and Beethoven. The dance forms that were popular in New England during the colonial era were centered primarily on contra dancing, which involves two lines facing each other as the dancers execute the particular dances. But the list goes on and on, for line dancing has a great legacy the world over.

Line dancing has the potential to introduce people to dance in a nonthreatening environment. When music is selected that the dancers like, motivation and success levels go higher. Most of the time, line dances are executed as partnerless dances done in lines. They are usually conducted without touching. They thereby can assist with the transition to dances with partners and with skill warm-ups for numerous sports. Line dancing also is a great follow-up to the starter activities found in chapter 2.

Music selection is simple. Use music that you and your students like, and you will always meet success. Some of the dances in this chapter are named for a particular piece of music, but may be danced to other songs. In fact, changing songs and tempos creates interesting results. It pushes your students to new and higher levels of achievement both with movement and in cognitive ability.

This chapter contains enough line dances to keep any group of dancers active for quite some time. Several classics are included as well as some dances that are more recent. They will add excitement and fun to any class. They have been categorized by the various components that contribute to learning, such as locomotor movements, combination movements, slow and fast movements, turns, vine steps, development of movement in all directions, and leading with both feet rather than with predominately one or the other. Line dancing can contribute quite heavily to overall motor development in a very inclusive manner.

▷ LINE DANCE ACTIVITIES

Rhythmic Lead-Up 1: Line Start

▷ Description

Line Start is a rhythmic lead-up activity designed to help get students ready for the lesson. The line start technique is also an excellent way to learn a multitude of dance steps and increase the confidence levels of the less skilled members of the class. It truly promotes inclusion in an "entry level by skill level" approach that is developmentally appropriate for this lesson. Virtually any of the line dances can be taught with this approach and, moreover, should be taught this way to ensure that all students have the opportunity to be up to speed with the rest of the class.

Music   Vary the tempos of the music selected for the lesson. Give your students extended opportunities to feel and move to the basic beat, or pulse, of the music—in place, side to side, and front to back.

Formation   Students form lines. The "line start" cue lets students know it is time to move out into the teaching space and spread out in parallel lines facing the teacher. Students will already know the formation from many of the starter activities from chapter 2. Periodically move the front line group to the rear, the sides to the center, and rotate the class around. Any dance step or movement can be learned from this formation.

▷ Counts and Steps

This exercise can really help get students ready to move in line formations in any direction. For instance, you may want to try four steps forward and hold for four counts and then four steps backward and hold for four counts. This progression should then be repeated to both sides as well. Another challenge is to use vine steps and then to add turns (quarter-turns, half-turns, full turns, and double turns) as you try this technique, always remembering to have students lead into the movements starting with one foot and then the other. Suggest that students move to the beat and hold it for four counts. This technique allows everyone the opportunity to catch up and raises immensely the success levels of your students.

In addition, it is strongly encouraged that you try this approach with all of the locomotor and combination movements. In fact, this teaching technique fits quite well with any combination of movements you can think to try. When ready, leave out the "four count and hold" sequence. Then slow down the music and gradually increase the tempo to vary the movement qualities and enhance skill development.

▷ Variations

- Try starting the dance on the foot opposite of the one the students started to further increase their ability with as many of the dances as possible. This can increase the students' motivation as they challenge themselves to learn the movements in a different direction or at a different tempo. Also, you can practice building line dance routines in multiples of eights. Groups can make up their own from the skills that they learn in your lead-up sessions to the dances that follow.

- One final variation with this line start technique is to use music that in the beginning is slower, such as 100 BPM, and then go to music that has a higher tempo. This will greatly enhance the success of your students and will continue to help them build better skills. In addition, it is a great way to increase the challenge for the more talented students in the class.

▷ Teaching Tips

Line dancing is a great way to increase fitness in the classroom in a pleasurable manner, particularly when you can use music that is age-appropriate and inviting to your students. After all, the whole idea is to keep your students moving on task and thereby helping to develop lifelong skillful, fit, and joyful movers!

Rhythmic Lead-Up 2: Entry Level by Skill Level

▷ Description

Provide an "entry level by skill level" activity for your students as you constantly raise the difficulty of the activity to teach more and more skills. Students should learn basic walking steps in the beginning of this line dance, later moving to other combination movements to widen their skill level with this form of dance. In addition, this activity should introduce turns, varying tempos, vine steps, and development of a wider range of laterality skills.

Music   Begin with music that is approximately 100 BPM, and move the tempo up as the skill level of your students increase. Whenever possible, try 2/4-, 3/4-, and 4/4-meter music. This is yet another way to improve students' skills with rhythmic movements.

Formation   Form the students into lines. This is a one-wall dance (that is, it is completed while facing only one direction) with warm-up combinations that can start with either foot; add more walls later.

▷ Counts and Steps for Rhythmic Pattern A

Students walk in sets of eight counts, in place, forward and then backward. They step on every count.

   1-8 Walk or march while standing in place.

  9-16 Walk or march while moving forward.

17-24 Walk or march while moving backward.

Variations

- Step on every other count, alternately step on only odd-numbered counts and hold on even-numbered counts, and then reverse it to hold on the odd-numbered counts and step on the even numbered counts

- Substitute different locomotor and combination movements, such as running, leaping, jumping, hopping, skipping, galloping, sliding, and so on.

▷ Counts and Steps for Rhythmic Pattern B

Students walk to the side in sets of four counts, alternating steps and holds.

   1-4 Side-step with the right foot, close the left foot beside the right, side-step with the right foot, close the left foot beside the right, and touch.

   5-8 Keep the feet still and hold for four counts.

 9-12 Side-step with the left foot, close the right foot beside the left, side-step with the left foot, close he right foot beside the left, and touch.

13-16 Hold for four counts.

Variations

- Add arm movements during the hold portions (keeping the feet stationary).

- Eliminate the hold portions and modify the pattern to combine any two locomotor movements, such as three side-steps and a jump, hop, or touch.

- Add direction changes with a new pattern to move to the right side, left side, forward, and backward.

- Combine rhythmic patterns A and B in an alternating manner for the length of one song.

- Add quarter-turns to repeat while facing a new wall (to create a four-wall dance).

▷ Teaching Tips

Make sure you demonstrate the movements and encourage the students to respond to the challenge of learning something new. Repetition is the answer to mastery. Practice this dance and the variations over and over, and the benefits will be seen later in your dance unit.

▷ LINE DANCE UNIT PLANNING

Your line dance unit will incorporate many of the line dances listed in this chapter along with those that you create in class. The following is a vocabulary list for the contents of the chapter. Remember that the directions for each dance are only suggestions to get you started. Get your students to come up with different variations, such as changing the tempo, changing the starting foot, adding more turns, and so on.

Line Dance Vocabulary

- Locomotor movements—walk, run, jump, hop, and leap
- Combination movements—skip, gallop, slide, polka, and schottische
- Rhythmic elements—**accent**, rhythmic pattern, even rhythmic pattern, uneven rhythmic pattern
- Selected dance steps—vine, hustle, side touch, step-kick, step-touch, rock step

Eight Count

▷ Description

This is an 8-count, one-wall dance that uses a vine step as well.

Music   Any strong, medium-speed (120 BPM) music will work for this.

Formation   Form students into lines.

▷ Counts and Steps

Students start with the right foot.

1 Right foot touch forward.
2 Right foot touch backward.
3 Right foot touch sideways.
4 Right foot touch beside the left foot.

Now do a four-count vine step to the right, starting with the right foot.

1 Right foot step to the side.
2 Left foot behind right.
3 Right foot to the side.
4 Right foot touch beside the right foot.

Repeat the dance using the left foot to begin.

1 Left foot touch forward.
2 Left foot touch backward.
3 Left foot touch sideways.
4 Left foot touch beside the right foot.

Do a vine step to the left, starting with the left foot:

1 Left foot step to the side.
2 Right foot behind left.
3 Left foot to the side.
4 Right foot touch beside the left foot.

Repeat the dance from the beginning.

▷ Teaching Tips

This dance teaches many of the basics of line dancing and is a great starting point for your classes. It can be used for interdisciplinary lessons with geometric lines and counting. Quarter-turns can be added to this dance on the third step of the vine to bring in the possibility of discussing fractions as well.

Grapevine or Vine

▷ Description

A 16-count line dance using the grapevine or vine step quarter-turns. We recommend using the word *vine* to cue the students while they are doing the steps, as it is faster to say.

Music   Any strong, medium-speed (120 BPM) music will work for this.

Formation   Form the students into lines.

▷ Counts and Steps

Vine to the right, starting with the right foot:

1. Right foot step to the side.
2. Left foot behind the right.
3. Right foot to the side.
4. Left foot touch beside the right.

Now vine to the left, starting with the left foot:

1. Left foot step to the side.
2. Right foot behind the left.
3. Left foot to the side.
4. Right foot touch beside the left.

Now the class can do several rock-steps forward and backward, ending with a quarter-turn to the left for a total of eight more counts.

1. Step forward on the right foot.
2. Rock backward on the left foot.
3. Rock forward on the right foot.
4. Step forward on the left foot.

Rock to the other side with a quarter-turn to the left.

1. Rock backward on the right foot.
2. Rock forward on the left foot.
3. Rock backward on the right foot.
4. Rock forward on the left foot, turning a quarter-turn to the left.

Now repeat the dance.

▷ Teaching Tips

Try this dance using the line start approach and holding pattern after each four-count sequence without turning on the last step to the left. When the students have mastered this dance without the quarter-turns, add them into the dance. Next, teach the dance to the left and reverse the dance movements to enhance laterality skills. Another change that can be added when your students are ready is to put in a full turn with the vine step.

The Hard Way

▷ Description

This is a 16-count, four-wall line dance that uses heel touches and shuffles, walking, vine steps, and quarter-turns. It was created by New Jersey square dance caller Mike Gilden.

Music Faith Hill, "The Hard Way," *Faith*, Warner Brothers, or any strong medium-speed (120 BPM) music will work for this.

Formation All students face front.

▷ Counts and Steps

Start on the right foot.

1-8 Right heel forward, right foot returns beside the left foot; left heel forward, left foot returns beside the right foot; repeat.

Next part to the dance is a vine to the right starting on your right foot, ready:

1-4 Vine step to the right; right foot step to the side, left foot step behind the right, right foot step to the side, and kick the left foot forward with a quarter-turn right.

5-8 Step backward four steps—left foot, right foot, left foot, right foot—touching the right foot next to the left foot on the last count.

Repeat the dance.

▷ Teaching Tips

This dance is another simple one; it reinforces counting and fractions with the quarter-turns.

I Got a Girl

▷ Description

This dance is done in a conga line. Participants place their hands on the hips or shoulders of the person in front of them or simply follow that person. As the music plays, the leader moves around the room, creating the step and body-movement pattern that others are to emulate for as long as this same person is the leader. On a preset signal from the teacher, the leader goes to the end of his or her respective line and the next person in the line leads the group. Lines can be of any length. In a class of 25, lines that are five persons long are fun, as are lines that are made up of 10 or more. The shorter the lines, the more times each student gets to lead.

Music Lou Bega, "I Got a Girl," *A Little Bit of Mambo*, RCA, or any medium-speed music will work well.

Formation Students form lines that will work their way through the room in a path chosen by their leaders.

▷ Counts and Steps

Here is a basic pattern to use with this dance.

1-4 Step; step; step; and then leap, jump, hop, or kick.

Also encourage students to try combination movements, such as the skip, slide, gallop, and polka steps in multiples of fours and eights. This can be a great time to add in vine steps and other dances that the leaders see fit to use.

▷ Teaching Tips

Give your students ideas for varying the dance, such as using different locomotor patterns and different combination patterns and moving the hands and arms more when leading. Suggest that they follow curved, straight, and zig-zag paths as well. This particular formation works extremely well with music of varying tempos.

Sixteen Count

▷ Description

This is a 16-count, four-wall line dance with walking steps and quarter-turns.

Music   Any strong, medium-speed (120 BPM) music will work for this.

Formation Form students into lines.

▷ Counts and Steps

Start with a walking step forward with a quarter-turn to the left, starting on the right foot.

1 Right foot step forward.
2 Left foot touch beside the right.
3 Left foot step forward.
4 Right foot touch beside the left.
5 Right foot step forward.
6 Left foot touch beside the right.
7 Left foot step forward, making a quarter-turn to the left.
8 Right heel scuff on the floor.

Back up for four counts and come forward for four counts, making a quarter-turn to the left.

1 Right foot step backward.
2 Left foot step backward.
3 Right foot step backward.
4 Left foot touch beside the right.

Now step forward.

1 Left foot step forward.
2 Right foot step forward.
3 Left foot step forward, making a quarter-turn to the left.
4 Right heel scuff on the floor.

Now repeat the dance.

▷ Teaching Tips

This is a very simple variation on the other dances discussed up to this point. It can provide a little variety and at the same time promote lots of success early on in the line dance unit. It also can be used to enhance counting and fractions with the quarter-turns. Remember to try these dances by starting on the other foot to enhance development of laterality skills!

Alley Cat

▷ Description

This is a 16-count, four-wall, American novelty dance with quarter-turns. Its origin is uncertain.

Music   Bent Fabric, "Alley Cat," *Ultimate Party Survival Kit*, Sony; or similar music.

Formation   All students face front.

▷ Counts and Steps

This dance starts by touching the right foot out to the side two times and then doing the same with the left foot.

1-2   Extend the right foot to the right side to touch the toe to the floor and close the right foot to the left foot.

3-4   Extend the right foot to the right side to touch the toe to the floor and close the right foot to the left foot, making sure to shift weight to the right foot.

Now with the left foot repeat the side touch.

5-6   Extend the left foot to the left side to touch the toe to the floor and close the left foot to the right foot.

7-8   Extend the left foot to the left side to touch the toe to the floor and close the left foot to the right foot.

Now repeat the same motion to the rear, extending the right foot to the back twice and the left foot to the back twice.

1-4   Repeat first set of counts 1 to 4 with right foot extended back.

5-8   Repeat the second set of counts 5 to 8 with the left foot extended back.

Now come knee lifts—twice on the right and twice on the left.

1   Lift the right knee straight up; let the foot hang naturally about 8 inches (20 centimeters) from the floor as if you are marching in place.

2   Touch the right foot to the floor.

3   Bring the right knee straight up again.

4   Bring the right foot to the floor by closing it to the left; shift your weight to right foot.

5-8   Repeat the first action of the first four counts with the left knee.

Do the same sort of knee lifts, but only once on each side this time.

1-2   Repeat counts 3 and 4 with the right foot.

3-4   Repeat these steps with the left foot.

Now comes the ending.

5-6   Clap your hands one time and hold count 6.

7-8   Jump on both feet to make a quarter-turn to the right and hold count 8.

Repeat the dance. The dance is done eight times through in the same way. On the ninth time every movement is halved as follows:

1-2   Extend the right foot to right side (1) and close (2).

3-4   Extend the left foot to the left side and close.

5-6   Extend the right foot back and close.

7-8   Extend the left foot back and close.

1-2   Lift the right foot and close.

3-4 Lift the left foot and close.

5-6 Clap hands and hold.

7-8 Make a quarter-turn and bow.

▷ Teaching Tips

Try this dance using the line start and holding pattern without turns and then add turns. Next, teach the dance to the left and reverse the movements to enhance laterality skills. Always go for music your students can relate to with these early line dances in your program.

Hustle

▷ Description

This is a classic 24-count, four-wall line dance with quarter-turns and an added twist.

Music Van McCoy, "The Hustle," *Pure Disco, Volume 2*, Utv Records; Harold Faltermeyer, "Axel F," *Beverly Hills Cop: Music From the Motion Picture Soundtrack*, MCA.

Formation Students form into lines.

▷ Counts and Steps

The first part of the dance simply involves walking four steps backward and then four steps forward.

1-4 Walk backward, starting with the right foot.

5-8 Walk forward, starting with the left foot.

Next the dancers grapevine to the right four counts and then back to the left four counts.

1-4 Vine to the right.

5-8 Vine to the left.

Next comes a hustle step to the right and then a hustle step to the left.

1-4 Hustle right; step right together with left foot, step right, touch with left foot beside right foot.

5-8 Hustle to the left; step left together with right foot, step left, touch with right foot beside left foot.

The last part of the dance proceeds as follows:

1-2 Snap the fingers two times overhead.

3-4 Stomp the right foot two times.

5-8 Right toe forward, backward, side; raise the knee high and make a quarter-turn left.

Repeat the dance.

▷ Teaching Tips

Try this dance using the line start approach and holding pattern without turns, and then add turns. Next, teach the dance to the left and reverse the dance movements to enhance laterality skills. Always start with slow counting and then add slow music. This process is gradually lengthened to keep the students active for longer periods of time in order to build cardiovascular endurance and fitness. At this point, go for more arm involvement and faster tempos to increase the heart rate. Another change that can be added when your students are ready is to put in quarter-, half-, and full turns in a logical progression. Always go for music that your students can relate to in your line dance unit. This greatly enhances motivation and students' acceptance of the activity. This dance is lots of fun done to the old disco song titled "The Hustle."

The Scoot

▷ Description

This is a nice 16-count, four-wall, modern country-western line dance with quarter-turns as well.

Music   Choose a medium-tempo modern piece.

Formation   Students form lines.

▷ Counts and Steps

Now that you can vine left and right, here is a dance that starts with a vine to the right and then back to the left.

1-4 Vine to the right.

4-8 Vine to the left.

9-12 Back up three steps starting with the right foot and **chug** forward on the right foot.

13-16 Step forward with the left foot and close together with the right; make a quarter-turn left and scuff right.

Repeat the dance.

▷ Teaching Tips

Try this dance using the line start approach and holding pattern without turns, and then add turns. Next, teach the dance to the left and reverse the dance movements to enhance laterality skills. Always start with slow counting and then add slow music. This process is gradually lengthened to keep the students active for longer periods of time in order to build cardiovascular endurance and fitness. At this point, go for more arm involvement and faster tempos to increase the heart rate. Another change that can be added when your students are ready is to put in quarter-, half-, and full turns in a logical progression. Always go for music that your students can relate to early in your line dance unit. This greatly enhances motivation and students' acceptance of the activity.

Jessie Polka

▷ Description

This is a fun, old-time 16-count dance done to country music.

Music   Adolph Hofner, "Jessie Polka," *South Texas Swing*, Arhoolie Records.

Formation   Dancers form four or five lines that radiate out from the center, each line facing the backs of the line in front, like the spokes of an old wagon wheel. They then move counterclockwise around the room.

▷ Counts and Steps

This dance starts with an 8-count heel-and-toe sequence.

1 Left heel forward.

2 Step the left foot beside the right foot.

3 Right toe back.

4 Touch the right foot beside the left foot.

5 Right heel forward.

6 Step the right foot beside the left foot.

7 Left heel forward.

8 Cross the left foot in front of the right foot.

The last half of the dance is made up of four two-steps forward, or step-close-step sequences, starting on the left foot.

1-8 Start on the left foot to do the four two-steps.

Repeat the dance.

▷ Teaching Tips

Try this dance using the line start and holding pattern without turns, and then add turns. Next, teach the dance to the left and reverse the dance movements to enhance laterality skills. Always go for music that your students can relate to for these early line dances in your program.

Scuffin'

▷ Description

This is a real nice 16-count, four-wall, modern line dance with quarter-turns that adds hip rocks into the dance very appropriately.

Music   A medium-speed modern piece works well.

Formation   Students form lines.

▷ Counts and Steps

The dance starts with a vine and scuff to the right and then a vine and a scuff to the left.

1-4 Vine to the right and scuff with the left foot.

5-8 Vine to the left and scuff with the right foot.

For the last half, step back on right foot and rock hips twice, step forward on left with a right scuff, repeat this again with a quarter turn on the end.

9-12 Step backward on the right foot and rock the hips two times; step forward on the left foot and scuff with the right.

13-16 Step backward on the right foot and rock the hips two times; step forward on the left foot with a quarter-turn to the left and then scuff with the right.

Repeat the dance.

▷ Teaching Tips

Try this dance using the line start approach and holding pattern without turns, and then add turns. Next, teach the dance to the left and reverse the dance movements to enhance laterality skills. Always start with slow counting and then add slow music. This process is gradually lengthened to keep the students active for longer periods of time in order to build cardiovascular endurance and fitness. At this point, go for more arm involvement and faster tempos to increase the heart rate. Another change that can be added when your students are ready is to put in quarter-, half-, and full turns in a logical progression. Always go for music that your students can relate to early in your line dance unit. This greatly enhances motivation and students' acceptance of the activity.

Old Flame

▷ Description

This is an easy 32-count country line dance with quarter-turns done to an old-time classic country tune.

Music   Frank Sinatra, "Love and Marriage," *The Very Best of Frank Sinatra*, Reprise Records.

Formation   Students form lines.

▷ Counts and Steps

Begin with a hustle to the right and then to the left.

1-4   Step with the right foot to the side and close to the left foot; shift your weight to the left foot; step with the right foot to the side and close left to the right foot.

5-8   Step with the left foot to the side and close to the right foot; shift your weight to the right foot; step with the left foot to the side and close right to the left foot.

Next, do four bleking steps with the heel–toe sequence.

1-8   Right heel forward and close, left heel forward and close; right heel forward and close, left heel forward and close.

Now comes the vine.

1-8   Vine with the right foot to the right, four steps; and vine with the left foot to the left, four steps.

Finish as follows:

1-8   Four two-steps forward (step-close-step sequence), ending up making a quarter-turn right on the fourth two-step.

Repeat the dance in lines, turning together.

▷ Teaching Tips

Try this dance using the line start approach and holding pattern without turns, and then add turns. Next teach the dance to the left and reverse the dance movements to enhance laterality skills. Always start with slow counting and then add slow music. This process is gradually lengthened to keep the students active for longer periods of time in order to build cardiovascular endurance and fitness. At this point, go for more arm involvement and faster tempos to increase the heart rate. Another change that can be added when your students are ready is to put in quarter-, half-, and full turns in a logical progression. Always go for music that your students can relate to early in your line dance unit. This greatly enhances motivation and students' acceptance of the activity.

Margie Dance

▷ Description

This 32-count line dance was choreographed in honor of Margie Hanson and presented at a retirement tribute for her at the 1992 American Alliance for Health, Physical Education, Recreation and Dance National Convention.

Music   The Hillside Singers, "I'd Like to Teach the World to Sing," *I'd Like to Teach the World To Sing*, Folk Era Records.

Formation   Students form lines.

▷ Counts and Steps

1-2   Sway with the body or hands to the right and left. Each sway represents one count.

3-4   Put the hands in the air and sway to the right and left.

5-8   Walk to the right and give a high-five greeting to the nearest person on the final step.

1-4   Walk to the left and give a high-five greeting to the nearest person on the final step.

5-8   Put the hands in the air and sway to the right, left, right, and left.

1-4   Join and slowly raise the hands (4 counts).

5-8   Slowly lower the hands (4 counts).

1-4   Say, "thank you" in sign language (see figure 5.1), two times.

5-8   Say, "I love you" in sign language (hold the two middle fingers down and keep the pinky, index finger, and thumb up) and raise hands.

Repeat the dance three more times. At the end, hug your neighbors and give them some N and Gs, which means tell them some "nice and good things."

Figure 5.1   "Thank you" in sign language.

▷ Teaching Tips

Try this dance using the line start and holding pattern without turns, and then add turns. Next, teach the dance to the left and reverse the dance movements to enhance laterality skills. Enjoy this dance during celebrations.

Popcorn

▷ Description

This is an easy, 16-count, four-wall line dance with quarter-turns that goes well with different kinds of music.

Music   Gershon Kingsley, "Popcorn," *Music to Moog By*, Dagored Records.

Formation   Students form lines.

▷ Counts and Steps

Dance starts with a grapevine to the right and then one to the left.

1-8 Vine to the right and left.

Next, step-hop forward with the right foot and then the same on the left foot. Then walk backwards with a kick on the fourth beat of this sequence.

1-2 Step forward on the right foot and hop.

3-4 Step forward on the left foot and hop.

5-8 Step backward on the right foot, left foot, right foot, and kick with the left foot.

The final eight counts include rocking forward and backward and walking forward with a quarter turn to the left.

1-2 Rock forward on the left foot, two bounces.

3-4 Rock backward on the right foot, two bounces.

5-8 Walk three steps forward on the left foot, right foot, left foot; and make a quarter-turn on the left foot to the left.

Repeat the dance.

▷ Teaching Tips

Try this dance using the line start approach and holding pattern without turns, and then add turns. Next teach the dance to the left and reverse the dance movements to enhance laterality skills. Always start with slow counting and then add slow music. This process is gradually lengthened to keep the students active for longer periods of time in order to build cardiovascular endurance and fitness. At this point, go for more arm involvement and faster tempos to increase the heart rate. Another change that can be added when your students are ready is to put in quarter-, half-, and full turns in a logical progression. Always go for music that your students can relate to early in your line dance unit. This greatly enhances motivation and students' acceptance of the activity.

Reggae Cowboy

▷ Description

This is a 24-count, four-wall country-western line dance with quarter- and half-turns.

Music   Choose a medium-tempo modern piece.

Formation Students form lines.

▷ Counts and Steps

This dance starts with sideways steps for two counts a piece. This is a little different than how most dances begin.

1-4 Step right, close left, step right, close left.

5-8 Step left, close right, step left, close right.

1-4 Step left, close right, step left, close right.

Next the dance adds in rocking forward and backward movements, two half-turns, and one quarter-turn.

5-8 Rock forward on the right foot right and back on the left; step backward on the right foot and forward on the left.

1-8 Step forward with the right foot and make a quarter-turn with your weight on the left foot; do this three times; close the right foot to the left and clap.

Repeat the dance.

▷ Teaching Tips

Try this 24-count dance using the line start and holding pattern after each 8-count segment. Next, teach the dance to the left and reverse the dance movements to enhance laterality skills. Always go for music that your students can relate to with these early line dances in your program.

Hallelujah

▷ Description

This can be a sing-along dance. It is 32 counts and uses some very nice lateral movements and introduces a jazz square.

Music   Parker and Penny, "Hallelujah," Hit Parade Records, or another upbeat medium tempo piece.

Formation   Students form lines.

▷ Counts and Steps

The dance starts with four body sways and walking to the right and back to the left.

1-4   Do four body sways—left, right, left, right—as the hands raise.

5-8   Walk to the right, stepping first with the right foot, then left, right, and left.

1-4   Facing front, do four body sways—left, right, left, right—as the hands raise.

5-8   Walk to the left; stepping first on the left, then right, left, and right.

Next, walk forward and backwards raising and lowering the hands.

1-4   Walk forward with the left foot, right foot, left foot; touch the right heel forward and lean backward, with the palms upraised in praise.

5-8   Walk backward with the right foot, left foot, right foot; touch the left toe backward and lower the arms.

The last sequence involves doing two jazz squares.

1-4   Step forward with the left foot, cross over with the right, step backward with the left, and step to the side with the right.

5-8   Repeat the jazz square again.

Repeat the dance.

▷ Teaching Tips

Try this dance using the line start and holding pattern after each 8-count segment. Next, teach the dance to the left and reverse the dance movements to enhance laterality skills. Always go for music that your students can relate to with these early line dances in your program.

New York, New York

▷ Description

This is a 32-count line dance that is a show classic. It has the potential to greatly add to your program.

Music   Frank Sinatra, "The Theme from New York, New York," *The Very Best of Frank Sinatra*, Reprise Records.

Formation   This can be done by individuals or in lines.

▷ Counts and Steps

Dance starts with four step-kicks starting on a step to the left.

1-8   Step with the left foot to the side, kick with the right foot, step with the right foot to he side, and kick with the left foot; repeat once more (see figure 5.2).

Next are four walking steps backward and forward with kicks on counts four and eight starting on the left foot.

1-4   Walk backward left, right, left; kick the right foot.

5-8   Walk forward right, left, right; kick the left foot.

Four **step-ball-changes** follow, starting on the left foot.

1-8   Step the left foot to the side and do a ball change on the right foot to land on the left; step with the right foot to the side and do a ball change on the left foot to land on the right; repeat once more.

The final sequence is a full turn to the left in four counts and then a full turn to the right in four counts.

1-4   Make four steps to the left and do a full turn starting with the left foot, right foot, left foot; touch the right foot beside the left.

5-8   Make four steps to the right and do a full turn starting with the right foot, left foot, right foot; touch the left foot beside the right.

Repeat the dance.

Figure 5.2   Step-kicks start out New York, New York.

▷ Teaching Tips

This dance lends itself quite well to being reversed, starting the dance on the right foot instead of the left.

Simple 32

▷ Description

This is a high-energy, 32-count, one-wall line dance.

Music   Alan Jackson, "Don't Rock the Jukebox," *Don't Rock the Jukebox*, Arista Records.

Formation   Students form lines.

▷ Counts and Steps

The first part of the dance involves stepping to the right four step-closes and then to the left four step-closes. Each direction takes eight counts to complete.

1-8 Step with the right foot to the right and close with the left foot four times.

1-8 Step with the left foot to the left and close with the right foot four times.

Next is four step-kicks in place starting with the right foot.

1-8 Do four step-kicks in place—step with the right foot, kick with left foot; step with left foot, kick with the right foot; repeat.

The last part of the dance involves three steps forward with a kick on count four and then three steps backward with a kick on count eight of this sequence.

1-4 Walk forward three steps with the right foot, left foot, right foot; kick the left foot one time.

5-8 Walk backward three steps with the left foot, right foot, left foot; kick the right foot one time.

Repeat the dance.

▷ Teaching Tips

This dance lends itself quite well to being reversed and starting on the left foot instead of the right.

Little Black Book

▷ Description

This is a classic 20-count, four-wall line dance that can be done individually or with a partner.

Music Jimmy Dean, "Little Black Book," *The Best of Jimmy Dean*, Sony.

Formation Students form lines or grab a partner.

▷ Counts and Steps

The dance begins with a vine to the right and then to the left.

1-8 Vine to the right on the right foot and then to the left on the left foot.

Now two step-hops forward starting on the right foot and then run forward three, again starting on the right foot, kick left foot on count four and put in a quarter-turn to the right and back up four to get ready to start the dance over again.

1-4 Do two step-hops forward on the right foot and then on the left foot.

5-8 Run forward on the right foot, left foot, right foot; hop, make a quarter-turn clockwise, raising the left knee on the final count.

1-4 Step backward three steps on the left foot, right foot, left foot; on the final count begin the dance again on the right foot.

Repeat the dance.

▷ Teaching Tips

This dance lends itself quite well to being reversed and starting the dance on the left foot instead of the right.

Continental

▷ Description

This is an old-time line dance from the 1950s. It was originally done in 20 counts but could and probably should be altered to be done in a variety of multiples of fours and eights. It is a four-wall dance.

Music   Elvis Presley, "Good Luck Charm," *Elvis: 30 #1 Hits*, RCA.

Formation   Students form lines.

▷ Counts and Steps

First comes a vine to the right and then a vine to the left.

1-8   Vine with the right foot to the right four steps and then with the left foot to the left four steps.

Next is four running two-steps straight ahead.

1-8   Perform four running two-steps straight ahead, starting on the right foot (step-close-step four times).

Last comes four kicks alternating feet, starting on the right foot. By the time the fourth kick has occurred, a quarter-turn to the right will have been completed.

1-4   Make three kicks alternating the right foot, left foot, and right foot while making a quarter-turn clockwise; after the third kick, cross the right foot in front of the left foot; the right toe touches the floor on the final count.

Repeat the dance.

▷ Teaching Tips

This dance lends itself quite well to being reversed and starting the dance on the left foot instead of the right.

The Stroll

▷ Description

This is a great line dance that was popular in the 1950s and 1960s. It is a social dance with two lines facing and individuals partnering up to dance down the middle of the lines. The basic step along the sides is an 8-count vine.

Music   Diamonds, "Stroll," *Diamonds Collection*, Stardust, or modern music with a medium or slow tempo.

Formation   Two lines face each other with girls in one and boys in the other. The dance progresses up the hall and dancers "freestyle" down the center all the time.

▷ Counts and Steps

This first part involves two crosses and then a vine step to the side to finish the 8-count sequence. Girls do the opposite footwork.

1-8   Cross the right foot over the left and then return to the starting position; cross the right foot over the left one more time and then come back to the right; repeat by crossing with the left for four more counts.

Now the same movement as above is repeated, but this time to the opposite direction.

1-8   Cross the left foot over the right and then return to the starting position; cross the left foot over the right foot one more time and then come back and to the left; repeat this to the left for four more counts.

Note: While this is going on, the group moves their lines to the head of the hall, and the boy and girl at the head of their respective lines freestyle down the middle to take their places at the end of the line (see figure 5.3).

Figure 5.3   Stroll formation.

▷ Teaching Tips

Encourage creativity as students dance down the middle with a new partner each time. This is a time for students to strut their stuff.

Have You Seen Her

▷ Description

This is a 32-count line dance that is made challenging by putting in turns in the second half of the dance.

Music   Choose a slow, modern piece.

Formation   Students form lines.

▷ Counts and Steps

The dance starts with a full turn to the right for four counts and back to the left for four counts.

1-8   Make a full turn right, stepping right, left, right, and ending with a touch of the left foot beside the right; they then make a full turn left, stepping left, right, left and ending with a touch of the right foot beside the left.

Next are step touches from side to side beginning to the right and back to the left.

1-8   Step sideways with the right foot and touch the left; step sideways with the left foot and touch the right; repeat.

The last part of the dance is walking forward and backward twice, but to make it more challenging, put in full turns with the movements.

1-8   Walk forward four steps starting with the right foot and backward four steps.

Repeat the entire dance.

▷ Teaching Tips

This dance lends itself quite well to being reversed and starting the dance on the left foot instead of the right.

Bus Stop

▷ Description

This is a classic 32-count, four-wall line dance that is always fun to do.

Music   Bob Seger, "Old Time Rock & Roll," *Bob Seger—Greatest Hits*, Capitol.

Formation   Students form lines.

▷ Counts and Steps

The first 16 counts involve heel clicks, toe touches, a quarter-turn to the left, and a walk to the back.

1-4   Begin with the feet together; click the heels together two times.

5-6   Put the right heel forward and touch two times.

7-8   Put the right toe backward and touch two times.

1-4   Put the right heel forward, the right toe backward, and then right toe to the side; raise the right knee high while making a quarter turn on the left foot; place the right foot beside the left.

5-8   Walk backward right foot, left foot, right foot, left foot.

Next comes a full turn to the right in four counts and then a full turn to the left in four counts.

1-4   Make a full turn to the right; step right foot, left foot, right foot, and touch the left foot beside the right.

5-8   Make a full turn to the left; step left foot, right foot, left foot, and touch the right foot beside left.

The last segment of the dance utilizes a hustle step to the right in four counts and then a hustle step back to the left in four counts.

1-4   Hustle right—step right foot to the side, step together with the left foot, step right foot to the side, touch left foot beside right.

5-8 Hustle left—step left foot to the side, step together with the right foot, step left foot to the side, touch right foot beside left.

Repeat the dance.

▷ Teaching Tips

A real challenge for this dance would be to try to reverse the way that the directions are given for the dance.

The Freeze

▷ Description

This dance was originally 20 counts, and this is how it is presented here. It would help the dance to add in 12 more counts to make it a 32-count dance. It is a fun-filled dance to do with country music.

Music   Tanya Tucker, "San Antonio Stroll," *The Upper 48 Hits: 1972–1997*, Raven.

Formation   Students form lines.

▷ Counts and Steps

1-4 Vine to the right and lift the left foot on the final count.

5-8 Vine to the left and lift the right foot on the final count.

1-4 Walk backward right foot, left foot, right foot; lift the left foot on the final count.

5-8 Rock forward on the left foot for two counts and backward on the right foot for two counts.

1-4 Walk forward left, right, left; lift the right foot while making a quarter-turn to the left on the left foot.

Repeat the dance.

▷ Teaching Tips

Try this one adding in turns everywhere that you can. It makes it much more challenging and more fun as well. This could be made into a 32-count dance by adding at the beginning a side-touch right and side-touch left four times for eight more counts and walking forward four extra steps at the end before the turn.

Sport Dance

▷ Description

This is a 64-count, four-wall dance that includes a combination of sport moves.

Music   Alabama, "Dancin', Shaggin' on the Boulevard," *Dancin' on the Boulevard*, RCA.

Formation   Students form lines.

▷ Counts and Steps

The first 16 counts is a carioca or vine step right and left.

1-16 Vine to the right, beginning on the right foot, for eight counts; vine to the left, beginning on the left foot, for eight counts.

The next sequence is a slide, step-close-step, two-step sequence with rock-steps which is done four total times, twice to each side.

1-4   Do a two-step on the right foot to the right side and rock-step backward on the left foot; step forward on the right foot.

5-8   Do a two-step on the left foot to the left side and rock-step backward on the right foot; step forward on the left foot.

1-8   Repeat the two-steps to the sides, starting back to the right.

Next are quarter-pivots both counterclockwise and clockwise.

1-8   Make four quarter-turns counterclockwise to complete a full turn.

1-8   Make four quarter-turns clockwise to complete a full turn.

The final eight counts are a schottische step forward and backward—just like shooting a lay-up shot in basketball.

1-4   Schottische step forward—step forward on the right foot, left foot, right foot, and hop on the right foot.

5-8   Schottische step backward—step backward on the left foot, right foot, left foot, and hop on the left foot.

Repeat the dance.

▷ Teaching Tips

This is a great dance to start line dancing. It incorporates many sport skills and helps to connect your students to the movements. It also lends itself to different kinds of music. It would be a good one to start to the left instead of to the right.

Struttin'

▷ Description

This is a really fun and modern 40-count, four-wall line dance.

Music   Choose a medium-speed modern piece.

Formation   Students form lines.

▷ Counts and Steps

The first part is to walk backward for four counts and then forward four starting on the right foot.

1-4   Walk backward right, left, right, and close the left foot beside the right.

5-8   Walk forward left, right, left, and close the right foot beside the left.

Next walk to the right starting on the right foot and turning back with a half-turn to walk back to the start position and make a quarter-turn to the right.

1-4   Walk sideways to the right on the right foot and then the left; make a half-turn on the right foot and close with the left foot beside the right.

5-8   Walk back to the left on the left foot then the right and left; make a quarter-turn to the right and close with the right foot beside the left.

This is followed by two kick ball changes and a lowering the head down to the right and left like going under an electric fence.

1-4   Do a kick ball change, which involves kicking the right foot out, stepping with the right foot beside left, and then stepping with the left; do this twice; the kick ball change is counted 1-and-2, 3-and-4.

5-8 Skate or do the "electric fence" to the right and to the left by lowering the head down to each side for a total of four more counts; this is counted as five and six to the right, seven and eight to the left.

Now students get to have some fun, showing some struttin' style.

1-8 Point with the right index finger to left knee and then up in the air four times (see figure 5.4).

The final sequence is to roll the hands around like an "egg beater" in front of your body and then follow the turning directions and end up facing one quarter of a turn to the left from the original start position.

1-8 Roll the hands around like egg beaters in front of your body for two counts (roll hands around each other and bend over forward); click the heels twice; right heel forward, backward, sideways, and kick forward with a quarter-turn to the left from the starting position.

Repeat the dance.

Figure 5.4   Struttin'.

▷ Teaching Tips

This dance will be lots of fun for your students. It will push them to learn more steps and to combine them into a given dance. Teach this dance in 8-count segments.

Rise

▷ Description

This is a 64-count dance that will challenge your students to proceed to a higher level with their dancing. It is a dance with a nice tempo that was very popular in the 1970s.

Music   Herb Alpert, "Rise," *Rise,* A&M Records.

Formation   Students form lines.

▷ Counts and Steps

Part A

First, students will hustle right and left twice.

1-4   Hustle right—step with the right foot, together with the left; step again with the right foot and touch beside the left.

5-8   Hustle left—step with the left foot, together with the right; step again with the left foot and touch beside the right.

1-4   Repeat the steps for counts 1 to 8.

This next segment uses a very nice static balance on count four of each measure with a walking step followed by the hustle step to the right and to the left again.

1-4   Step forward with the right foot, left foot, right foot, and hold for one count.

5-8   Step forward with the left foot, right foot, left foot, and hold for one count.

1-4   Hustle right—step with the right foot, close beside the left; repeat.

5-8   Hustle left—step with the left foot, close beside the right; repeat.

Part B

The first part of B is the three step sequence and the hold on count four beginning on the right foot.

1-4   Step backward with the right foot, left foot, right foot, and hold for one count.

5-8   Step backward with the left foot, right foot, left foot, and hold for one count.

Next, with feet spread about shoulder width apart, swing hips side to side while you "rock down" for four counts and then back up for four counts.

1-8   Rock side to side; go down four counts and up four counts. Note: The feet should be shoulder-width apart; swing the hips side to side while you rock down for four counts and then back up for four counts.

The final segment is made up of two sets of four quarter-pivots, so that the body is turned all the way around twice.

1-8   Step with the right foot forward; make a quarter-pivot counterclockwise with the right foot and repeat this three times to return to the original position.

1-8   Step with the left foot forward; make a quarter-pivot clockwise with the left foot and repeat this three times to return to the original position.

Repeat the dance.

▷ Teaching Tips

The slowness of this piece greatly increases the students' chances for success. It can certainly be danced at a faster tempo, and direction changes and locomotor patterns can be altered with very little effort.

Celebration Time

▷ Description

This is a 32-count dance that was created by John Bennett while at the North Carolina Department of Public Instruction. It is a great dance to do at celebration times and is really quite easy to do. It can be done as a four-wall dance or as only a one-wall dance.

Music   Kool & the Gang, "Celebration," *The Very Best of Kool & the Gang*, Mercury/Universal.

Formation   Students form lines.

▷ Counts and Steps

The first part involves pointing to the right and to the left.

1-2   Extend the right arm with the palm down and point two times to the right.

3-4   Extend the left arm with the palm down and point two times to the left.

5-6   Extend the right arm with the palm up and point two times to the right.

7-8   Extend the left arm with the palm up and point two times to the left.

Now hitchhike two times with right thumb and two times with the left thumb.

1-2   Point two times over the right shoulder with the right thumb.

3-4   Point two times over the left shoulder with the left thumb.

Next roll hands in front while bending over for two counts and roll the hands back up for two more counts.

5-6   Roll the hands in front, similar to the motion made when winding yarn into a ball, while bending downward.

7-8   Roll the hands in front while straightening up, then bending backward.

Next comes a pointing and slapping sequence.

1-2   Point two times with the right hand to the left knee.

3-4   Point two times with the left hand to the right knee.

5   Point one time with the right hand to the left knee.

6   Point one time with the left hand to the right knee.

7   Slap the right hip one time with the right hand.

8   Slap the left hip one time with the left hand.

Simply walk around in a circle for the final eight counts strutting your stuff.

1-8   Walk around in a circle for all eight counts back to your original starting position.

Repeat the dance, making a quarter-turn right after the sequence so that four times through makes it a four-wall dance.

▷ Teaching Tips

This is a "must-learn" line dance for your classes. Kids of all ages like this one. It is a high-energy dance that all of your students will love to do.

▷ SUMMARY

Line dances give students the opportunity to dance solo in a very nonthreatening manner. The flexibility of the dances in this chapter will allow students to be successful and give them the confidence to dance in social settings.

Create Your Own Line Dance

This is an opportunity for students to do both individual and group work, depending on your preference and needs. Creating their own dances allows students to develop critical thinking and socialization skills.

Checklist for Creating a Line Dance

- Instruct students to create their own line dances.
- Stay developmentally appropriate. Beginners can start by creating simple line dances, such as one with 16 counts, before progressing in stages to a line dance with 24, 32, or even 64 counts—if your students are especially sharp.
- Challenge students to choreograph the dance to face four walls.
- Have them incorporate different directions and turns into their dance.
- Have the students try this alone and with partners or small groups to change the social dynamic and increase their development of social skills.
- Require students to write up their descriptions to emphasize the language aspects of dance.

Rubric

Now that you have your students into creating their own dances, here is an example of a rubric that could work for this particular activity or for others with modifications.

4 Points—Exemplary	The student choreographed the assigned number of counts to create a four-wall line dance with variety and movements that was executed well to the music.
3 Points—Acceptable	The student choreographed the assigned number of counts to create a four-wall line dance with some variety and movements that was sometimes executed to the music.
2 Points—Needs improvement	The student choreographed the assigned number of counts to create a four-wall line dance with no variety; movements were rarely executed to the music.
1 Point—Unacceptable	The student choreographed fewer than the assigned number of counts in the line dance, it was not a four-wall dance, and there was no clear rhythmic pattern established.

 # Review Questions

Have students submit questions for the class to answer or have them answer questions similar to these that follow. In addition, these could be used as a homework assignment, as an in-class assignment, or for class discussion.

1. Make a list of the benefits of line dancing.
2. Trace the history of line dancing.
3. When creating line dances, what is the main number that is critical to developing such dances?

4. Collect and write up several line dances from other sources.
5. Describe the physiological benefits received from line dancing.
6. When creating line dances, what are some of the important things that you should be sure to include?
7. What is the great appeal of line dancing?

▷ **Observation Questions** ◁

The following are some suggestions for what to watch for while observing your students learning and performing line dances. You can challenge them to watch for these things as well and thereby introduce a new way of learning by observation.

1. List the different locomotor movements that you observed in this activity.
2. Describe how to do the hustle step.
3. List the combination movements that you observed in this activity.
4. How many walls did the dancers face during the dance?
5. What caused you to face different walls during the dance?
6. What was the tempo of this dance?
7. Which dance was an 8-count dance?
8. Did the movement of the participants reflect the theme and attitude of this dance? Please describe your observations.
9. Did the participants raise their heart rates to meet their target for aerobic benefits?
10. Was there an opportunity for the dancers to develop movements in all directions?
11. Was there an opportunity for leading with different feet? Please describe the level at which this occurred.
12. Was the dance developed in multiples of 4, 8, 16, 32, or 64 counts?
13. Was the music selection appropriate for your class?

▷ CHAPTER 6

Folk Dances

Folk dances reflect the cultures of many lands. They will pump life and excitement into our programs. There are enough dances in this chapter to keep any teacher active for quite some time. Through our study of folk dance we can help to preserve our array of cultural heritages.

The chapter begins with a description of folk dancing and tips for starting your folk dance program. It then proceeds to descriptions of the dances, which have been grouped primarily by the region of the globe from which they come.

▷ DESCRIPTION OF FOLK DANCING

Folk dancing is the oldest form of dance and probably one of the earliest forms of communication. The inherent self-expression that embodies folk dancing separates it from the functional aspects of games and gymnastics in our physical education programs.

Dance is the expression of oneself through rhythmic movement. Folk dance, which is also the expression of oneself, is an expression through patterned movements. This patterning traditionally separates folk dance forms from other dance forms. Probably this characteristic of folk dance has turned off many youngsters to dance; they perceive that they are unable to perform a complete set of patterned movements.

This brings up the argument, discussed in chapter 1, regarding whether to modify a particular dance for a group. Many say that it is not the proper thing to do because it destroys the integrity of the dance. For this very reason you may want to have two levels of folk dance for your students. There is a need for a modified level to promote and ensure success, and there is also a need to preserve a dance completely intact for its built-in values. Simplify your dances to raise the success level of students, then teach them the prescribed pattern for a given dance. This modification will allow you to bring along all of your students and will give them the chance to see and perform the complete dance.

Importance of Folk Dancing

Folk dance should be an integral part of all dance programs. The teacher must know when to modify and when to preserve a dance or the students can be lost to dance forever. Knowing what to do at the proper times comes with experience, a willingness to learn, and a desire to promote dance for everyone. It can be any of these three elements or a combination of them that has caused some teachers to feel negatively about teaching dance.

Folk dance can be the easiest form of dance to teach. However, not knowing how to modify a dance has probably caused us to turn off young students and perhaps even ourselves. Experiment, simplify, and teach in small segments. Don't be afraid to modify or change the directions to raise success levels. If we believe that education should be child centered, then folk dance must be modified in the beginning to fit the needs of students. We must not try to form the student to fit the activity. We all have an obligation to educate youngsters beyond simply developing movement skills. All children have feelings and thoughts that must be nurtured. We must focus on total development.

When starting dance with children, they need success immediately. Provide activities around basic movements that they have done before, and begin focusing on rhythmic movement. Don't even call it dance in the beginning. Be sure to cover all the nonlocomotor, locomotor, and combination movements; then work on phrasing. Youngsters need to internalize phrasing without the pressure of fouling up a patterned dance. Percussion instruments and music can help with this early movement. Contrasts in movement should be the focus with this process of exploration. Contrast is an important element of expression at all levels of dance. If you as a teacher feel more comfortable, you can do exercises to music as preparation for dance concepts later. The results of a lesson are important to the teacher but probably more important to the student. Remember that feelings, creativity, and movement are fundamental to all dance forms.

Starting the Program

Rhythm is the basis of all movement activities, and the key to success hinges on the proper rhythmic execution of any skill. Look for the basic patterns of dance found in nearly every sport. Certainly, these can be useful as lead-ins to your folk dance lessons or any other dance forms.

True dance must have soul, express passion, and imitate nature. Writers in the late 1800s sing the praises of folk dances, which to them "barely veil the wooing of the sexes in rhythmic movements, expression of deep feelings, and imitation of every even the smallest aspects of human nature" (Sachs, 1937, 429).

The following selection provides a variety of folk dances to choose from. This allows you maximum flexibility in meeting your programmatic needs. There is plenty here for everyone. Although all the dances are relatively easy, they are arranged progressively according to area. If you are a beginning teacher, this organization will assist you by commencing with the easiest dances to ensure success for both you and your students.

▷ AFRICAN

Fanga

▷ Description

The fanga dance originated in West Africa and is now danced throughout most of Africa. It is intended to welcome people and is performed at happy occasions. Fanga actually means "welcome." This dance was shared with us by Joy Kagendo Wells.

Formation   Both boys and girls dance in one straight line. The girls usually line up in the middle of the formation with the men on the sides playing drums and other percussion instruments.

▷ Counts and Steps

1-8   "Welcome one, welcome all": Stand with the hands in front as if holding a beach ball. Step back with the right foot as if making a semicircle and let the right hand follow the right foot around and up over the head. Step back with the left foot and place it beside the right foot. Repeat this one more time and then repeat the steps and arm movements to the left side. (See figure 6.1.)

1-8   "We welcome you with open hands": Raise both hands up (palms facing you) to your right a bit just above the head with your eyes following the hands. Next, move the hands diagonally toward the left hip and tap once on the side of the hip as if hitting a drum. Lift hands up again diagonally, only this time do two short lifts. The pattern that you should duplicate in this part of the dance is that of the hands going up to the right once and down to the left once, up to the right twice and down once, up once, and down twice (up, down, up, up, down, up, down, down).

1-12   "We welcome you from the north, south, west, and east": The right foot goes out to the side and both hands go up; the right foot comes back in and the left foot goes out to the side as the hands come down. The right foot goes out again and the right hand

Figure 6.1   Welcome one, welcome all.

makes a circle that is completed when the right foot returns back to its original position. The left foot goes out and in as the left hand is raised and makes a circle with this foot movement.

13-16 "We bear no arms": Both hands come from the chest and go out to the right side. This movement is repeated to the left side. This movement calls for the foot on the side to which you are moving to step out as the hands go to the chest.

1-4 "Let's celebrate": Lift the right hand up once as if to wave, then lift the left hand and wave. Switch back to the right side, and this time wave twice on the right side and then on the left side.

Repeat each movement four times.

▷ Chant

Fanga Alafia, Ashei, Ashei (two times)

We welcome you with all our heart, Ashei, Ashei (two times)

We welcome you from the North and South, Ashei, Ashei (two times)

We welcome you from the East and West, Ashei, Ashei (two times)

Fanga Alafia, Ashei, Ashei

▷ Meanings

Fanga (pronounced FAHN-ga) means "we welcome you with open arms."

Alafia (pronounced A-LAH-fee-a) means "we welcome you with love."

Ashei (pronounced A-SHAY) means "that's right, we agree."

▷ Teaching Tips

This dance provides a great opportunity to study African culture and discuss the positive forms of socialization exhibited in the movements. It can involve the entire student body of the school if you so desire.

▷ AMERICAN–NORTH

La Bastringue

▷ Description

This is a French Canadian couple mixer for all ages. It is designed for total inclusion. It has a different organizational pattern in that the girls line up in a single circle on the left-hand side of their male partners instead of the right-hand side.

Music Jean Carnigan, "La Bastringue," Worldtone Records; or another hoedown selection.

Formation Students form a single circle; partners are formed with girls to the left of boys.

▷ Counts and Steps

Pattern 1: Forward and Back

1-4 Everyone joins hands and walks to the middle of the circle right, left, right and then touches the left foot to the right.

5-8   Everyone walks backward from the center left, right, left and then touches the right foot to the left.

Repeat both the first and second sets.

Pattern 2: Two-Step to Left and Right

1-8   Do four two-steps to the left (clockwise)—left-right-left, right-left-right, left-right-left, right-left-right—counted as 1-and-2, 3-and-4, 5-and-6, 7-and-8; you can also do step-close-step four times

1-8   Do four two-steps to the right (counterclockwise)—right-left-right, left-right-left, right-left-right, left-right-left.

Pattern 3: Swing

1-4   The boy turns his partner once under his raised left hand for a four-count **swing**. She turns to face the next boy on her left and the boy faces the next girl on his right.

5-16   The new partners execute a **buzz swing** and end up ready to **promenade** the circle facing counterclockwise.

Pattern 4: Promenade

1-16   Couples promenade, doing eight two-steps beginning on the right foot; on the last two-step couples turn to face the center and join hands with everyone to repeat the dance with new partners.

▷ Teaching Tips

Take time to practice this rather odd way to get a new partner and to organize a dance formation with the girl on the boy's left side instead of on his right. This dance can be done to most popular dance music to increase motivation in the beginning.

The Hokey Pokey 10

▷ Description

This is a dance for all ages that is very simple and performed without a partner. It was designed for total inclusion and fulfills that objective extremely well. It is primarily a dance for younger children involving identification of body parts but is often danced at social occasions by all ages.

Formation   Students stand in a single circle, partnerless, and facing the center (see figure key.4, page xvi).

▷ Counts and Steps

Part A

1-4   Standing in a circle, all sing the first line of Verse 1. Extend the right hand to the center of the circle.

5-8   All sing the second line of Verse 1, and extend their right arms away from the center.

1-8   All sing the final line of Verse 1, extending their hands back to the center and shaking them.

Part B

1-8   All sing the first line of the chorus, holding up their arms and turning around for four counts to face anyone nearby.

1-8 All sing the last line of the chorus. Everyone slaps their thighs twice, claps their own hands twice, and then claps hands with the other person three times.

Repeat this process with the following verses:

Verse 2: Left hand

Verse 3: Right foot

Verse 4: Left foot

Verse 5: Right elbow

Verse 6: Left elbow

Verse 7: Head

Verse 8: Backside

Verse 9: Whole self

Verse 10: Hokey Pokey—Bend down and straighten up again while singing. Do it again on the second count. On the third, kneel down on hands and knees, and pound on the floor. Stand up again on the last count.

▷ Teaching Tips

This is a simple dance that is very inclusive and easy to learn. It is a lot of fun, and people of all ages really seem to enjoy it. So, pull it out at any time for any group and it will be a definite hit.

Amos Moses (Hully Gully) 11

▷ Description

This is a novelty 8-count dance. It is a very short and simple line dance that everyone can perform. It is performed without a partner. The dance was developed in connection with an old song by Jerry Reed but can be done to any medium-tempo 4-count rhythm.

Formation Students stand anywhere on the floor and face front. This is called an open formation.

▷ Counts and Steps

1-2 Right heel forward and close.

3-4 Left heel forward and close.

5 Step forward on right.

6 Step left foot behind right foot.

7 Step forward on right with a quarter-turn right.

8 Step forward on left and close beside right.

Repeat until the song ends.

▷ Teaching Tips

This is a fun dance that will not take a lot of time to teach. It gets everyone going quickly and is an easy dance for which to create variations.

Jump Jim Jo

▷ Description

This is a couples dance that contains a progression of partner exchanges. It can be done by persons of all ages.

Formation   Couples form a circle with the boy's back to the center of the circle; both hands are joined (see figure key.3, page xv).

▷ Lyrics

"Jump, jump, oh jump, Jim Jo,

Take a little whirl, and around you go,

Slide, slide, and stamp just so,

You're a sprightly little fellow

When you jump, Jim Jo."

Alternate words for the last two lines:

"Then you take another partner

And you jump, Jim Jo."

▷ Counts and steps

"Jump, jump, oh jump, Jim Jo."

1-4   Dancers jump to the side in a counterclockwise direction with two slow jumps, followed by three quick jumps in place (counts 1, 2, 3-and-4).

"Take a little whirl, and around you go."

5-8   Drop the hands to the sides; each partner turns in place to the right to make a full turn with four slow jumps (counts 5, 6, 7, 8). Alternate version: The boy twirls the girl under joined right hands.

"Slide, slide, and stamp just so."

1-4   Couples rejoin hands and slide slowly counterclockwise twice, then they stamp their feet three times (counts 1, 2, 3-and-4).

"Then you take another partner, and you jump, Jim Jo."

5-8   Each dancer moves right with four light running steps and then jumps quickly three times (counts 5, 6, 7-and-8).

Repeat the dance from the beginning with a new partner.

▷ Variation

Instead of the two slow slides in a counterclockwise direction, couples may run around in place with both hands held and stay with the same partner for the three quick jumps.

▷ Teaching Tips

This is an excellent dance to help students memorize words and to move while reciting them.

Bunny Hop 13

▷ Description

This is a conga-style dance for all ages. It was first developed in the United States in the 1950s and is often seen at weddings and other social occasions.

Formation Students form a line, standing in single file with the hands on the hips of the person in front of them. You may wish to alternate boys and girls, placing either a boy or girl at the head of the line (see figure 6.2). This is a line dance, of sorts, from the party times after World War II. Everyone can be included in this dance.

▶ **Figure 6.2** Single-file formation for the Bunny Hop.

▷ Counts and Steps

1-4 Start with both feet together, put the left foot out to the side, and close; do this twice.

5-8 Put the right foot out to the side and close; do this twice.

1-2 Jump forward once and hold.

3-4 Jump backward once and hold.

5-8 Jump forward three times and hold.

Repeat the dance.

▷ Teaching Tips

• This a great dance for parties! It is very easy and can be done with several lines circulating around the room.

• If students are too squeamish about placing their hands on each other's hips, an alternative is to have them place their hands on the shoulders of the person to their front.

Ten Pretty Girls 14

▷ Description

This dance does not require partners and can be done in many forms. It is appealing to members of any age group. It is said to have originated in Texas, but no real proof has been found. It is an easy dance for young students to learn, but it works quite well for older students as well.

Formation   Any number of dancers stand side by side in a circle or in lines. They may hold hands or place their hands behind each other's backs.

Counts and Steps

Part A

1-and   Start on the right foot, place right toe forward, and pause.

2-and   Place the right toe to the right side and pause.

3-4   Take three steps, moving sideways to the left—right foot, left foot, right foot; step with the right in back of the left while moving sideways on the first count (counts 3-and-4).

5-and   Place the left toe forward and pause.

6-and   Place the left toe to the left side and pause.

7-8   Take three quick steps, moving sideways to the right—left foot, right foot, left foot; step with the left in back of the right on the first count (counts 7-and-8).

Part B

1-4   Everyone moves forward four steps, strutting—right foot, left foot, right foot, left foot.

5   Vigorously kick the right foot forward and lean the body back.

6   Kick the right foot backward and lean the body forward; make a half-turn to face the opposite direction.

7-8   Stamp the feet in place lightly three times—right foot, left foot, right foot (counts 7-and-8).

Repeat the dance, starting with the other foot each time.

Teaching Tips

This is a very easy dance. Take time to walk through it without musical accompaniment in the beginning. Then you will be ready to do the entire dance with music.

Skip to My Lou 15

Description

This is a circle dance done by those of all ages to the well-known folk song with the same name. This is a typical early-American folk song that had a dance set to it.

Formation   Students form a double circle with boys on the inside circle; couples join inside hands, facing the line of direction (see figure key.2, page xv).

Counts and Steps

Part A

1-16   All sing, "Skip, skip, skip to my Lou; skip, skip, skip to my Lou; skip, skip, skip to my Lou; skip to my Lou, my darling." While singing, couples join inside hands and skip counterclockwise 16 times.

Part B

1-16   All sing, "Lost my true love, what'll I do; lost my true love, what'll I do; lost my true love, what'll I do; skip to my Lou, my darling." Couples release hands. While singing, the boys make a half-turn and skip clockwise 16 times. The girls continue with 16 skips counterclockwise.

Part C

1-16 All sing, "Found another one, prettier'n you; found another one, prettier'n you; found another one, prettier'n you; skip to my Lou, my darling." While singing, each boy finds a new partner and swings her in place with a **two-handed skipping swing**. He puts her on his right side and repeats the dance. Those without partners go to the center of the circle for "lost and found," find a partner, and join the circle.

▷ Teaching Tips

Let the students have time to get the lyrics and movements without any pressure to perform perfectly in the beginning.

Red River Valley 16

▷ Description

This dance is performed in groups of three and is designed to include everyone at the dance. This is actually a folk dance that was popular in the early years of westward migration in the United States. It was probably done by those in the early wagon trains heading out to settle new territories.

Formation Students circle in sets of six that break into two facing lines of three dancers. Trios are formed by one boy and two girls or one girl and two boys. The three join hands. All sing with great gusto while dancing the action indicated in the words of the song (see figure key.6, page xvi).

▷ Lyrics

Oh, you lead right down in the valley,

And you circle to the left, go once around,

Now you swing with the girl in the valley,

And you swing with your Red River Gal.

Oh, you lead right down in the valley,

And you circle to the left and to the right,

Now the girls star right in the valley,

And the boys do-si-do so polite.

Oh, you lead right down in the valley,

And you circle to the left and to the right,

Now you lose your girl in the valley,

And you lose your Red River Gal.

▷ Counts and Steps

Part A

1-8 Lines of three walk forward, bearing right and passing the opposite set of dancers, to meet a new line of three.

1-8 Join hands with the new line to form a circle of six; walk eight steps.

1-8 The center dancer in each set of three then swings the dancer to her or his right.

Part B

1-16   Repeat the steps from the first two sets of counts in part A.

1-8   Four girls (or the four people on the ends of the two lines) join right hands across in the center between the two lines to form a **right-hand star**; walk clockwise once around; drop back into place on the last two counts to clear the way for the next eight counts.

1-8   The two center dancers **do-si-do;** partners face and walk around each other, starting right shoulder to right shoulder.

Part C

1-16   Repeat the steps for first two sets of counts in part A.

1-8   The two dancers on the right of the three-person lines facing one another change places by passing on the right shoulder diagonally across the set.

1-8   The two dancers on the left of the lines change places by passing on the right shoulder diagonally across the set.

Repeat the entire dance with new partners each time.

▷ Teaching Tips

Take some time to introduce this dance. It has a new formation that, while very simple, is different enough to throw off your students. A drawing of the new figures helps them to visualize this new formation and execute the dance.

La Raspa *9*

▷ Description

La Raspa is a novelty dance, rather than one of Mexico's traditional dances. In the United States it is quite often called the Mexican Hat Dance. Some say that it is the national folk dance of Mexico. It is a dance for all ages. *La raspa* means "the file." The opening step is a bleking step, which is done by thrusting one foot out with the heel down and the toe up while the participant lands on the opposite foot from which she or he sprung to begin the step.

Formation   Students form a single circle with partners facing each other (see figure key.9, page xvii).

▷ Counts and Steps

Part A: Chorus

1-4   Partners hold both hands and do a bleking step—hopping on the left foot and sending the right foot forward with the heel down and toe up (counts 1, 2), then hopping on the right foot and sending the left foot forward with the heel down and toe up (on counts 3, 4).

5-8   Partners repeat the bleking step described in the first set of counts, starting with the right foot forward (on counts and-5), repeat it again while starting with the left foot forward (counts and-6), repeat it once more with the right foot forward (counts and-7), finish with a double clap (counts and-8).

Repeat this three times.

Part B:

1-8 Hook right elbows, take eight running steps clockwise, and release elbows to clap on the eighth step.

1-8 Hook left elbows, take eight running steps counterclockwise, and release elbows to clap on the eighth step.

1-16 Repeat the steps for both of these sets.

Repeat the dance from the beginning.

Part B, variation 1

1-32 Skip 16 steps with the right elbows linked and 16 steps with the left elbows linked. Do not repeat.

Part B, variation 2

1-32 Assume the closed ballroom dance position and do a polka around the ring for 16 steps.

Part B, variation 3

1-32 Face your partner (all should be in a single-circle formation for this version) and do a grand right and left around the circle; at the end of the chorus take a new partner and repeat the dance from the beginning. (See the Lucky Seven lesson in chapter 7 and figure 7.1 for a description of grand right and left.)

▷ Teaching Tips

Walk through this slowly. The bleking step is very unique for those who have never done it before. Be adventurous and try the variations; they are lots of fun. This is a great introduction to Mexican culture.

Salty Dog Rag 17

▷ Description

This is a couples or line dance that is very popular in folk dance groups. It moves right along and presents a good challenge for the dancers. It is based on an old folk ballad that is still sung across the country by folk singers.

Formation   Couples begin side by side in the skaters' position (see figure key.2, page xv).

▷ Counts and Steps

Part A

1-8 Schottische step—step right foot to the side, then left foot, and then right foot, and hop; then left foot, right foot, left foot, and hop; move to the right side and return. Dancers move to the right side for four counts, and then back to the left for four counts.

1-8 Make four step-hops forward.

1-8 Repeat the steps in the first set of counts.

1-8 Repeat the steps in the second set of counts.

Part B

1-8 Face your partner and hold hands. Do the schottische step right and left as described in the first set of counts in part A.

1-8 Holding right hands, make four step-hops in a circle clockwise.

1-8 Face your partner and hold hands. Do the schottische step right and left again as in the first set of counts in part A.

1-8 Holding left hands, make four step-hops in a circle counterclockwise.

Repeat the dance.

▷ Line Dance Modification

Part A

1-8 Schottische step right and left.

1-8 Four step-hops in place.

1-8 Schottische step right and left.

1-8 Four step-hops in place.

Part B

1-16 Go forward four steps and backward four steps, two times.

1-16 Right heel forward, close; left heel forward, close; right heel forward, close; clap, clap, clap (counted 1, 2, 3, 4, 5, 6, 7-and-8—the 7-and-8 counts are the three claps at the end of the sequence). Repeat this sequence.

Repeat the dance.

▷ Teaching Tips

This is a really fun dance with good variations. Be sure to try them. Your students will enjoy the challenges.

Solomon Levi

▷ Description

This is a four-couple square dance. It is a sung dance that dancers of any ability enjoy participating in at a very easy level.

Formation Four couples hold inside hands and start in a square (see figure key.5, page xvi).

▷ Counts and Steps

Part A

1-8 One couple separates and turns back to back; each partner walks around the outside of the group, going in opposite directions.

1-8 Pass your partner on the opposite side of the group and pass her or him again coming back home.

Part B

1-8 Bow to your **corner**; bow to all the partners by bowing forward.

1-8 Swing your partner round and round and promenade the hall by getting into skater's position and walking around the circle back to the starting position.

Part C

1-8 Promenade with your partner around the formation and end up back home while you sing, "Hey, Solomon Levi, tra la la la la la la la la la la."

1-8   Repeat this movement while you sing, "Poor Solomon Levi, tra la la la la la la la la la.

Note: The tune plays through nine times. Add variety by having the **heads, sides**, and all four do the figure at the same time, or repeat for each couple. In this formation, the heads are couples 1 and 3 on the circle; the sides are couples 2 and 4 on the circle.

▷ Teaching Tips

The variations can be confusing, so walk through them slowly at first and then bring them up to tempo. The participants will really enjoy their success with the various figures.

Virginia Reel 19

▷ Description

This is a contra dance that was modified from an English variation known as Sir Roger de Coverly. It was changed from its original to avoid being connected back to the Old World that the early American settlers had left behind. All ages danced this particular dance. It is probably the most popular of the contra or "longway" dances. The Virginia reel is usually done in family style with all participants active throughout. It is performed to many tunes.

Formation   Students form longways sets of six couples facing one another; all girls are on the left and all boys on the right in relation to the head couple (see figure key.8, page xvii). The head couple is closest to the music or caller and the "head" of the call.

▷ Counts and Steps

Part A

1-8   "Forward and back"—both lines take four steps to the center, bow to their partners across from them in the other line as they take the fourth step on count four, and then take four steps back.

1-8   "Right hand around"—partners meet, join right hands, swing once around clockwise, and return to their original spot.

1-8   "Left hand around"—repeat using the left hand and swinging counterclockwise.

1-8   "Both hands around"—repeat using both hands and turning clockwise.

Part B

The counts depend on the number in the set.

- "Head couple down and back"—the head couple joins both hands and sashays down the set and back to the head position; the sashay is done with quick, but smooth, sliding side-steps.

- "Reel the set"—the head couple hooks right elbows, turns once and a half around, then separates and goes to opposite line; the head boy turns the second girl once around with a left **elbow turn**, as the head girl does the same with the second boy.

- The head couple meets in the center for a right elbow turn and continues to the third girl and boy for a left elbow turn.

- The head couple continues down the set in this fashion, making left elbow turns to the set and right elbow turns in the center until it has "reeled" the entire set.

- At the foot of the set, the head couple swings halfway around so the boy and girl are on the correct side; joins hands, and sashays back to their original place at the head of the set.

Part C

The counts, as in part B, depend on the number in the set.

- "Cast off to the foot"—the head couple leads to the outside, proceeding to the foot of the line; boys go to the left and girls to the right; they are followed by line of dancers on the side on which each is dancing.
- "Form the arch"—upon reaching the foot of the set, the head couple joins hands to form an arch; the others, now led by the second couple, join hands and sashay through the arch; the second couple leads to the head of the set, where it now stands as head couple for the next figure.

When all couples have gone through the arch, the head couple drops hands and steps back to become the foot couple. In this manner, after six changes (so long as there are six dancers in each line), each couple will have had its turn as head couple.

▷ Teaching Tips

This is a great historic dance that lends itself to many different types of music. Try some different tunes.

Winston-Salem Partner Dance 20

▷ Description

This is a partner dance with many smooth-flowing figures that came from the Southern District AAHPERD Convention when it was held in Winston-Salem, North Carolina. It was actually created at the conference and is danced quite a lot by dancers in the southeastern United States.

Formation   Couples are scattered throughout the room; partners are side by side, holding inside hands.

▷ Counts and Steps

1-8   Begin with the outside foot; boys place the left heel out at a diagonal, girls place the right heel out at a diagonal, and close; repeat on the inside foot; repeat from the beginning.

1-8   **Balancé** away and together two times; this involves doing a step-ball-change to one side and a step-ball-change again to the other.

1-4   Partners face each other and vine to the boy's left for four steps.

5-8   Take a full turn in four steps back to place and a closed position.

1-8   Do four two-steps for a full turn.

Repeat the dance.

▷ Variation

This can be done as a mixer with one circle. Boys move forward counterclockwise during the two-step turn to the next girl in the circle.

▷ Teaching Tips

This dance is especially fun as a progressive dance. Take time to walk through it to be sure that the dancers understand it correctly before the music is added. It is an easy dance for which to find a variety of music. "I Just Called to Say I Love You" by Stevie Wonder is popular, or choose a current piece of music at about 100 BPM.

Miserlou

 21

▷ Description

This is a Greek-American line dance with no partners. Miserlou is a girl's name that means "beloved." The dance uses typical Greek steps, and it was popularized by the dancers at Duquesne University in Pittsburgh, Pennsylvania.

Formation   Students form an open (or broken) circle or a line. A leader starts at the right end of the formation. Participants bend elbows and join hands in a manner that makes the arms resemble a W. Right foot is free and ready to take weight as the dance starts (see figure 6.3).

Figure 6.3   Open or broken circle formation for the Miserlou.

▷ Counts and Steps

1-4   Step sideways right with the right foot and pause; point the left toe across in front of the right foot and pause.

5-8   Swing the left leg around in an outward arc to cross and step with the left foot behind the right; step sideways right with the right foot, cross, and step with the left foot in front of the right; turn on the ball of left foot to face slightly left; swing the right leg around in front.

1-4   Facing slightly left and moving that direction, do one two-step right and forward; raise the right heel, bending the left knee slightly.

5-8   Two-step left and backward and pivot on the ball of the left foot to face center.

▷ Teaching Tips

This is an elegant dance that takes balance and practice to execute. Don't be in a hurry to learn this one.

Cotton-Eyed Joe 22

▷ Description

This is a Texas-style dance with two versions, the original and a modern one. It can be danced as a large group dance or with a partner and can be performed by all ages.

▷ Counts and Steps (Original)

Formation   Form a double circle with partners facing (see figure key.3, page xv). Girls do the opposite.

Part A

1-4   Left heel and toe and step left and close with right; step counterclockwise.

5-8   Right heel and toe and step right, and close with left; step counterclockwise.

1-4   Repeat movements for the first set of counts.

5-8   Repeat movements for second set of counts.

Part B

1-8   Boys go left, or counterclockwise, by doing four two-steps; girls go right, or clockwise, by doing four two-steps; couples then face.

1-8   Step left foot and close, four times.

1-8   Step right foot and close, four times.

1-8   Turn face to face then back to back; do four two-steps.

Repeat the dance.

▷ Counts and Steps (Modern)

Formation   Partners stand side by side and make a formation resembling the spokes of a wagon wheel; form four or five lines that radiate out from the center, each line facing the backs of the line in front.

1-2   Bring the left toe up to cross the right knee and kick forward.

3-4   Do one two-step backward, starting on the left foot.

5-6   Bring the right toe up to cross the left knee and kick forward.

7-8   Do one two-step backward, starting on the right foot.

1-8   Repeat the steps in the first four sets of counts.

1-16   Do eight two-steps forward, starting on the left foot.

Repeat the dance.

▷ Variation

Another challenge is to start on the right foot and reverse the entire dance.

▷ Teaching Tips

Learn this one in parts and repeat it several times before trying the full dance. Try the variation to challenge your students.

▷ AMERICAN–SOUTH

Carnavalito 23

▷ Description

This is a Bolivian festival dance done primarily at carnival time, hence the name. It is danced by all ages and is found in most South and Central American countries.

Formation   Students form a circle, a broken circle, or lines (which may be shaped like an S; see figure 6.4). They join hands and make a quarter-turn to the right to face a leader.

Figure 6.4   Carnavalito street dance formation.

▷ Counts and Steps

Part A

1-4   Take four steps forward, starting with the right foot; bend forward and hold.

5-8   Take four steps forward, starting with the left foot; bend forward and hold.

1-8   Repeat the steps for the first two sets of counts, always moving forward.

Part B

1-16   Change the forward steps to step-hops; the leader pulls-line into a big circle with eight step-hops.

1-16   The circle reverses as the person at the opposite end of the line pulls it for eight step-hops.

Reverse direction and start from the beginning.

▷ Teaching Tips

This is a fun dance that gives students an opportunity to experience and dance a special celebration dance from another country.

Ciranda 24

▷ Description

This is a typical northern Brazilian folk dance. It is danced by all ages at the same time. It provides an opportunity for leadership to spring forth. You will have lots of fun seeing what moves the participants come up with during the Ciranda. It definitely promotes individuality and creativity.

Formation   Students form a circle with no partners (see figure key.4, page xvi).

▷ Counts and Steps

This is a follow-the-leader type of dance. All movements are created on the circle by a leader for multiples of eight counts. When someone else on the circle is ready to become the leader, this person calls out "change" and everyone takes up the step that this new leader demonstrates. Everyone does this new step until another person calls out "change" and introduces a new step for the group to dance. This continues until the group is ready for a new dance.

▷ Teaching Tips

Dancing the Ciranda provides yet another great occasion to get a sense of another culture. Encourage students to try new things while you are building their confidence levels.

▷ ASIAN

Hora (Hava Nagila) 25

▷ Description

The hora may well be the national dance of Israel, and the hora step is the basic step for dances in such countries as Greece, Romania, Bulgaria, and Yugoslavia. It is, therefore, a dance that all folk dancers should learn. There is an old and a new hora. The new hora, as done in Israel, is more energetic, with dancers springing high in the air and whirling around with shouts of ecstasy. The music we have selected can be used for either version. There are many tunes to which the hora is done, but the melody of "Hava Nagila" is perhaps the most popular.

Formation   Students form a circle of dancers with no partners and with their hands on each other's shoulders (see figure key.4, page xvi).

▷ Counts and Steps (Hora)

1-4   Do a vine step to the right.

5-6   Step with the right foot, then kick the left foot diagonally in front of the right.

7-8   Step with the left foot, then kick the right foot diagonally in front of the left.

Repeat the step to the left.

This step is repeated over and over. The circle may also move to the right, in which case the same step is used but beginning with the right foot.

▷ Teaching Tips

The vine step is best taught with everyone facing the front of the room and then moving into a circle. This is a great opportunity to do some teaching of culture and history to raise the students' awareness of what life is like in this part of the world.

Tinikling Dance Variation

▷ Description

Stretch Bands evolved from the Tinikling Dance that comes from the Philippines. It provides a creative approach to this rhythmic activity. According to the LIKHA Pilipino Folk Ensemble (2005), Tinikling is considered to be one of the oldest dances from the Philippines. This dance originated on Leyte in the Visayan Islands and uses bamboo poles to imitate the tinikling bird, which walks around between the tree branches and grass stems.

Music   The original dance uses 3/4 time and is very much fun that way. When teaching students to do this dance I use 4/4 time. I use any four-count, moderate-tempo music. The selection needs to be stimulating and exciting, music the children like. We cannot emphasize this enough. If the children do not like the music, it will be a challenge to motivate them, which will in turn increase your frustration and stress. The students will detect this, which will of course lead to a lack of success.

Formation   Two lines of students face each other.

- One student ties the elastic band, stretch rope, or nylon pantyhose to one ankle and ties another one to the other ankle.
- Have the student directly across from him or her face him or her and tie the other ends of the bands to his or her ankles. The students thereby will be connected at the ankles by the bands (left ankle to right ankle and vice versa).
- The connected students stand across from each other with a slight degree of tension on the stretch ropes. These students are the band jumpers.
- A third student becomes the jumper or dancer. This student is the jumper.

▷ Counts and Steps

1-2   The band jumpers jump two times with their feet together.

3-4   The band jumpers jump two times with the feet apart (creating the rhythm of "together-together-apart-apart" or "in-in-out-out" in 4/4 time). At the same time, the jumper will jump using the same pattern. The jumper will do the exact opposite in between the two stretch bands and between the band jumpers.

▷ Variation 1

- Students can jump in pairs.
- Students can jump criss-cross.
- Students can jump with three jumpers between anchors, or two jumpers jumping inside and one jumper jumping outside.
- Students can jump to any music with which they can easily feel a beat; it should be slow enough for them to be successful in their jumping effort.

▷ Variation 2

- Two band jumpers join another set of band jumpers (see figure 6.5).
- Students form a cross equidistant from each other.
- Students jump around the outside of the square figure in between the bands as well as in the center of the square.
- Four students enter the jumping activity from each corner.
- Students jump between the bands, moving either counterclockwise or clockwise. This is quite an adventure!

Figure 6.5 Making this formation becomes a challenge as well as making it even more fun!

▷ Variation 3

- One band jumper stands between two other band jumpers.
- The one band jumper will be facing one of the two other band jumpers and will have her or his back to the other band jumper.
- The one band jumper will put the bands from the other two on her or his ankles. The three band jumpers are now in a line and are all connected by the bands.
- This "train effect" can continue until a large unbroken circle of all the band jumpers in the class is formed. The jumpers can be either on the inside or on the outside of the circle. Since this is a variation, the jumpers continue to do the same step used in the previous dances.

▷ Teaching Tips

After using these variations, it is time for the students to use their creativity to combine band jumpers into various geometric shapes and grids. This will add another level to this fun-filled fitness rhythmic activity.

Tanko Bushi 26

▷ Description

Tanko Bushi is a Japanese folk dance that is very old. Many people in Japan made their living digging coal. It was usually the women in the early years that did the mining, but both men and women dug coal for a living. There are many coal-mining dances in Japan. The actions in the dance thereby are intended to resemble the coal-mining process; it is meant to remind people of the difficulty of this work and that they should have reverence for it and all of the things that coal mining provided for the Japanese people.

The Tanko Bushi is to be executed slowly and smoothly with lots of form. As is the case in much of Japan, clapping is included in celebrations, and clapping originally may have begun this dance and ended this dance. Today it retains some of this element and has 14 counts.

Formation Students may form an open or closed circle that can move either counterclockwise or clockwise. Four main movements are depicted in the dance that describe the actions of the coal miner as she or he digs, throws the bag over the shoulder, looks up at the moon, and pushes the heavy coal cart.

▷ Counts and Steps

1-2 Touch with the right foot and imitate digging on count 1 and then step with the right foot on count 2.

3-4 Touch with the left foot and imitate digging on count 3 and then step with the left foot on count 4.

5-and-6 Touch with the right toe forward on the first half of count 5, and on the second half step with the right foot; on count 6 touch with the left foot forward while imitating throwing the bag of coal over your shoulder.

7-and-8 Touch with the left toe backward on the first half of beat 7, and on the second half step with left foot; on count 8 touch backward with the right foot; during these counts the dancer looks up at the moon.

9-10 Step forward with the right foot and then forward with the left while imitating pushing the coal cart.

11-12 Step backward with the right foot and then backward with the left to bring both feet together; clap at the same time that the feet are brought together.

13-14 Clap on both beats of this sequence.

Sometimes there are more claps before repeating the dance over again. Repeat the dance.

▷ Teaching Tips

This dance takes time to master. It is a slow dance but be patient with it. It affords another great opportunity to enrich students' cultural and historical awareness of this part of the world.

▷ EUROPEAN-EASTERN

Savela Se Bela Loza 28

▷ Description

This is a Serbian dance performed to celebrate the grape harvest for making wine. The name of the dance translated into English is "A pretty grapevine entwined itself."

Formation Students form a line or open circle with no partners and a leader at the right end.

▷ Counts and Steps

Part A

1-20 Facing slightly right, take 20 small running steps.

21-40 Facing slightly left, take 20 small running steps back the other way.

Part B

1-4 Vine right.

5-8 Vine left.

Repeat the vines four more times for a total of six times and then repeat the dance.

▷ Teaching Tips

This is a simple folk dance from another part of the world. It will provide a wonderful introduction to Serbian culture and give your students a different look at life as it is reflected through another country's folk dances.

Biserka 29

▷ Description

This is a Serbian dance for closing an evening. It is danced as a way to say "thanks for the evening" to the hostess and host. All of those in attendance dance out of respect for the persons sponsoring the party.

Formation   Students form a single circle facing the line of direction and hold hands with those adjacent to them (see figure key.10, page xvii).

▷ Counts and Steps

1-2   Step right (counterclockwise) with the right foot and then the left.

3-4   Two-step forward (right, left, right).

5-6   Face center; step in on the left foot and back on the right.

7-8   Two-step clockwise (left, right, left).

Repeat the dance.

▷ Teaching Tips

Stress the social aspects of dances such as this one. It is intended to honor others, something that we need to do more often. It is a very simple dance with lots of power.

Troika 27

▷ Description

This is a Russian mixer dance with a formation that is meant to imitate a sleigh drawn by three spirited horses.

Formation   Three students stand in a straight line with the hands joined (see figure key.6, page xvi).

▷ Counts and Steps

Part A

1-4   Make four running leaps forward, diagonally and to the right.

5-8   Repeat these leaps to the left.

1-8   Make eight running leaps forward.

1-8   Keep the hands joined; the left dancer runs in place as the right dancer runs through an arch formed by the left and center dancers; the center dancer then follows under his or her own left arm (see figure 6.6).

1-8   Repeat as the right dancer runs in place while left dancer does the figure.

Part B

1-32 Three dancers join hands in a circle; run 12 steps clockwise and stamp three times, repeat counterclockwise; and face direction of the large circle. Dancers one and three form an arch while dancer two runs through to next couple. The dancer in the middle threesome runs counterclockwise up to the next set of dancers on the circle and now dances with the two new partners.

Repeat the dance.

Figure 6.6 Troika arches.

▷ Teaching Tips

This dance provides a great opportunity to be physical and get heart rates up. It involves group work, so you need to pace the lesson to allow students to become comfortable with one another in order to dance together smoothly.

▷ EUROPEAN–WESTERN

Danish Dance of Greeting 30

▷ Description

This is a Danish circle dance for couples. It is a very simple dance performed by those of all ages. It is excellent for promoting positive socialization.

Formation Students form a single circle of couples, facing the center (see figure key.4, page xvi).

▷ Cues

Clap, clap, bow.

Clap, clap, bow.

Stamp, stamp.

Turn yourself around.

▷ Counts and Steps

Part A

1-2   Clap the hands twice and bow to your partner.

3-4   Clap the hands twice and bow to your neighbor.

5-6   Stamp twice in place, left foot then right, facing the center.

7-8   Turn once in place with four running steps.

1-8   Repeat the steps for the first four sets of counts.

Part B

1-16 All join hands and circle to the left with 16 light running steps.

Part C

1-16 Circle right with 16 light running steps.

▷ Teaching Tips

Teaching this dance provides an excellent opportunity to discuss social behavior in a very positive manner. Take time to discuss greeting others with respect, as this is what this dance is all about.

German Wedding Dance 31

▷ Description

This dance is very typical of the dances that come from southern Germany. Everyone who attends the celebration at which the dance takes place is welcome to take part. There are lots of opportunities to insert some fun into this dance for a very enjoyable evening.

Formation   Boys stand in one line facing the girls in another; the dancers move to the top (the end closest to the music or dance teacher) of the set when their turns come up (see figure key.8, page xvii).

▷ Counts and Steps

There are no specific counts for this dance.

- The head couple forms an arch with the inside hands.
- The head couple walks down the girls' line (see figure 6.7) and up the boys' line.
- They drop hands and the boy in the head couple chases the girl to the bottom of the set.
- A new head couple repeats the dance.

Figure 6.7 German wedding dance.

▷ Teaching Tips

Teach about the social aspects of this dance and its use for celebrations. It is fun and easy, so jump right into it.

Chimes of Dunkirk 32

▷ Description

This is a French-Belgian circle dance for couples.

Formation   Students form a single circle of couples with partners facing (see figure key.9, page xvii).

▷ Counts and Steps

Part A

1-4   Stamp three times in place, beginning on the left foot, and then pause for count 4.

5-8   Clap the hands three times and pause for count 8.

Part B

1-8   Join both hands with your partner, turn clockwise once around with eight running steps, and bow.

Part C

1-16   All join hands and circle left with 16 running steps; end with a bow.

▷ Teaching Tips

The chimes of Dunkirk is a simple dance that can be lots of fun. Take time to talk about the French-Belgian part of the world.

Kinderpolka 33

▷ Description

The kinderpolka is a German dance done with a partner. It promotes cooperation and fun while dancing with a partner.

Formation Partners form a single circle with the girl on the boy's right; they face each other, join both hands, and extend the hands sideways to shoulder height (see figure key.9, page xvii).

▷ Counts and Steps

Part A

1-2 Take two side-steps toward the center; the boy starts the side-steps with his left foot and the girl with her right, stepping and then closing on both occasions (counts 1-and-2-and).

3-4 Stamp lightly three times; the boy stamps with his left foot and the girl with her right (counts 3-and-4).

5-6 Take two side-steps away from the center; stepping and closing (counts 5-and-6-and).

7-8 Stamp three times (counts 7-and-8).

1-8 Repeat the steps for the first four set of counts.

Part B

1-4 Partners face and clap their own knees one time, their own hands one time, and then their partner's hands three times (the count is: clap knees, 1; clap hands, 2; clap partner's hands, 3-and-4).

5-8 Repeat the steps for the sixth set of counts.

Part C

1-2 Spring lightly in place on the left foot; place the right heel forward, toe up; and shake the right forefinger at the partner, "scolding" (counts 1-and-2).

3-4 Do the same with left heel and left forefinger (counts 3-and-4).

5-8 Turn around in place with four steps, face your partner, and stamp three times (counts 5, 6, 7-and-8).

▷ Teaching Tips

This is a very typical dance with slapping and clapping. Teach your students to know this common characteristic of a good number of German folk dances.

La Candeliere 34

▷ Description

This Italian wedding dance is also known as the candle dance. It provides everyone at the party the opportunity to have lots of fun and can be done to a waltz or polka.

Formation Students form two lines, with the boys in one and the girls in the other, facing each other. Dancers move to the top of the set when their turn comes up. Two boys and one girl stand at the head facing down the center (see figure key.8, page xvii).

▷ Counts and Steps

There are no specific counts in this dance. You can use a bouquet of flowers instead of a candle.

- The head girl gives a candle to one of the head boys and dances down the center to the bottom of the set with the other boy.
- Two new girls come in and the boy gives a candle to one and dances with other.
- Repeat this pattern over and over.

▷ Teaching Tips

Give students plenty of time to enjoy this dance with their classmates.

Carousel 35

▷ Description

This is a Danish couples dance. It is designed to mimic the old park carousels with the wooden animals.

Formation   A double circle of couples face the center. Girls join hands in the center of the circle with the boys behind them. Boys place both hands on their partners' shoulders.

▷ Counts and Steps

Part A

1-16 All take 16 slow sliding steps to left (clockwise).

1-16 As the music speeds up, take 16 fast sliding steps left.

Part B

1-16 Take 16 fast sliding steps to the right (counterclockwise).

1-16 Take 16 fast sliding steps to right; at the end, the boys quickly change places with the girls, placing them in the front.

Repeat the dance from the beginning.

▷ Teaching Tips

Teach about the old carousels and discuss the Danish culture when you are doing this dance.

Shoemaker's Dance 36

▷ Description

This is a Danish couples dance. A fun dance for all ages. The movements of the dance are a reminder of the activities of the cobbler in olden times.

Formation   Students form a double circle with partners facing (see figure key.3, page xv).

▷ Lyrics

Wind, wind, wind the bobbin, wind, wind, wind the bobbin.

Wind, wind, wind the bobbin, wind, wind, wind the bobbin.

Pull, pull, pull, pull, clap, clap, clap (or tap, tap, tap).

▷ Counts and Steps

Part A

1-2 With the arms bent at shoulder height and the hands clenched to form fists, circle one fist over the other in front of chest, "winding the bobbin" (counts 1-and-2-and).

3-4 Reverse the circle and "wind" in the opposite direction (counts 3-and-4-and).

5-6 Pull the elbows back vigorously twice, "pulling and tightening the thread" (counts 5-and-6).

7-8 Clap your own hands three times (counts 7-and-8).

1-8 Repeat the steps for first four sets of counts.

Part B

1-16 Partners face counterclockwise with the inside hands joined; skip 16 times forward, ending with a bow on the last count.

Repeat the dance.

▷ Variation

In this variation dancers move their feet more than in the first version. This version requires the dancers to have a little more coordination.

Variation Lyrics

Heel and toe and away we go.

Heel and toe and away we go.

See my new shoes neatly done.

Away we go to have some fun.

Part A Counts and Steps

1-2 Place the heel of the outside foot forward.

3-4 Point the toe of the outside foot behind you.

5-8 Take three running steps forward; start with the outside foot and pause.

1-8 Repeat the pattern for the first eight counts, starting with inside foot.

Part B Counts and Steps

1-16 Repeat steps for first two sets of counts 1 to 8.

▷ Teaching Tips

Talk about how dances reflect the nature of society. This is a great time to discuss why we need to preserve these traditional folk dances from around the world.

Seven Jumps 37

▷ Description

This Danish dance was originally danced by men only. Any number of people may participate. Dancers must hold position for the duration of the note. This dance may be danced by persons of all ages and most certainly should be danced by those of both sexes.

Formation   Students form a single circle and join hands. The dance may be done as a couple formation with partners joining both hands for the chorus and facing each other for the figures (see figure key.4, page xvi).

▷ Counts and Steps

Part A

1-16   Chorus—begin the dance with the chorus and return to it after each of the seven figures (parts); the chorus consists of seven step-hops to the left with a jump on the eighth count.

1-16   Repeat step-hops and jump to the right; step-hop by stepping and then hopping on one foot as the opposite leg swings forward and across; the jump may be left out for general use, and dancers may instead do eight step-hops to the left, then eight to the right.

For the seven figures, stand motionless only on the last sustained note of the music.

Part B

1   Figure 1, right foot: On the first sustained note, place the hands on the hips and raise the right knee; do not lower the knee until the second note, and stand motionless throughout the third note.

2-32   Repeat the chorus with the steps for both sets of counts in part A.

Part C

1-2   Figure 2, left foot: repeat figure 1 with the left knee.

3-32   Repeat the chorus with the steps for both sets of counts in part A.

Part D

1-3   Figure 3, right knee: Repeat figures 1 and 2 and kneel on the right knee.

4-32   Repeat the chorus with the steps for both sets of counts in part A.

Part E

1-4   Figure 4, left knee: Repeat figures 1, 2, and 3 and then kneel on the left knee.

5-32   Repeat the chorus with the steps for both sets of counts in part A.

Part F

1-5   Figure 5, right elbow: Repeat figures 1, 2, 3, and 4 and then place the right elbow on the floor.

6-32   Repeat the chorus with the steps for both sets of counts in part A.

Part G

1-6   Figure 6, left elbow: Repeat figures 1, 2, 3, 4, and 5 and then place the left elbow on the floor.

7-32   Repeat the chorus with the steps for both sets of counts in part A.

Part H

1-7   Figure 7, head: Repeat figures 1, 2, 3, 4, 5, and 6 and then place the head on the floor.

8-32   Finish the dance with a final chorus.

▷ Teaching Tips

This dance presents a great opportunity to discuss gender roles in society since it was originally danced only by men. It is also possible to focus on how other cultures have dealt with gender issues. Have students think about why it was originally danced only by men.

Bleking 38

▷ Description

This is a Swedish couples dance with a step that is quite common in Swedish folk dances.

Formation   Students form a double circle with partners facing and arms extended forward at shoulder height; partners join both hands (see figure key.3, page xv).

▷ Counts and Steps

Part A

1-2   Bleking step—hop on the left foot and place the right heel forward, thrusting the right arm forward and pulling the left elbow back vigorously; make a slight jump onto the right foot and place the left heel forward, thrusting the left arm forward and pulling the right elbow back vigorously (counts 1-and-2).

3-4   Repeat these steps in double time, making three quick changes by alternating right heel, left heel, right heel forward (counts 3-and-4).

5-8   Repeat the steps in the first two sets of counts, reversing footwork and arm movements (counts 5-and-6, 7-and-8).

1-8   Repeat the steps in the first three sets of counts; finish facing your partner with both arms extended sideways with the hands joined.

Part B

1-8   Turn clockwise with your partner by doing eight step-hops; move the arms down and up in a windmill gesture with each step-hop.

1-8   Turn counterclockwise with your partner by doing eight step-hops as described in the last set of counts.

▷ Teaching Tips

There are many countries that use the bleking step, including Mexico and the United States. This is a good time to make comparisons and connections to other cultures.

Gustaf's Skoal 39

▷ Description

This is a Swedish four-couple dance. It is designed to be a simple and inclusive dance.

Formation   Students form squares of four couples, as in American square dancing; they face center joining inside hands (see figure key.5, page xvi).

▷ Counts and Steps

Part A

This is a four-sided square dance where couples 1 and 3 are heads while couples 2 and 4 are sides.

1-4   With inside hands joined, head couples one and three walk forward four steps and bow deeply on the fourth.

5-8   Walk four steps backward to place.

1-8   Side couples repeat these steps.

1-8   Head couples repeat the steps from the first set of counts.

1-8   Side couples repeat these steps again.

Part B

1-8   As side couples raise their joined hands to make arches, head couples skip forward.

1-8   Head couples separate, go under the arch, and return home.

1-8   Each couple joins hands and swings with skipping steps.

1-8   Side couples do same skipping action as head couples take their turn to make arches.

▷ Teaching Tips

This dance from another culture provides an excellent opportunity for discussion about social relations and inclusion in activities.

Bummel Schottische 40

▷ Description

This dance originated in Mecklenburg, Germany. Everyone in attendance would join in on the fun. The lyrics were usually sung with the movements.

Formation   Couples begin in the sweetheart position. Girls stand in front of boys with the hands raised to shoulders and the palms forward. He takes her hands in his.

▷ Lyrics

Mother Witch, Mother Witch, just look at me!

How well I dance just look and see!

First on my heels, then on my toes.

O Mother Witch, how well it goes.

Chorus: Tra-la-la and so on.

▷ Counts and Steps

Part A

1-4 Touch the left heel then toe in front and do a step-close-step to the center (counted 1, 2, 3-and-4).

5-8 Touch the right heel then toe in front and do a step-close-step to the center (counted 5, 6, 7-and-8).

1-8 Repeat; when moving to the right the second time, the girl turns out to the right to face her partner in a shoulder-waist position, with her hands on his shoulders and his hands on her waist.

Part B

1-16 Dance the schottische around the room left-right-left-hop, right-left-right-hop, step-hop, step-hop, step-hop, step-hop.

1-16 Repeat the steps for first three set of counts.

▷ Teaching Tips

Here is another opportunity to discuss cultures and preservation of their dances. It also provides an excellent time to teach cooperation with others and socialization skills.

Scandinavian Polka 31

▷ Description

This is a couples dance that uses parts of the polka step. It is a great dance to do with partners of all ages.

Formation Couples start facing each other, holding hands, and scattered around the room; girls do opposite footwork.

▷ Counts and Steps

Part A

1-4 Step to the side with the left foot, close with the right foot, step to the side again with left foot, and kick the right foot.

5-8 Step to the side with the right foot, close with the left foot, step to side again with the right foot, and kick the left foot.

1-8 Repeat.

Part B

Partners are facing each other in a closed position for this 8-count polka and then they turn and repeat it for eight more counts; boys start with the left foot and girls with the right.

1-8 Step, close, step, hop; step, close, step, hop (counted 1-and-2-and-3-and-4-and).

1-8 Step, close, step, hop; step, close, step (counted 1-and-2-and-3-and-4).

Repeat entire dance.

▷ Teaching Tips

This is a good chance to practice polka steps and work with or without a partner. Teach the dance without partners and then add partners. Introduce an 8-count break in the dance for students to find a new partner.

Farmer's Jig 41

▷ Description

This is an English contra dance. It is done to a jig or reel and is lots of fun for the dancers.

Formation Students stand lengthwise in a set of four couples; another such line is facing them. Partners are not next to each other in line but are actually facing one another. That is, one partner is in one line and the other is across from him or her in the other (see figure key.8, page xvii).

▷ Counts and Steps

Part A

1-16 All four couples advance up the room eight steps dancing away from the music, turn, and go back eight steps.

1-16 All four couples gallop up the room away from the music for eight steps and back eight steps.

Part B

1-16 Two pairs of partners (first and second couples; third and fourth couples) make right- and left-hand stars for 8 counts, each with appropriate hands joined to form a star.

1-16 The head couple casts by turning to the outside of the line and forming an arch with their joined hands as the others follow, go under the arch, and back to their new positions in the set. The boys will go left and the girls right, following the previous couple up the center.

Repeat the dance.

▷ Teaching Tips

It is time to learn a new formation from another culture. Take time to introduce the new figure—the star—as it alone will throw off your dancers.

▷ SUMMARY

This chapter has shown the cultural diversity of several regions of the world. The method used to introduce the dances discussed here is an important aspect of teaching them. You can challenge students to be eager for knowledge of other countries, and this chapter gives enough information to interest the students in learning more about the dances. It lends itself quite well to serving as a resource for the integration of geography and social studies. On a final note, through the study of folk dance, dancers can become involved in the preservation of the vast array of cultures found around the world.

Create Your Own Folk Dances

Having given the students the tools they need to learn the steps, the logical progression is to have them create their own folk dances to enhance their desire to create and be successful. This phase of the requirements can give students self-confidence and produce immense self-esteem, and it allows for the development of students' critical thinking and social skills.

Checklist for Creating Your Own Folk Dance

- Instruct students to create their own folk dance based on the skills and steps that they have learned.
- Ask students to come up with a 32-count folk dance with variety and movements that are executed well to the music. To start, students can create dances that are similar to the ones that they have already learned and then branch off into creating their own folk dances.
- Allow students to do both individual and group work, depending on your preference or needs.
- Instruct students to write up their descriptions and turn them in to you to practice language, reading, and writing skills. As part of this assignment, students who have progressed to creating new folk dances can describe the community that their dance will represent. It can be one of their own communities or one that they have invented. Imagination is key!

Rubric

Now that you have your students into creating their own folk dances, here is an example of the rubric that could work for this particular activity or for others with modifications. Just by changing a few words, this rubric could work with other aspects of your warm-ups.

4 Points—Exemplary	The student created a 32-count folk dance with variety and movements that were executed very well to the music.
3 Points—Acceptable	The student created a 16-count folk dance with some variety and movements that were sometimes executed to the music.
2 Points—Needs improvement	The student created a 16-count folk dance with no variety, and movements were rarely executed to the music.
1 Point—Unacceptable	The student created fewer than 16 counts for the folk dance or did not establish a clear rhythmic pattern.

 # Review Questions

Have students submit questions for the class to answer, or have them answer questions similar to these in the following list. In addition, these could be used as a homework assignment, as an in-class assignment, or for class discussion.

1. Make a list of the benefits of folk dancing.
2. Trace the history of folk dancing in a particular continent or country.
3. When creating folk dances, what is the main number of counts that is critical to developing such dances?
4. Collect and write up several folk dances from other sources.

5. Describe the physiological benefits received from folk dancing.

6. When creating folk dances, what are some of the important things that you should be sure to include?

7. What is the great appeal of folk dancing?

 Observation Questions

1. List the different locomotor movements that you observed in this activity.

2. List the combination movements that you observed in this activity.

3. What formations were used in this dance?

4. What was the tempo of this dance?

5. Did the actions of the participants reflect the theme and attitude of this dance? Please describe your observations.

6. Did the participants raise their heart rates to target work zones for aerobic benefits?

7. Was there an opportunity for the dancers to develop movements in all directions?

8. Was there an opportunity for leading with different feet? Please describe the level at which this occurred.

9. Was the dance developed in multiples of 4, 8, 16, 32, and 64 counts?

10. Was the music selection appropriate for your class?

> CHAPTER 7

Mixers

The mixer is one of the more exciting forms of rhythmic activities. Virtually all cultures have their special mixers. They provide an opportunity to meet and greet people in an open, non-threatening environment that focuses on the individual. This is a wonderful by-product of rhythmic and dance activities.

As people mature, they need to find balance mentally, emotionally, physically, socially, and spiritually to ensure a lifetime of healthful living. Mixers provide many benefits in these areas, but perhaps their greatest contribution comes in the social realm. Their main purpose is to provide a nonthreatening environment for people to grow socially and safely. They carry as a focus the concept of inclusion for all. They provide a great opportunity to build confidence and self-esteem. Give them a try; you may discover or rediscover that they have potential to enrich your program.

The following are all easy mixers for your classes. They will provide you with a wealth of information and enough depth to meet the needs of your program. They are all quite easy, so you can use them at virtually any level.

The dances have been grouped by different formations (to see illustrations of these formations, please see the key to diagrams, pages xv to xvii). The selections for inclusion in the book have been made to assist you in helping students to learn a variety of organizational formats that can be used with folk dances as well. Also, the variety of organizational patterns can provide a challenge to your students as you have them create their own mixers. Remember that the musical arrangements listed with the mixers are only suggestions and that mixers lend themselves quite well to other four-count music, particularly those your students know best and listen to the most.

▷ HISTORY OF MIXERS

As a dance form, mixers have been around as long as humankind. Mixers can be found in countries around the world as far back as records exist. And it is quite obvious that nearly all cultures highly value this social form of interaction even today. Just look at the abundance of mixers currently found all around. Mixers as a dance style have found a wonderful place in programs for all ages.

▷ TEACHING SOCIAL MIXERS WITH THE ROUND-ROBIN WAVE

This is a very popular approach to ease students into the social arena. The round-robin wave is a fantastic fitness and rhythmic activity that requires concentration, teamwork, memory, and sequencing. It provides just the sort of challenge that students will want to tackle, and they will always leave the gym laughing.

Round-Robin Wave

The wave effect is created by having each step performed by a group of students, in the order of the dance steps. Choose a dance that you want the students to learn. Determine how many steps it has. Write the directions for each step or movement on a 5-inch by 8-inch (13-centimeter by 20-centimeter) index card. How many cards you make for each step will depend on the number of children you are teaching.

If you have 36 students, and you are teaching "Oh, Johnny" (which has six steps), for example, you will divide the students into clusters of six to match the number of steps in the dance. There will be six students in each cluster. Make six cards each for the same step. Since this is a mixer, you will want to have the number of boys and girls as even as possible. Have three cards or each step in a pile from which the boys will select and three cards in the pile from which the girls will select. That will make the numbers of boy–girl connections roughly even.

Designate where each step will be practiced. Have the stations for each step dispersed in a circular formation around the gym in the order of the dance. Make it very clear that these steps are an important piece of a bigger rhythmic puzzle that the students are going to put together. Emphasize the importance of being a member of a team.

Wave station 1: "Well, you all join hands and you circle the ring." Demonstrate the movement needed for this piece of the puzzle.

Wave station 2: "You stop where you are and give her a swing." Demonstrate the swing that you prefer to ease partners into working together.

Wave station 3: "And then you swing that girl behind you." Boys swing the girl to his left or behind him. The corner is the girl to the boy's left in the circle.

Wave station 4: "And then you go back home and you swing your own." Swing your partner. This station calls for the same movements as wave station 2. You do not actually need to repeat the movement, but make sure that your students are aware that this is the next part of the puzzle and what the caller will call.

Wave station 5: "It's allemande left with the corner gal." Boys extend their left hand to their corner girl and walk around her back to their original spot. Demonstrate the allemande left to ensure the boy gives his left hand to the corner girl. Girls extend their right hand to the boy.

Wave station 6: "Do-si-do 'round your own." Walk around your partner, passing right shoulders, and then moving back to back before returning to your original spot. Have the students raise their arms to chest level and cross them with one arm over the other.

Wave station 7: "And then we all run away with that sweet corner maid, singing 'Oh, Johnny, Oh, Johnny, Oh.'" Promenade counterclockwise.

▷ Practice

Once the students have learned the puzzle piece on which they are working, turn on the music and let the students hear the words. They will then see how the piece fits together with the music. Make them aware of when to begin each movement. The dance is anchored in the music. Listening is essential for success.

Once the students can perform the movements learned at a particular station, have the students rotate to the next station. This will continue until all the students have rotated to each station. Once students have learned each step or movement, have one square (four boys and four girls) try to perform the entire dance together.

After the class views how the dance is performed, have four squares form and watch the fun. Have one student not taking part in the dancing be the keeper of the music and another the caller. Give the caller a card with the cue words on it and let her or him call out the directions. All students are now familiar with the dance and will eagerly want to test their skills. There will be very little anxiety or uneasiness because the dance will have become so familiar that they will forget they are attempting a *new* dance.

▷ Teaching Tips

This square dance contains skills that are fundamental to the dance form. With success at this dance, students thereby will learn valuable dance steps for other square dances. When the students start the square-dance unit, they will be very happy about being so capable!

▷ SINGLE CIRCLE FACING CENTER WITH A PARTNER

Circassian Circle 42

▷ Description

This is an English circle mixer that is very simple and includes everyone in the room on any given occasion. Perhaps it gets its name from the circassian walnut tree that is found in England.

Formation   Students form a single circle facing center (see figure key.4, page xvi).

▷ Counts and Steps

Part A

1-16   Walk forward into the circle and walk back out of the circle; do this two times.

1-8   Girls walk to the center of the circle and back.

1-8 Boys walk to the center and back out to a new partner—his left-hand girl; the left-hand girl is the girl to the boy's left on the circle.

Part B

1-8 New partners swing by interlocking right elbows.

1-8 Partners swing again by interlocking left elbows.

1-16 Promenade around the ring.

Form a circle and repeat the dance.

▷ Teaching Tips

This dance has a nice, smooth progression. Practice the progression over and over again as this is the part of the dance that usually confuses the dancers.

Lucky Seven 43

▷ Description

This is a fun circle mixer that mixes up the group well and promotes inclusion from the start.

Formation Students form a single circle facing center (see figure key.4, page xvi).

▷ Counts and Steps

Part A

1-8 Circle left.

1-16 All participants step to the middle and back two times.

Part B

1-16 Do a grand right and left (see figure 7.1). Partners face one another and join right hands; they pull that person toward and past them and then extend a left hand to the next

Figure 7.1 Grand right and left in the Lucky Seven.

person in the circle, pulling that person toward and past them. They do this until the seventh person is reached; boys go counterclockwise and the girls clockwise. See also figure 8.23 on page 200.

1-8   All boys swing their seventh girl.

Part C

1-16   Promenade.

Repeat the entire dance.

▷ Teaching Tips

Lucky Seven is a very nice dance with a new move, the grand right and left. Getting it right requires much patient practice. While it is a rather simple movement, it is very different from anything that they have done before.

Bingo 44

▷ Description

This is a waltz-tempo American circle mixer. We don't see many waltzes when it comes to mixers, but this is one of the best. It mixes the group very well and is always fun for the dancers.

Formation   This is a partner dance in which all begin by holding hands and facing center; girls are on the right of the boys (see figure key.4, page xvi).

▷ Counts and Steps

Part A

1-3   Balancé in by stepping to the center and close.

4-6   Balancé out by stepping back and close.

1-6   The boys roll their partner across by allowing her to turn left to face him; then the boy will proceed to a new position by moving one partner to his right.

1-36   Repeat the first three sets of counts three more times.

Part B

1-24   Boys face the girl on their right, and girls face left as they do two slides to the center and two slides back two times.

Part C

1-24   Grand right and left on "B, I, N, G, O." Partners are still facing, join right hands, and begin the movement. Everyone shouts "B" while taking right hands, "I" while taking left hands, "N" with right hands, and "G" with left hands. When meeting the fifth girl, boys swing her and shout "OOOH!"

Repeat all parts of the dance.

▷ Teaching Tips

This is a new tempo: the waltz. Because of this, it will require a bit of practice just to get a feel for 3/4 time. Also the grand right and left may still require extra practice time.

Oh, Johnny 45

▷ Description

This is an American singing circle mixer that is lots of fun for the dancers. It has numerous partner exchanges and allows everyone to be a part of the dance.

Formation Students form a single circle of couples facing center.

▷ Counts and Steps

1-8 "Well, you all join hands and circle the ring." Circle left.

1-8 "You stop where you are and give her a swing." Boys swing their partner.

1-8 "And then you swing that girl behind you." Boys swing their corner, or the girl to the boy's left.

1-8 "And then you go back home and you swing your own." Boys swing their partner again.

1-8 "It's allemande left with the corner gal." Boys give their left hand to their corner girl, walk around her, and go back to their original spot.

1-8 "Do-si-do 'round your own." Walk around your partner passing right shoulders, going back to back, and proceeding back to your original spot.

1-8 "And then we all run away with that sweet corner maid, singing 'Oh, Johnny, Oh, Johnny, Oh.'" Promenade counterclockwise for eight more counts.

Repeat the dance.

▷ Teaching Tips

The dance has a lot of turns and requires some practice to get the flow of the dance to be smoother. This would be a good time to use the connections activity from chapter 2, page 35, using the various turns. This is the dance described to do the Round Robin Wave on page 164.

Nine Pin 46

▷ Description

This is an eight-person circle mixer done with an extra girl in the center of the circle. It is designed to get everyone dancing and provides lots for fun for all of the participants, no matter what their age may be. The Nine Pin perhaps came into being before the settlement of the American colonies.

Formation Students form a circle composed of four couples with an extra girl—the nine pin—in the center (see figure key.4, page xvi).

▷ Counts and Steps

Part A

1-32 Each boy swings his partner in the center of the circle.

Part B

1-4 Boys go to the center of the circle with backs to the center and join hands.

5-8 All five girls to outside of the circle, facing in and joining hands.

1-16 All circle left.

1-8 When the word "swing" is heard, girls take a boy and go back home; the leftover girl in the center is the new nine pin.

Repeat the dance.

▷ Teaching Tips

This dance provides for positive interaction. Try it with popular music to raise motivation levels. Consider the lyrics of the music chosen.

Teton Mountain Stomp 47

▷ Description

This is an American mixer that is not particularly old, but it certainly resembles those mixers of the past. It is designed for everyone to take part, no matter what their ability.

Formation Students form a single circle with partners facing and holding hands (see figure key.9, page xvii).

▷ Counts and Steps

1-4 Begin on the inside foot; step, close, step, and stamp.

5-8 Repeat with the outside foot.

1-2 Move in, step and stamp.

3-4 Move out, step and stamp.

5-8 Walk counterclockwise for four steps with your partner, right hip to right hip; the boy moves forward as his partner backs up.

1-4 Each person does a half-turn continuing counterclockwise with the boys going backward four steps and the girls forward four steps.

5-8 Reverse and walk clockwise four steps back toward original spots.

1-4 Each person does a half-turn with boys going backward four steps counter clockwise to their original spots and girls clockwise forward four steps.

5-8 Each person walks forward four steps to meet a new partner.

Repeat the dance.

▷ Teaching Tips

This is a fun dance with lots of turns. Try it with modern music and watch the motivation levels skyrocket!

▷ DOUBLE CIRCLE FACING LINE OF DIRECTION

Riga Jig 48

▷ Description

This is an English circle mixer that can include any number of participants. As with others already covered, it gets individuals together and interacting with each other through the medium of dance.

Formation Students form a double circle, facing the line of direction (see figure key.2, page xv).

▷ Counts and Steps

Part A

1-16 Promenade for 16 steps and face your partner.

1-4   Clap your hands three times and hold.

5-8   Slap your knees three times and hold.

1-8   Do-si-do, if you please (see figure 7.2).

Part B

1-4   Move to the right; each person steps to her or his right side to meet a new partner.

5-8   Shake right hands with your new partner.

1-8   Say, "Hello, hello, hello my name is _____."

Repeat the dance.

Figure 7.2   Do-si-do in the Riga Jig.

▷ Teaching Tips

This dance provides an excellent way to meet people, and it has cultural roots that can be shared in class. This is another one that lends itself to modern music.

Angus Reel

▷ Description

This is an American mixer that is great for large groups of all ages. It probably was an early American dance done on the wagon trains going west to settle this great big country.

Formation   Partners form a double circle, facing the line of direction (see figure key.2, page xv).

▷ Counts and Steps

1-8   Promenade eight steps and face your partner.

1-4   Back away from your partner with four steps.

5-6 Stamp three times left, right, left (counts 5-and-6).

7-8 Clap three times (counts 7-and-8).

1-8 Do-si-do with your partner.

1-8 Do-si-do with your corner. The corner is the girl to the boy's left on the circle.

Repeat the dance with your corner as your new partner.

▷ Teaching Tips

This dance still can be seen in dance halls. Music can be varied to raise motivation levels.

Five-Foot Two 50

▷ Description

This is an American mixer with fun music. It was developed rather recently. Undoubtedly, the originator understood how to have fun with a mixer-type dance!

Formation Students form a double circle, facing the line of direction and in the **varsouvienne** position with the girl beside the boy, holding left to left hands in front and right to right hands behind the girl's right shoulder (see figure key.2, page xv).

▷ Counts and Steps

1-8 Two-step left, two-step right, walk four steps forward.

1-6 Two-step left, two-step right, walk two steps.

7-8 Release left hands and form a circle; boys face out, girls face in.

1-4 Balancé forward and balancé back; to balancé means to step forward or backward and to close with the other foot and then reverse the movement.

5-8 Turn with the right hand, halfway around.

1-4 Balancé forward and balancé back.

5-8 Partners release right hands, and boys take the hand of the girl behind them.

Repeat the dance.

▷ Teaching Tips

Practice the progression without music to improve the flow of the dance. This will pay off later. Progressions by themselves create confusion. Students are not used to such organizational patterns.

Sweet Georgia Brown 51

▷ Description

This is an American mixer that people of all ages like because of the music. It hasn't been around too terribly long, but it is one of those fun-filled dances for everyone.

Formation Students form a double circle, facing the line of direction (see figure key.2, page xv).

▷ Counts and Steps

1-4   Walk four steps forward counterclockwise.

5-8   Partners step apart four steps.

1-4   Partners step together four steps.

5-8   Partners do a right elbow turn in four steps; elbow turns simply involve locking the same elbow with the partner and doing a 360-degree walk around them.

1-4   Walk four steps forward counterclockwise.

5-8   Do a right elbow turn in four steps.

1-4   Do a left elbow turn in four steps.

5-8   Boys move ahead to the next girl in four steps.

Repeat the dance.

▷ Teaching Tips

Practice the patterns in this dance thoroughly before adding the accompaniment. This is a good one with which to try different music to raise interest levels.

 CJ Mixer 52

▷ Description

This exciting American mixer coordinates a lot of group action. This is a really fun one.

Formation   Students form a double circle, facing the line of direction and in the varsouvienne position (see figure key.2, page xv).

▷ Counts and Steps

1-8   Walk forward three steps, turn halfway around, and walk backward three steps; this will all go in the same direction.

1-8   Walk forward three steps, turn halfway around, and walk backward three steps; this will land the students back where they started.

1-6   Do a left-hand star for six steps with girl in the lead; this involves putting the left hand into the center and walking around 360 degrees in a "star" formation.

7-8   Release hands and turn toward the reverse line of direction.

1-6   Do a right-hand star for six steps.

7-8   Boys take the next girl in the circle and turn toward the line of direction.

Repeat the dance.

▷ Teaching Tips

There are some very nice patterns in this dance! Practice them thoroughly to help the dancers understand the flow of the dance completely.

Sicilian Circle 53

▷ Description

This is another great English circle mixer. It mixes the group extremely well.

Formation   Students form a double circle with two couples facing each other (see figure key.7, page xvi).

▷ Counts and Steps

Part A

1-16   All join hands in the circle and circle left for 16 counts; this will take them fully around the circle twice.

1-8   Do a right-hand star.

1-8   Do a left-hand star.

Part B

See chapter 8 for descriptions of the courtesy turn (page 204) and chain (page 205).

1-8   Girls chain over and do a courtesy turn to finish the move.

1-8   Girls chain back and do a courtesy turn to finish the move.

1-8   All move forward again and pass on through to the next couple.

This is an English piece with English cues. With a double circle, couples facing, "four hands, twice around" is for each foursome. "Right hands 'round" is right hands joined like an American right-hand star, same for left. The "pass through" is simply a walk forward passing the opposite couple to meet the next couple in the circle.

Repeat the dance.

▷ Teaching Tips

There are some new movements in this dance. Practice them to help the dancers adjust.

▷ DOUBLE CIRCLE PARTNERS FACING

Bouquet of Flowers and Scarf 54

▷ Description

This is an old-time American mixer that uses a scarf and a bouquet of flowers. It is lots of fun to pull out to change things up a bit. Your students will enjoy this one as it promotes and provides opportunities for leadership.

Formation   Partners form a circle with the boys on the inside facing out.

▷ Counts and Steps

There are not precise counts for this mixer. Instead, all couples dance. Two individuals, a girl holding a bouquet of flowers and a boy holding a scarf, wander inside the circle of dancers (see figure 7.3). The girl gives her bouquet to another girl, and the boy gives his scarf to

Figure 7.3 Starting formation for the Bouquet of Flowers and Scarf mixer.

another boy. Then they dance with that person's partner. The new carriers repeat this procedure, both selecting someone else. Since the suggested music, "Moon River," is a waltz, everyone waltzes to the music. However, a polka, a two-step, or anything else that you prefer could be applied to this dance. This mixer may also be combined with other mixers to add excitement and make the activity a success.

▷ Teaching Tips

This dance provides a wonderful opportunity to promote leadership among your dancers. Push them to involve everyone in the figure.

Fun Mixer 55

▷ Description

Here is a mixer that allows dancers to call for themselves. This is another great opportunity for students to display some leadership without feeling self-conscious in front of the entire group.

Formation Students form a double circle facing the line of direction, with any number of dancers standing in the middle of the circle. Students take turns calling the dance, and partners on the circle hold hands (see figure key.2, page xv).

▷ Counts and Steps

1-4 Begin with the feet together; the caller may call for the inside or outside circle to move up or back for two, three, or four steps—or any other fitting number thereof.

1-16 Dancers go to the other side of the circle and swing whomever they choose when the caller calls for the "cheaters swing."

1-16 Dancers in the center now move to the circles and replace a partner; the replaced person goes to the center to call.

1-16 Everyone now promenades the hall.

Repeat the dance.

▷ Teaching Tips

Push your students to be creative in their calls. Have the students meet in clusters to create a call. Then have each cluster put their creation in the music.

Paul Jones 31

▷ Description

This is an American polka with many opportunities to be active and meet new people. This is a really fun dance for everyone.

Formation   Students form a double circle; girls are on the inside holding hands with each other and facing out; boys are on the outside holding hands with each other and facing in (opposite figure key.3, page xv).

▷ Counts and Steps

Part A

1-16 All circle left.

Part B

1-32 Boys freestyle or polka with their partner (the girl he is facing) around the room when the caller says "Paul Jones."

Part C

1-16 Back to the center and circle left. (Since everyone is off doing their thing with the new partner, this call brings everyone back to the original formation.)

Repeat the dance.

▷ Teaching Tips

This dance provides excellent practice for the polka. You can change the music so that students get new partners, do a swing dance, waltz, or whatever step.

Jiffy Mixer 56

▷ Description

This is an American mixer by Jerry and Kathy Helt. While this is not all that old, as far as dance goes, it has provided lots of fun for dance groups of all ages for many years.

Formation   Students form a double circle with the boys facing out and in the **butterfly** position. Girls do the opposite footwork.

▷ Counts and Steps

1-8 Left heel touch forward, left toe touch back beside the right foot, left heel touch forward, left toe touch back beside the right foot; step left to the side with the left foot (counterclockwise), right close, step left again, right touch.

1-8 Right heel touch forward, right toe touch back beside the left foot, right heel touch forward, right toe touch back beside the left foot; step right to the side with the right foot (clockwise), left close, step right again, left touch.

1-8   Chug away from your partner—clap, chug, clap, chug, clap, chug, clap. (A chug is when knees are slightly bent and quickly straightened with a short slide forward or backward, depending on the directions.)

1-8   Everyone walks to her or his right, 2, 3, 4; turn your new partner for four counts.

Repeat the dance.

▷ Teaching Tips

Chugs are new. Be sure to explain and practice them thoroughly. This dance readily lends itself to other music.

Patty-Cake Polka 57

▷ Description

This is a high-energy American circle mixer that requires clapping coordination. It has been around for quite some time and probably has roots that go back to the western European countries that first settled this county.

Formation   Students form a double circle with partners facing (see figure key.3, page xv).

▷ Counts and Steps

1-4   Left heel out in front and cross to touch the left toe in front of right foot. Repeat.

5-8   Slide counterclockwise three times.

1-4   Right heel out in front and cross to touch right toe in front of left foot. Repeat.

5-8   Slide clockwise three times.

1-8   Patty-cake right hands three times with your partner and pause, patty-cake left hands three times, and then patty-cake both hands three times; patty-cake on your own knees three times.

1-4   Do a right elbow turn one time around.

5-8   Move onto the next dancer on the circle to your left, walking for four to the next person coming from the left.

Repeat the dance.

▷ Teaching Tips

This dance takes some coordination with the claps and slaps. Work out the flow before beginning the dance itself.

Barn Dance 58

▷ Description

This is an American mixer for parties and is lots of fun. Use this one with groups and you will be richly rewarded.

Formation   Students form a double circle with boys facing out and holding hands with their partners. Girls do opposite footwork (see figure key.3, page xv).

▷ Counts and Steps

1-8   Hustle left and right—step left, close right, step left, and close right with a touch; then step right, close left, step right, and close left with a touch.

1-8   Boys hustle left and right again while girls do a turn under their partner's raised left hand going each direction.

1-8   Face the line of direction, hold inside hands, and do four step hops in the line of direction by starting on either foot.

1-4   Turn and face your partner; boys back away toward the center of the circle and girls back away from the center for four steps.

1-4   Do an eighth-turn to the left and progress on to the next person, walking four steps forward to meet them.

Repeat the dance.

▷ Teaching Tips

This dance has some new patterns to practice before turning your dancers loose. This one lends itself quite well to an array of musical forms.

▷ FREE OR OPEN

Broom Dance 59

▷ Description

This is an American mixer that is fun for all ages. It is another one of those that can get participants mixing.

Formation   Open.

▷ Counts and Steps

There are not precise counts for this mixer. Couples dance while the music plays. One person holds a broom as if dancing with it. When this person drops the broom on the floor, everyone switches to a new partner, including the person holding the broom. Whoever is left over is now the new broom holder (see figure 7.4).

▷ Teaching Tips

Use this one to promote socialization in a very nonthreatening situation. It lends itself to variety in the music selection. The dance may be changed so that the broom is passed instead of dropped if needed.

Figure 7.4   Broom dancing.

Clap and Stamp Three Times 60

▷ Description

This is an American mixer that can always motivate a group.

Formation   This dance is open with partners.

▷ Counts and Steps

1-2   Clap hands three times (counted 1-and-2).

3-4   Stamp either foot three times (counted 3-and-4).

5-6   Repeat steps for counts 1 to 2.

7-8   Repeat steps for counts 3 to 4.

1-8   Take your partner's hands and walk eight steps forward in any direction.

1-8   Slide with your partner eight times in another direction.

1-8   Slide with your partner four times in the opposite direction, release your partner's hands, and walk four steps to a new partner.

Repeat the dance.

▷ Teaching Tips

This dance can be done on a circle. It lends itself to variety in the music.

▷ SUMMARY

Mixers focus on the important element of social fitness. The mixers in this chapter have been arranged for your students to be comfortable with the progressions in the dances. They will meet many other students without staying with any person a long time. These dances are simple, so students will have a high level of success and will come back wanting more.

▷ Create Your Own Mixer ◁

Having given the students the tools they need to learn the purpose of a mixer, the next logical progression is to have them create their own mixers to enhance their desire to create and be successful. This phase of the requirements can give students self-confidence and produce immense self-esteem. It even allows for the development of students' critical thinking skills and, once again, those all-important social capabilities.

Checklist for Creating Your Own Mixer

- Instruct students to create their own mixer based on the skills and steps that they have learned.

- Ask students to come up with a 32-count mixer with variety and movements that are executed well to the music. The mixer should be simple and fun, and it should use one of the formations they have learned in this chapter. It likewise should require participants to work with multiple partners.

- Allow students to do work as a group to enhance the social aspects of the activity.

- Instruct students to write up their descriptions and turn them in to you to practice language, reading, and writing skills.

Rubric

Now that you have your students creating their own mixers, here is an example of a rubric that could work for this particular activity or for others with modifications. Just by changing a few words, you can make this rubric work with other aspects of your warm-ups.

4 Points—Exemplary
: The student created a 32-count mixer with variety and movements that are executed well to the music. The mixer is simple and fun, and it uses one of the formations they have learned in this chapter. It requires participants to work with multiple partners.

3 Points—Acceptable
: The student created a 32-count mixer with variety and movements that are executed well to the music. The mixer uses one of the formations learned in this chapter but only requires participants to work with one partner.

2 Points—Needs improvement
: The student created a mixer with less than 32 counts and not a lot of variety, but it is still fun and requires work with one partner.

1 Point—Unacceptable
: The student created a mixer with less than 32 counts, no variety, and barely any partner work.

Review Questions

Have students submit questions for the class to answer, or have students answer questions similar to these in the following list. In addition, these could be used as a homework assignment, as an in-class assignment, or for class discussion.

1. Make a list of the benefits of mixers.
2. Trace the history of mixers in a particular continent or country.
3. Describe the physiological benefits received from performing a mixer.
4. When creating mixers, what are some of the important things that you should be sure to include?
5. What is the great appeal of dancing a mixer?
6. What purpose did and do mixers serve in society?
7. Find or create a new mixer and bring it to share with the class.

Observation Questions

1. List the different locomotor movements that you observed in this activity.
2. List the combination movements that you observed in this activity.
3. What formations were utilized in this dance?
4. What was the tempo of this dance?
5. Did the activity of the participants reflect the theme and attitude of this dance? Please describe your observations.
6. Did the participants raise their heart rates to their target work zones for aerobic benefits?

7. Was there an opportunity for the dancers to develop movements in all directions?

8. Was there an opportunity for leading with different feet? Please describe the level at which this occurred.

9. Was the dance developed in multiples of 4, 8, 16, 32, and 64 counts?

10. Was the music selection appropriate for your class?

▷ CHAPTER 8

Square Dances and Clogging

American square dance is an integral part of our heritage in the United States. It is a popular dance form and has one of the highest participatory rates of all physical activities. Its followers are many, and for this reason we begin with a short, informative historical section. The history of American square dance helps us to revitalize, to reflect on our roots, and to see that we have historically been a nation of great dancers. Most important, we can bring our curriculum and heritage to life through dance. We then move into a section on teaching square dance to others. Here we deal with teaching suggestions, square dance calling, the square dance lesson, styling tips for the teacher and dancers, reminders for callers, and reminders for effective teaching.

The following sections deal with three forms of square dancing. The first form is Appalachian big set, also known simply as big set, big circle, big circle mountain, or Kentucky running set. This is square dancing in sets of four persons; it preceded the development of western square dance. The second form is western square dance. This section includes 10 lessons that will fit with all ability levels. It is in need of modification only if your group requires a slower or faster pace. The third form of square dancing is clogging. Dancers may clog dance in both the Appalachian big set form and the western square dance forms, depending on where they live. However, smooth dancing or simply walking through the figures is the predominant form of dancing in both Appalachian big set and western square dance.

The Suggested Resources section at the end of the book includes information about obtaining music and directions for the activities in this chapter.

▷ HISTORY OF AMERICAN SQUARE DANCE

On June 1, 1982, by act of the United States Congress, contemporary western square dance became the official American folk dance. The evolution of contemporary western square dance provides a history that parallels the development of our country.

Since most early settlers of the eastern seaboard wanted nothing to do with their mother countries, they developed and preserved the dances of their new country. In contemporary western square dance we have the vestiges of these early forms. The French quadrille was a circle of eight and was danced primarily with visiting couples. The Appalachian big set, which involves square dancing in circles of four, preceded the square of eight that we know today.

The Appalachian big set and the French quadrille were combined to form western square dancing. The term "western" was added because the dance was performed farther west as our country was settled. The western square dance of that early period had a circle of eight and evolved into our contemporary western square dance form. It is referred to as western square dance to differentiate it from other forms of square dancing that are alive today.

Since teaching the Appalachian big set helps students learn western square dance patterns, it is discussed before western square dance is discussed. It is a vehicle for working with groups that are new to square dance, so it provides a successful system for teaching square dancing to beginners.

During the evolution of the Appalachian big set and western square dance, dancers began stamping and shuffling their feet by using what was referred to as *clogging*. Clogging has roots in virtually all the countries from which settlers along the eastern seaboard came. It has been included after the western square dance section because of its prevalence in our country and its great physiological benefits. It is a fun alternative to the more common smooth dancing, or walking patterns, seen in contemporary western square dancing.

▷ BASICS OF TEACHING SQUARE DANCE

The following ingredients are important in developing your square dance program. They appear as follows in four sections: Teaching Suggestions, Square Dance Calling, Designing the Square Dance Lesson, and Styling Tips for Teachers and Dancers. The fourth section concludes with a checklist of reminders for callers.

Teaching Suggestions

You need to consider a number of points when teaching square dance. The following list has been compiled to assist you in making decisions about how to deliver your program.

- Start with the simplest move, then add the next simplest and see what variations you can do. Add a third move when appropriate, never teaching too many at one time.
- The caller should strive to be the best possible square dancer before teaching others.
- Moves should be taught, taught again, and reviewed in succeeding sessions to ensure that the dancers know them.
- Reinforce in a positive manner.
- Start with a big circle for teaching the early moves.
- To keep the dancers' attention, mix the squares regularly in the beginning.

- Learning time should be fun time, full of discovery and excitement at each session. Don't just say that square dancing is fun—show it!
- If possible, callers should avoid using cue cards; this allows them to keep their eyes on the dancers.
- Use costumes, scenery, and square dance songs to stimulate interest and a deeper understanding of the history and people who began this type of folk dancing.
- Teach the dance by phrases rather than by counts. This is less confusing to the dancers.
- Avoid spending too much time on one dance.
- Emphasize fun and enjoyment rather than the perfection of every skill.
- The caller must call within the framework of the dancers' knowledge.
- Discourage the dancers from clapping and stamping as their skills improve, so everyone can hear the calls and concentrate on the movements.
- When anyone in the square gets lost, instruct the dancers to return to their home positions and wait for the next call to start.

Square Dance Calling

Square dancing is directed by a caller. With very little practice, you can become proficient enough in square dance calling to conduct classes for beginners. There are two basic calls in square dance: the patter call and the singing call. In the patter call, the caller directs the dancers through many formations that eventually bring them back to their home positions. Patter calling presents an element of surprise to the dancers. They don't know what sequence the caller is following and this challenges their skills.

The second variation, the singing call, usually has seven choruses, all of which are sung. They have an opening figure, a main figure done by two head couples for two verses, a break, a main figure done by two side couples for two verses, and an ending. The opening, break, and ending contain the same figure with no **partner** change. The main figures have four partner changes to get dancers back to their original partners in their original positions.

It is quite easy to make up your own calls. However, samples have been included in this section, listed in a progressive order (the description of the steps appears later in this chapter). When making up calls, think about eight moves at eight counts a piece for a total of 64 counts. This is the usual length of a chorus in your music. When starting out, it is always good to start with the phrase "honor your partners and honor your corners." If possible, start calls on counts seven and eight of a phrase so that the desired movement starts on count one of the musical phrase. If students cannot complete their moves in eight counts, just wait until everyone has caught up before you make the next call.

Sample Call 1
This is a simple 64-count call.

- Honor your partners (4 counts) and your corners all (4 counts).
- Circle left (8 counts).
- Circle right (8 counts).
- Everyone forward and back (8 counts).
- Do-si-do your partner (8 counts).
- Do-si-do your corner (8 counts).
- Swing your partner (8 counts).
- Swing your corner (8 counts).
- Now everyone promenade; you have a new partner (16 or 32 counts).

Sample Call 2

All moves except the honors should be given eight to 16 counts. Both the honors can be completed in eight counts. In the beginning, do not rush your students through the figures. Eventually, as their level of expertise and confidence gets higher, you will be able to get your students completing the moves in eight counts.

- Honor your partners.
- Honor your corners.
- All join hands and circle left.
- Now circle to the right.
- You all go forward and back.
- Then do-si-do your partner.
- Promenade the set and swing at home.
- Allemande left, then turn your partner by the right.
- Allemande left, then do a grand right and left.
- Meet your partner, give her a swing and promenade home.
- Gents to the center with a right-hand star.
- Then back by the left for a star promenade.
- Break it all up with a corner swing and promenade home.

Sample Call 3

Do not hurry your students; allow plenty of time to complete these movements. Use the talk-through, walk-through, and dance-through method.

- Heads pass through.
- Split the couple, around one.
- Go into the middle (active couples only).
- Form a right-hand star.
- Turn it around 'til your corner comes up.
- Left allemande.
- First couple, go down the center.
- Split the ring, separate.
- Go back home and swing your own.
- Couples 1 and 3 go across the square.
- And separate, go around two people.
- Right back home and swing your own.
- Join hands and circle to the left.
- All four ladies rollaway with a half-sashay.
- And keep on circling.

Sample Call 4

- Couple 1 (2, 3, or 4) separates; they walk around the set, go back home, and swing their own.
- Circle left, then circle to the right.
- Boys, U-turn back for a left allemande.
- Heads pass through and U-turn back.

- Heads pass through and U-turn back once more.
- Head two girls chain across the set.
- Now the side two girls chain across the set.
- Then all four girls chain back home.

Sample Call 5

Remember to use a slow pace and allow plenty of time for dancers to complete the figures. However, normal completion time is eight beats of the music.

- Girls to the center with a left-hand star.
- Back by the right, but not too far.
- Meet your partner with a do paso.
- Turn him by the left and then a right to the corner.
- Then courtesy turn as you go back home.
- Couples 1 and 3 do the right and left through.
- Couples 2 and 4 do the right and left through.
- Once again, couples 1 and 3 do the right and left through.
- Couples 2 and 4 again do the right and left through.
- Boys allemande left the corner girl.
- Grand right and left and then promenade home.
- Couples 1 and 3 star through.
- Then pass through and split two.
- Separate and go around one.
- Walk down the middle and star through again.
- Then pass through, left allemande. (Repeat for side couples.)
- Couples 1 and 3 lead to the right.
- Head gents break and circle to a line.
- Go forward and back, then bend the line.
- All four girls chain across, then chain right back.
- Allemande left and promenade back home.

Sample Call 6

- Heads go forward and back.
- Now sides you do the same.
- It's all around your left-hand girl.
- Then you see-saw your pretty little taw.

Sample Call 7

- Head couples forward and back.
- Now forward again with a full square through.
- Allemande left with the corner girl.
- Couples 1 and 3 square through.
- Split two, go around one to a line of four.
- Forward and back with all eight.
- Left allemande.

- Head couples square through.
- Do-si-do the corner and do a left allemande.
- Come on back with the right and left grand.
- Sides face, grand square.
- Walk, two, three, turn; walk, two, three, turn.
- Walk, two, three, turn; walk, two, three, don't turn.
- Reverse, two, three, turn; walk, two, three, turn.
- Walk, two, three, turn; walk, two, three, you're home.

Designing the Square Dance Lesson

A lesson can be divided into three or four parts. Part 1 is a warm-up time, a review of the movements learned to this point, and perhaps a full dance with these basic movements. Parts 2 and 3 could be combined or separated. If done separately, part 2 is the introduction of new moves with a walk-through and practice calls. Part 3 involves one or more dances containing these new moves. Part 4 is the closing of the lesson. It is a time for the class to do previously learned dances and to request their favorites.

Styling Tips for Teachers and Dancers

Here are a few points regarding quality. *Quality* is the most important word to remember during your square dance time. How much you know is not as important as how well you know it. Dancers should be taught consideration for others. No roughhousing should be tolerated. Dancers should help each other rather than pulling someone along. Dancers need to discover that at first they must *learn to listen*. They can then *listen to learn*, which is the nature of all dancing.

The term *styling* refers to all the points mentioned so far. Styling gives your dancers and dances quality. It starts with posture. Dancers should be reminded to stand tall, with the "sitting room" tucked under and the "dining room" held in tight (the abdomen is held in and the sitter is held tight). This posture is maintained throughout the dance as the dancers use a movement called a **shuffle** to travel through the moves. The shuffle is an easy, light walk in time to the music with the weight kept on the balls of the feet. The feet will be lightly in contact with the floor throughout most of the dance, and dancers will be encouraged to take small steps. The shuffle is the predominant locomotor pattern for square dancing. Clogging, another locomotor pattern, will be discussed later in the chapter.

Before starting a dance, it is customary to honor your partner and your corner. It is often called "bow to your partners and corners." Usually the boys bow and the girls curtsy, or both can do a simple bow.

Use simple mixers in the beginning of lessons to get everyone dancing and having fun. Several simple mixers have been included in the western square dance section, not only to add variety and fun to a class but also to reinforce learned moves and introduce new moves.

The Appalachian big set is an excellent dance form with which to start your square dance lessons. The western square dance lessons will follow, and the clogging section will complete the chapter. The following lists serve as reminders for calling your square dance program. Follow these suggestions as you build your program.

Reminders for Callers
- Be a motivator.
- Be enthusiastic.
- Be a leader and a good host or hostess.
- Set achievable goals.

- Practice so you sound good from the start.
- Use variety in your calls.
- Change the inflection of words at the ends of phrases to avoid becoming monotonous.
- Make it sound nice.
- Use a cadence and rhythm that corresponds to the music.
- Practice until calling becomes easy.

As mentioned earlier, there are two kinds of calls, the patter call and the singing call. When using a singing call, remember that songs usually have a 64-count chorus or sometimes even an 80-count chorus. If the song being used has 80 counts, have the girls chain over and back to fill the extra 16 counts.

▷ APPALACHIAN BIG SET

Appalachian big set is designed to include any number of couples in a big circle, versus a square of four couples, as in western square dance. The big set is the ideal place to begin teaching square dancing fundamentals with all groups. It allows everyone to see each other, so everyone can learn from others. It thereby provides successful experiences from the beginning.

Many figures are done in this style of dancing. We are indebted to this form for giving us many of the western square dance figures we use today. For this reason, it goes well before your western square dance unit.

In the big set, the action goes around the set rather than across it. Movements for squares of eight can be separated from big set figures according to whether they are performed across the set or around it. However, numerous moves in western square dance go around the set.

Big set began with and still has a caller, which is America's only unique contribution to square dance. If the calling was conducted from within the set, it was quite simple and was considered a prompt. Calling from within the set means that the caller dances with the group. However, if the caller is outside the set, there is plenty of improvised patter added to the call.

A successful method of teaching square dance moves is known as the "talk-through, walk-through, dance-through" approach. This means that you describe what you want your dancers to do using a demonstration, if possible. Then everyone walks through the figure without music. Finally, we dance through it!

Big set usually has three parts: opening big set figures, small-circle figures consisting of four people, and closing big set figures. Everyone dances the big set figures together. Only two couples dance the small-circle figures together; this is also known as a four-person square.

- Big set figures: Big-circle figures involve everyone in one large circle. It is important to know which person does what in the dance, so your students should know about big set identification. The girl on the boy's immediate right is his partner, and the next girl to the right is his right-hand girl. The girl to his left is his corner or left-hand girl (see figure 8.1). Note that it is not imperative to pair boys with girls. Pairs can be boy–boy or girl–girl, or you can use colored pinnies (or vests, or ribbons, or scarves) to differentiate partners; then do the calls by colors.
- Small-circle figures: Small-circle figures are done with groups of four to eight people. When dancing small-circle figures and when two couples meet, they automatically join hands and circle left, even if the caller hasn't made the call. To establish circles of four, the caller may call, "odd couple out and circle up four," or "couple up four hands around." When dancing in small circles, couples can move into these circles of four in a variety of ways. One way is for couples to number off odd and even. One of the couples travels to the next couple to dance another figure. A second way is to couple up with four people. Those with their backs to the inside of the hall travel, and those on the outside stay in place. Third, the caller can have people couple up four hands (that is, four people) around and progress wherever they please or as the caller directs.

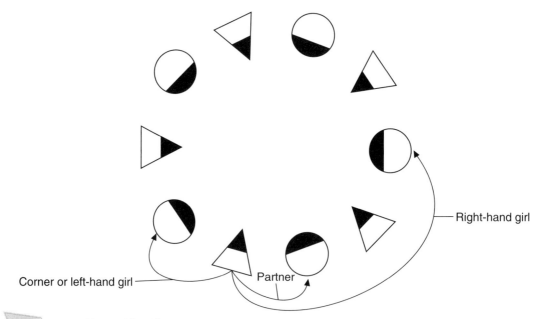

Figure 8.1 Big set identification.

• Square figures: A square consists of four couples facing center with the back of each dancer parallel to a different wall. Opposite couples are 7 to 10 feet (2 to 3 meters) apart from each other, and the girl is on the right of the boy. The couples are numbered 1, 2, 3, and 4 around the square in a counterclockwise direction, starting with the couple whose back is to the front of the hall and the caller (see figure 8.2). Couples 1 and 3 are the head couples, and couples 2 and 4 are the side couples. The girl on the boy's immediate right is his partner, and the next girl to the right is his right-hand girl. The girl across the set is his opposite, and the girl to his left is his corner or left-hand girl.

Note: The walk, honors, and square identification need to be included in the first session. The walk, or shuffle, and honors have already been described in the big set section.

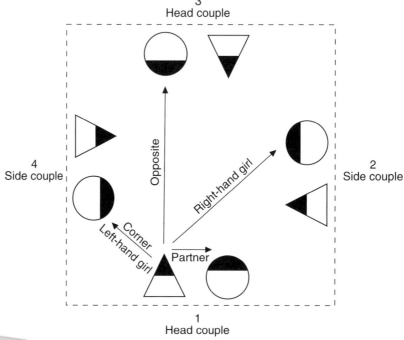

Figure 8.2 Square identification.

BIG-CIRCLE FIGURES

Circle Left and Right

▷ Description

Designated dancers join hands to form a circle and move clockwise to the left (see figure 8.3) or counterclockwise to the right. If the caller does not specify which direction to circle, couples automatically circle left.

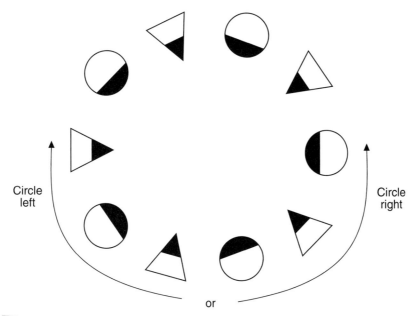

Figure 8.3 Circle Left and Right.

▷ Styling

When hands are joined, boys' palms are up and girls' palms are down. The elbows are bent comfortably so that the hands are above the elbows.

Forward and Back

▷ Description

The designated dancers move forward three steps, stop and touch (see figure 8.4); then they back up three steps, stop and touch.

▷ Styling

As couples come together holding inside hands, they may touch outside hands with the opposite couple on count 4, then back up.

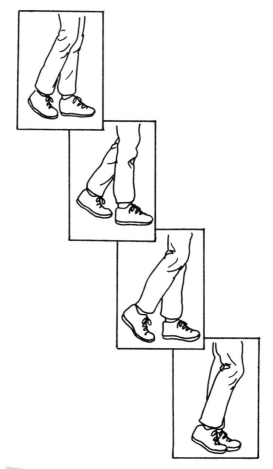

Figure 8.4 Forward and Back.

Do-Si-Do

▷ Description

Two dancers face each other. As they walk around each other back to where they started, they pass right shoulders first, then back to back, then left shoulders (see figure 8.5). This dance is done in eight steps.

▷ Styling

The arms are in a natural position throughout the movement.

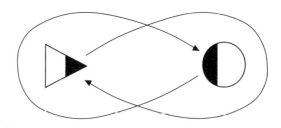

Figure 8.5 Do-Si-Do.

Swing

▷ Description

Two dancers standing right side to right side (hip to hip) and move forward and around, turning clockwise (see figure 8.6). Four steps are taken for one turn and eight for two turns.

▷ Styling

The swing is done with right hips adjacent in a modified closed position. The boy's left hand holds the girl's right, and the boy's right hand is just above girl's waist on her back. The girl's left hand is on the boy's right arm or shoulder. The buzz-step swing is a pivoting action around the right feet of the dancers, with the left foot acting as a pusher. The dancers lean back slightly and stay in close at the bottom. At the K-2 level, have students hold hands and walk around in a circle for their swing.

Figure 8.6   Keep your partner on your right side during your swing.

Couple Promenade

▷ Description

Two dancers walk in the skater's position—side by side with the left hands the right hands together in front of the dancers. The girl is on the right and moves around the set counterclockwise, unless otherwise indicated. Couples move back to their home positions and face the center of the set.

▷ Styling

In the promenade position (see figure 8.7), the boys' palms are up and the girls' are down. The boys' right forearm is over the girls' left arm. For K-2 children, holding hands works well for the promenade.

Figure 8.7   Promenade position.

Single-File Promenade

▷ Description

The dancers move one behind the other in a single circle (see figure 8.8) either right or left.

▷ Styling

The hands and arms are in a natural position while walking around the set.

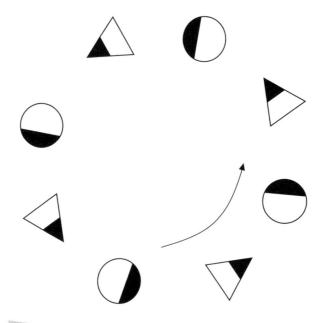

▼ **Figure 8.8**   Single-File Promenade.

Single-File, Girl in the Lead

▷ Description

This has the same call as Single-File Promenade, except the girl promenades in front of her partner around the circle counterclockwise (see figure 8.9).

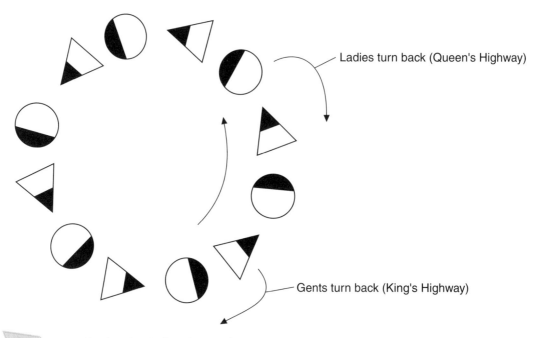

▼ **Figure 8.9**   Single-File, Girl in the Lead.

Ladies Turn Back or Queen's Highway, Gents Turn Back or King's Highway

▷ **Description**

Both of these calls are executed in the same manner as the Single-File, Girl in the Lead (see figure 8.9). Either the girls or the boys, depending on the call, do a half-turn to their right and promenade back around the outside of the circle clockwise until they meet their original partner or whomever the caller designates.

Girls to the Center, Boys to the Center, Everybody to the Center

▷ **Description**

Depending on who the call is for, the designated dancers take four steps to the center of the circle and four steps back (see figure 8.10).

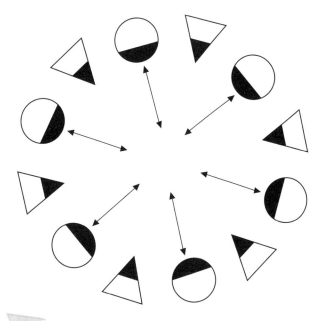

Figure 8.10 Girls to the Center.

Wind Up the Ball of Yarn

▷ **Description**

This call occurs when the caller indicates a designated dancer to "wind it up," as a snail's shell is wound—or like winding a ball of yarn from the outside in. The designated dancer releases his or her right hand to the next person, winds it up (the designated dancer begins making concentric circles inside the original big circle until all the dancers have formed a tight coil), turns in the opposite direction, and unwinds the figure (see figure 8.11).

Figure 8.11 Wind Up the Ball of Yarn.

Open Tunnel and London Bridge

▷ Description

For Open Tunnel, the lead couple turns back while promenading. All the couples behind them form an arch under which the leads are to duck (see figure 8.12). Each succeeding couple then turns and ducks under the arch. When the lead couple gets through everyone, they form an arch and come back over the other dancers. Each succeeding couple does the same thing.

If the call "London Bridge" is given, instead of going back under the arch, the lead couple turns and forms an arch with other couples following, just as is done in Open Tunnel.

Figure 8.12 Open Tunnel and London Bridge.

▷ SMALL-CIRCLE FIGURES

Birdie in the Cage

▷ Description

One girl, usually the traveling girl (the girl that is in the couple that is advancing around the set), moves in the center of the other dancers; they then circle around her (see figure 8.13). Then the call, "Bird fly out and crow hop in," may be given; the girl gets out of the circle. The traveling boy goes into the center, and the others encircle him with hands joined.

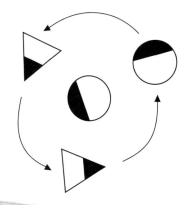

Figure 8.13   Birdie in the Cage.

Swing at the Wall

▷ Description

The partners in the inside couple (the couple with backs to the center) separate, walk around the outside couple on the circle, and swing at the wall (swing on the outside of the set) behind the outside couple; then the inside couple moves back through the outside couple and swings in the hall inside the circle (see figure 8.14).

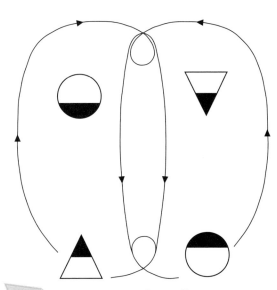

Figure 8.14   Swing at the Wall.

Take a Little Peek

▷ Description

The partners of the inside couple peek (take a look at their partner) around the sides of the outside couple, move back to the center, and swing; the partners of the inside couple peek once more, move back to the center, and then all four couples swing (see figure 8.15).

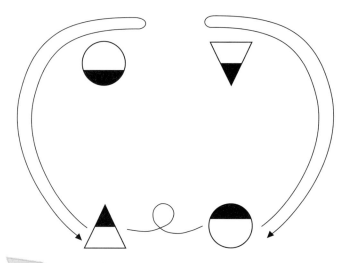

Figure 8.15   Take a Little Peek.

Mountaineer Loop

▷ Description

The partners of the inside couple drop inside hands and dive under and through an arch formed by the outside couple (see figure 8.16); the partners of the inside couple come back and join hands; then all circle left, and the figure is repeated by the outside couple under the inside couple's arch.

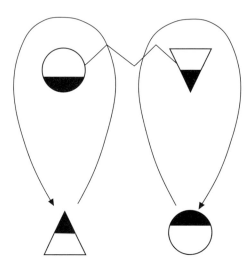

Figure 8.16   Mountaineer Loop.

Swing When You Meet

▷ Description

Inside couple around the outside couple, and swing when you meet; back to the center and inside couple swings (see figure 8.17). Inside couple around this couple once more and swing when you meet, back to the center, and swing all four.

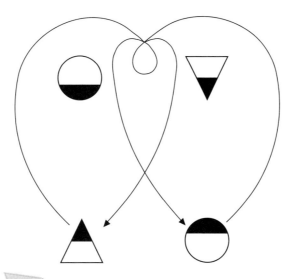

Figure 8.17   Swing When You Meet.

Couple Couples Swing

▷ Description

The inside couple moves through the outside couple and goes back home around the outside (see figure 8.18); couples swing their partners, then couple up four (the four join hands), circle four hands around (left).

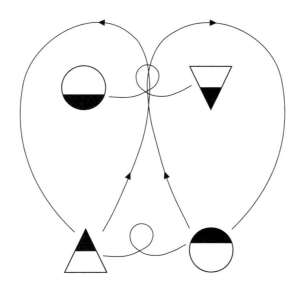

Figure 8.18   Couple Couples Swing.

Girl Around the Girl

▷ Description

The inside girl walks around the outside girl, and the inside boy follows (see figure 8.19a); then inside girl walks around the outside boy, and the inside boy doesn't follow (see figure 8.19b).

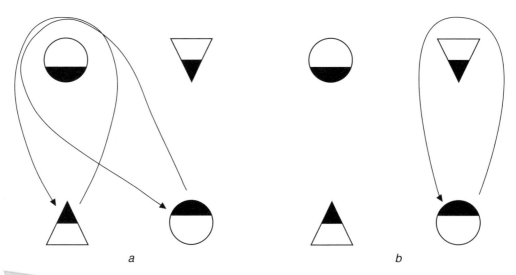

a   b

Figure 8.19, a and b   Girl Around the Girl.

Georgia Rang Tang

▷ Description

Turn your opposite partner with a right-hand around; turn your partner with a left-hand around (see figure 8.20); turn your opposite partner with a right and your partner with a left.

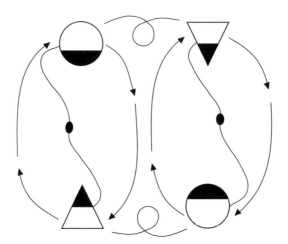

Figure 8.20   Georgia Rang Tang.

Allemande Left and Right

▷ Description

Two dancers, holding either left or right hands, walk around each other and back to place (see figure 8.21); the allemande left is done with one's corner.

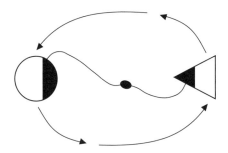

Figure 8.21   Allemande Left and Right.

Arm Turns, Left and Right

▷ Description

Two dancers, holding either left or right forearms, walk around each other and back to place.

▷ Styling

Dancers grasp each other just below the elbow for this turn and walk around each other (see figure 8.22).

Figure 8.22   Right-hand arm turn.

Grand Right and Left

▷ Description

Partners face and join right hands; they pull their partner by them and give a left hand to the next person; boys go counterclockwise and girls go clockwise; this pattern continues until each dancer meets her or his original partner (see figure 8.23).

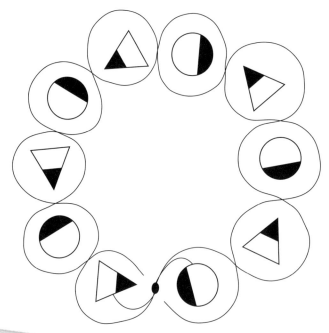

Figure 8.23 Grand Right and Left.

Weave the Ring

▷ Description

This is a grand right and left without touching hands.

▷ Styling

The hands and arms are in a natural position throughout the movement.

Star Right and Left

▷ Description

Designated dancers step forward, extend either the right or left hand to form a star, and walk forward in the direction they are facing (see figure 8.24, a and b). Stars may be directed to turn a quarter-, half-, three-quarter-, or full turn.

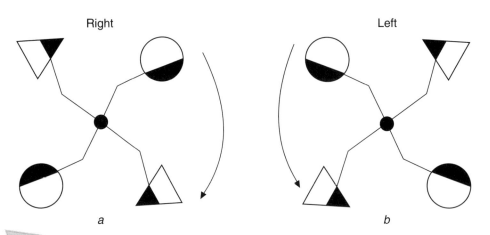

Figure 8.24, *a* and *b* Star position.

▷ Styling

Stars may be formed with the palms up and touching in the center or in the form of a wrist-hold in which each dancer holds the wrist of the person in front a little lower than shoulder-height.

Star Promenade

▷ Description

This is the same formation as that used for a four-hand star, except that those in the star place their arms around the designated dancer's waist and take that dancer with them (see figure 8.25).

▷ Styling

Both dancers put their arms around each other's waists in this movement.

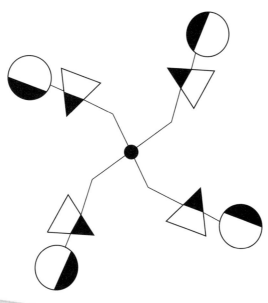

Figure 8.25 Star Promenade.

▷ SQUARE FIGURES

Many of these figures are done in big set dancing with modifications as well.

Pass Through

▷ Description

No hands are used in this movement. Two facing couples walk forward and pass their opposites. They pass right shoulders and remain back to back with relation to the other couple to receive the next call (see figure 8.26).

▷ Styling

Arms should be in a natural position.

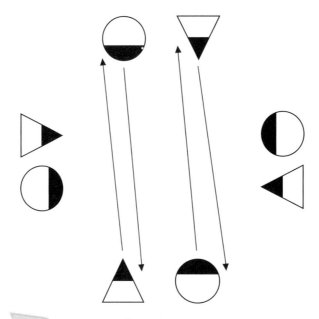

Figure 8.26   Pass Through.

Split the Outside Couple and Split the Ring

▷ Description

One couple moves forward to the opposite couple, going between and through them (see figure 8.27) with the next call indicating the direction to be followed.

▷ Styling

Split the Outside Couple usually involves two couples. Split the Ring, which is really the same move, may only involve one couple.

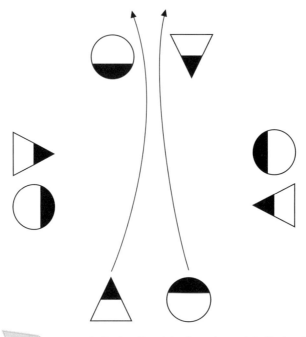

Figure 8.27   Split the Outside Couple and Split the Ring.

Rollaway Half-Sashay

▷ Description

The girl rolls across a full turn (360 degrees) in front of the boy. The result is that the girls have changed places (see figure 8.28).

▷ Styling

The boy gently pulls the girl across in front of him; she moves to the opposite side as he steps back and to the right.

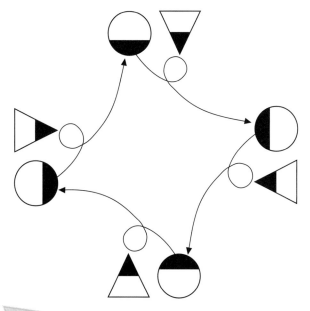

Figure 8.28 Rollaway Half-Sashay.

U-Turn Back

▷ Description

This is a single-dancer movement with a quarter-turn away from your patner to return back home (see figure 8.29). The designated couple goes across the set, divides the opposite couple, turns back to back, and goes home.

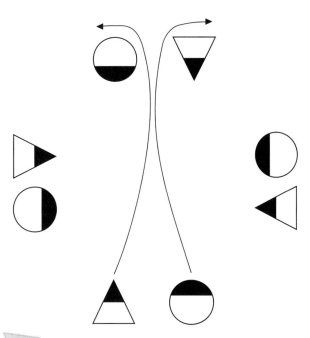

Figure 8.29 U-Turn Back.

Separate and Divide

▷ Description

Dancers turn back to back (separate) and on "divide" walk forward around the outside of the square, girls to the inside (see figure 8.30). Follow the next call.

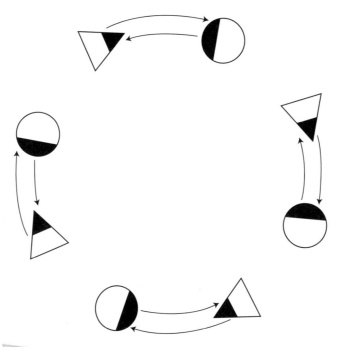

Figure 8.30   Separate and Divide.

Wrong Way Grand

▷ Description

This is the same as the grand right and left, but the boys move clockwise and girls move counterclockwise.

Courtesy Turn

▷ Description

The boy takes the girl's left hand; her palm faces down in his left hand, which is facing up. He places his right hand on the small of her back. Together they turn until they are facing the center as the boy backs up and the girl goes forward (see figure 8.31). She may either hold her skirt or put her free hand on her hip.

Figure 8.31   Courtesy Turn.

Two or Four Ladies Chain

▷ Description

Two indicated girls extend right hands to each other in the center. They pull by, extend their left hands to the opposite boy, and complete the move with a courtesy turn (see figure 8.32). With the four ladies chain, all four girls go to the center with a right-hand star; do a half-turn, and courtesy turn with the opposite boy.

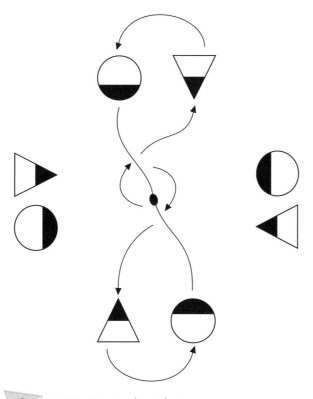

Figure 8.32   Two Ladies Chain.

Do Paso

▷ Description

Partners face and do a left forearm turn. Then they do a right forearm turn with their corners and a courtesy turn with their partners. At the end of the courtesy turn, they face the center of the set or follow the next call.

Lead Right

▷ Description

From a static square or starting formation, the designated couples move out to face the couple to their immediate right (see figure 8.33).

▷ Styling

Couples hold inside hands; outside hands are in a normal dance position.

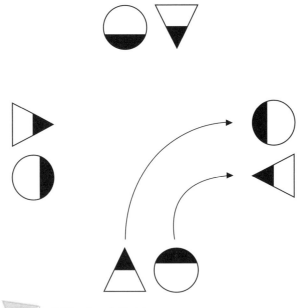

Figure 8.33 Lead Right.

Right and Left Through

▷ Description

Two facing couples go toward each other, join right hands, pull by, and give their left hands to their partners. The movement is completed with a courtesy turn. The result is that the couples end up facing across from where they started (see figure 8.34).

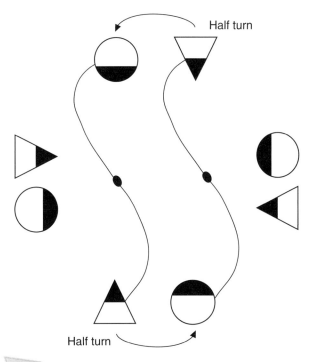

Half turn

Half turn

Figure 8.34 Right and Left Through.

Star Through

▷ Description

This movement begins with partners facing. The boy's right hand is placed against girl's left hand with the fingers pointed up to form an arch. The dancers move forward with the girl doing a quarter-turn left under the arch, while the boy does a quarter-turn to the right behind the girl (see figure 8.35). The dancers end up side by side with the girl on the boy's right.

▷ Styling

The hands should be up, palm to palm, with enough height for the girl to move comfortably under the arch.

Figure 8.35 Star Through.

Circle to a Line

▷ Description

Two facing couples circle left doing a half-turn. The boy indicated by the caller breaks the hold with his left hand but retains the right-hand hold (see figure 8.36, *a* and *b*). The released dancer moves forward under a raised arm arch (see figure 8.36*c*). The dancer becomes the right end in a line of four that is facing center. The line straightens out for the next call.

a   b   c

Figure 8.36, a-c   Circle to a Line.

Bend the Line

▷ Description

A line with an even number of dancers, usually four, all face the same direction and drop hand holds in the center. The ends move forward while the centers back up; both halves of the line are now facing (see figure 8.37).

▷ Styling

Use normal couple hand holds and quickly join hands in the new line.

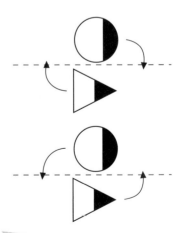

Figure 8.37   Bend the Line.

All Around the Left-Hand Lady

▷ Description

Begin with corners facing and walking around each other. Right shoulders are adjacent and remain so throughout the move. Dancers loop in a complete circle to return to face their partners (see figure 8.38).

▷ Styling

The arms are in a natural dance position.

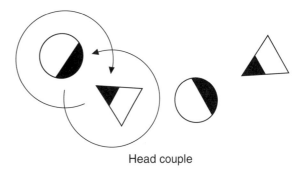

Head couple

Figure 8.38   All Around the Left-Hand Lady.

See-Saw (Your Taw)

▷ Description

Start with dancers facing, and in this case partners facing. Following the call, "All around the left-hand girl," move as required by walking forward and around your partner; keep left shoulders adjacent throughout the move instead of right shoulders (see figure 8.39).

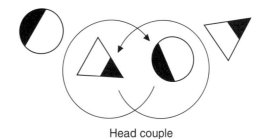

Head couple

Figure 8.39   See-Saw (Your Taw).

See-Saw is a Left-Shoulder Do-Si-Do

▷ Description

When not used with the call "All around the left-hand lady," this move is like a do-si-do, except that it starts with left shoulders passing first instead of right shoulders. When used with the call "All around the left-hand lady, and see-saw your taw" the moves combine into a flowing figure-8 pattern (see figure 8.40).

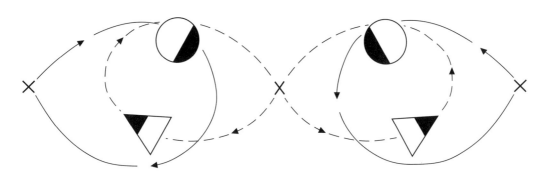

Figure 8.40   All Around the Left-Hand Lady and See-Saw Your Taw.

Grand Square

▷ Description

The heads and sides perform the movement in different directions (see figure 8.41) at the same time on the command, "Sides face, grand square." The heads move forward four steps, do a quarter-turn on the fourth step to face their partners, and back up four steps. Then they do a quarter-turn to face their opposites, back up to the corner in four steps, do a quarter-turn to face their partners, and walk home four steps. Do not turn; the action from this point is reversed (for a total of 16 counts). This is the halfway point. The heads now back away from their partners four steps, doing a quarter-turn on the fourth step to face opposites. They then walk forward four steps, and again on the fourth do a quarter-turn to face the center of the set and their partner. Walk forward four steps, do a quarter-turn on the fourth step to face opposite, and back up four steps to your home position. This is a 32-count move.

While the heads do their first 16 steps, the sides face their partners to back away and do the second 16 steps. Upon completion of the second 16, the sides do the first 16 steps, while the heads are doing the last 16.

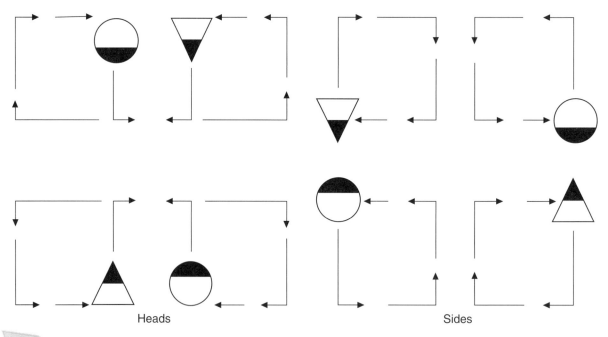

Heads   Sides

Figure 8.41   Grand Square.

Square Through

▷ Description

This may be called for one to five hands. It starts with couples facing, joining right hands, and pulling by one another (see figure 8.42). Then do a quarter-turn, join left hands, and pull by again. Half of the square through has been completed. Do a quarter-turn again, join right hands, and pull by once again. Do one last quarter-turn, join left hands and pull by for a final time, but do not turn.

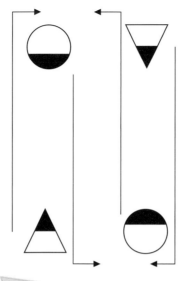

Figure 8.42   Square Through.

CLOGGING

Appalachian clog dance varies in form from geographic region to region, but it is truly an American folk art. It takes its roots from sources that include England, Ireland, Scotland, and Africa. Our earliest settlers brought these varieties, and because of this we cannot identify one source as the true source of clogging. Later, contributions came from Germany and France.

Perhaps clogging arose from the walking step used in Appalachian big set as the participants added foot stamping, shuffles, chugs, and heel–toe combinations to emphasize the rhythmic pattern of the music. While a couple waited to dance in the Kentucky running set, they would freestyle in place. The men would perform a solo jig, called a hoedown.

Black men added another form of flat-footed chugs and shuffles, called the buck dance. It was this buck dancing that found its way into minstrel shows and vaudeville. It eventually evolved into our modern tap dance and Charleston.

Clogging has continued to grow over the years. It has great appeal because of its relationship to American folk traditions, its exciting rhythms and steps, and its capacity to provide aerobic exercise. Its evolution parallels that of square dance, both the big set and western forms. Depending on the location, the participants might smooth shuffle or they might clog dance through the figures. Because of the popularity of clogging while square dancing, a short section on basics is included for you to try in your programs.

History

It is believed that the term *clogging* has its roots in the wooden-soled shoes used in old English clog dancing. Today, however, cloggers wear flexible leather-soled shoes and add taps to them to amplify the sound of the steps.

Clogging has moved from the Appalachian Mountains across the United States and has its own national association. It can be included as an alternative to walking through your figures and offers another challenge to add to your square dance program. Since clogging can be done either while square dancing or as a separate activity, these basics will add another colorful dimension to your program. In addition, it can help develop physical, mental, and social fitness!

Step Description

Many steps in clogging have strong regional ties, such as the Western North Carolina triple, Smoky Mountain variation, and the Tennessee walking step. However, despite all the regional differences, most cloggers recognize the following eight basic steps:

- Toe: a step or tap on the floor with the ball of the foot.
- Heel: a transfer of weight from the toe to the heel with a snap to make a distinct sound.
- Step: a flat-footed stamp with the heel and toe touching the floor simultaneously.
- Drag (also known as a backward chug): a slide back on one foot, with the weight on that foot, without lifting the toe or heel.
- Slide (also known as a forward chug): the same as the drag, except done going forward (similar to a skip).
- Rock (also known in modern tap as a step-ball-change): a step with the left foot that involves placing the ball of the right foot slightly behind the left foot, a transfer of weight to the right foot while lifting the left foot, and a step again on the left foot (can also be done starting on the right foot).
- Brush (also known in modern tap by the same-name): a brush of the floor with the foot that is done by placing the weight on one foot, lifting the other foot, and kick it forward so the ball of the foot slides across the floor and the heel makes no sound.
- Double toe (also known in modern tap as the shuffle): a double brush done with the weight on one foot, brushing the other foot forward and then back (knee will straighten slightly on the forward brush and bend slightly on the brush back).

It is from these eight steps that the more complex steps are developed. Steps that include big kicks, knee and foot slaps, heel clicks, and syncopated rhythms are just a few of these more-involved steps. The music is usually traditional, reflecting its rural heritage. However, today cloggers are dancing to just about anything.

Of course, this form of dancing is like all the rest; putting together combinations is what it is all about. The combinations are put together to make up eight-count phrases. Begin by practicing the basics in multiples of two, four, and eight. Repetition is the ingredient that will lead your dancers to rapid improvement.

Some sample practice routine ideas follow:

1-4 Tap your left toe three times and step on your left foot.

5-8 Tap your right toe three times and step on your right foot.

1-8 Do four drags (backward chugs) on one or two feet.

1-8 Do four slides (forward chugs) on one or two feet.

1-8 Repeat the first set of counts, but this time use the heel instead of the toe for the tapping.

1-16 Repeat the second and third sets of counts.

1-8 Rock or step-ball-change four times.

1-4 Brush the left toe forward and across in front of the right foot; bring the left foot back across in front of the right foot and step with the left foot.

5-8 Brush the right toe forward and across in front of left foot; bring the right foot back across in front of the left foot and step with the right foot.

The total counts in this practice routine is 64, and now the entire routine can be repeated over and over again. Try adding in new steps and variations in the same manner to challenge students to continue their personal growth with this new form of dancing.

SUMMARY

You should now be able to add some variety to your square dance program. Appalachian big set serves as a great lead-in to squares of eight. Clogging to the movements of the dances certainly can add variety to a program. Square dance forms are developmentally appropriate for your classes. The contents of this chapter have the potential to enliven your classes and have your students wanting more.

▷   **Create Your Own Square and Clogging Dances**   ◁

This is an opportunity for students to do both individual and group work, depending on your preference and needs. For instance, clogging can be done as an individual and group activity. Square dancing and Appalachian big set involve couples, squares of four and eight, and huge circles. This form of dancing really lends itself to lots of individual and group efforts.

Checklist for Creating Your Own Square or Clogging Dance

- Instruct students to create their own square or clogging dances.
- Stay developmentally appropriate. The dance should fill 64 counts of music and incorporate all of the factors of different directions and turns. Beginners can start by creating simple figures similar to some of the other figures in the chapter.
- Have the students try this alone and with partners or small groups to change the social dynamics and increase the development of social skills.
- Require students to write up their descriptions to emphasize the language aspects of dance.

Rubric

Now that you have your students creating their own square and clogging dances, here is an example of a rubric that could work for this particular activity or for others with modifications. Just by changing a few words, this rubric could work with other aspects of your warm-ups.

4 Points—Exemplary	The student created a 64-count dance with variety and movements that are executed well to the music.
3 Points—Acceptable	The student created a 32-count dance with some variety and movements that are sometimes executed to the music.
2 Points—Needs Improvement	The student created a 32-count dance with no variety and movements rarely executed to the music.
1 Point—Unacceptable	The student created fewer than 32 counts in the dance and there was no clear rhythmic pattern established.

▷   **Review Questions**   ◁

Have students submit questions for the class to answer, or have them answer questions similar to these suggested in the following list. In addition, these could be used as a homework assignment, as an in-class assignment, or for class discussion.

1. Make a list of the benefits of square dancing and clogging.
2. Trace the history of square dancing and clogging in the United States.

3. When creating figures, what is the main number of counts that is critical to developing such dances?

4. Collect and write up several square dances from other sources.

5. Describe the physiological benefits received from square dancing and clogging.

6. When creating square dances, what are some of the important things that you should be sure to include?

7. What is the great appeal of doing square dances at a party?

Observation Questions

1. List the different locomotor movements that you observed in this activity that are usually found in square dancing and clogging.

2. List the combination movements that you observed in the square dancing and clogging activities.

3. What are some of the formations used in square dancing and clogging?

4. What were the tempos of these dances?

5. Did the actions of participants reflect the theme and attitude of square and clog dance? Please describe your observations.

6. Did the participants raise their heart rates to the target work zone for aerobic benefits?

7. Was there an opportunity for the dancers to develop movements in all directions?

8. Was there an opportunity for leading with different feet? Please describe the level at which this occurred.

9. Was the square and clog dance developed in multiples of 4, 8, 16, 32, and 64 counts?

10. Was the music selection appropriate for your class?

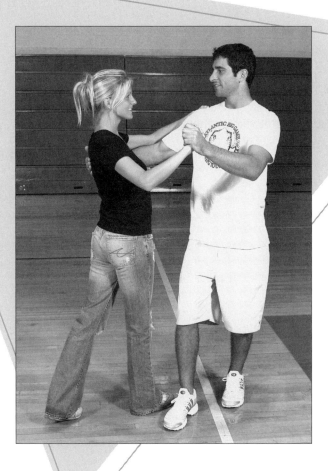

CHAPTER 9

Social Dances

Social dance is just what its name says it is: dance for society, dance for everyone. It is the social dances around the world that help to preserve the intangible cultural heritage of any society. This chapter focuses on dance forms that have come to be known as social or recreational dance. Social dance is very often characterized by having partners to do a particular style of dance.

It is not the intent of this chapter to cover all of the social dance forms that are known but rather to include several that will make an impact and be a hit with your students. In addition, the primary teaching technique to introduce these dances will be quite unique to most of you who are using this text. However, you can be sure that this approach has been used for a long time and it has been successful with students of all ages.

The social dances included in this chapter are the waltz, foxtrot, tango, merengue, salsa or mambo, rumba, and swing. More than enough material will be included to get any program started and to carry your students through a complete unit on social dance. It is these same social dances that have been further expanded to make up the ballroom and Latin dances that are performed around the world as well.

Did You Know?

Social Dance, Dance Sport, Ballroom, and Latin Dance Fact Sheet

- Ballroom and Latin dance are lifetime pursuits appropriate for all ages!
- More than 300 colleges have ballroom dance programs, and 1,000 more are being added.
- The first national primary, middle, and high school DanceSport championships were held in 1995 and now are held annually.
- The number of college student and junior DanceSport members more than doubled in the past two years. It is anticipated that there will be over 30,000 United States Amateur Ballroom Dance Association members by the year 2005, and more than 20 percent will be DanceSport athletes under age 20.

Source: United States Amateur Ballroom Dance Association, March 2001.

The primary organizational patterns for beginning to teach these dances will be ones that are very familiar to all of us. Some organizational patterns will be structured moves in lines, and then some learning patterns will promote movement in and through the spaces with turns and directional changes to more closely approximate the actual dance pattern being learned. This is always done first without partners and without musical accompaniment.

After an acceptable level of success is attained by your students, then the appropriate music is added while doing the same movements. All of the social dance forms will follow this sequence. The next step is to learn to "guard" a partner without a musical accompaniment: to mirror the partner's movements as if she or he is actually in an offensive and defensive pattern. The focus is the same in dance as in sports at this point; the feet must not be crossed and foot movements must mirror those of the person with whom you are dancing. Also, guard your partner closely. After students can execute guarding fairly smoothly, add the appropriate music.

Nothing is said about form, who partners with whom, and which foot to start with. In fact, everyone is expected to master the movements starting on either foot because this is important for teaching dance and sport techniques. Always introduce the social dance through the sport model. This is likely to help your students more readily identify with the movements and skills.

Once your students are really into the social dance, then use all of the normal teaching formations—lines facing, partners on circles, lines facing front, waves going the length of the room—and practice the basic steps of the social dance forms. For any of the steps a student is only required to know four basic movements: walking forward, walking backward, walking to the side, and doing rock-steps either forward or backward.

Probably my favorite drill is a "walking and turning" drill without and with musical accompaniment. This involves walking forward and backward in straight, curved, and zig-zagging lines and adding half-turns, full turns, and quarter-turns to simulate dance movements. Lots of students can be moving through your teaching space, and you can provide lots of feedback. An important teaching cue is "have your ankles and knees and thighs brush" to keep the legs from spreading out too much. Also, "keep your weight under your body for good posture while practicing and dancing." This can be done alone as well as with a partner, as social dancing really involves mirroring your partner. The better one can mirror his or her partner, the better he or she will dance socially. Two additional cues to use with the walking and turning exercise are, first, to tell students to slightly flex the knees to absorb and smooth out the activity (think "soft knees") and, second, to make contact with the floor with the feet moving just slightly above the floor so as to appear to glide over the surface of the floor. It is important to teach moves that start off on either foot. But as your students progress, let them know that boys lead with the left foot and girls with the right foot just about all of the time.

These drills provide a great opportunity to practice the heel–toe technique found in the waltz, foxtrot, and tango and the ball–flat technique found in the meregue, rumba, salsa or mambo, and swing.

Each of the social forms that is included in this chapter will start with a short historical discussion of the dance form and is followed by several specific dance steps for each form. After this, all that must be done is to have your students learn the individual dance steps. At that point, they are dancing and even creating on their own.

One other teaching tip that you may want to try is to find current popular music for the age group that you are teaching. Introduce the style that you are going to teach through the progression described previously. This allows you, the teacher, to hook your students into a particular dance form, and the student doesn't even know that she or he is dancing.

▷ SMOOTH AMERICAN-STYLE DANCES

The styles selected for inclusion in this category are the waltz, foxtrot, and tango. The heel–toe technique is the dominant characteristic of these styles.

Waltz

Probably none of the other ballroom and Latin dances is more deserving to be named the queen of the ballroom and Latin dance scene today than is the waltz. It may be the most elegant of all of the dances performed today. It was the waltz that both revolutionized and scandalized dance in the 1700s. After all, it was the first time that dancers had faced each other in public to dance. Moreover, dancers danced in very close proximity to one another with the man's arm around the waist of his partner in what really appeared to be an embrace. This was a major change as dancers previously danced mostly in lines and side by side to entertain the onlookers more than the dancers. Until then, this type of behavior in public was strictly taboo. It actually was so scandalous that it was banned as a dance form from public ballrooms for many years.

The roots of the waltz go back to the Middle Ages in Europe, receiving influence from the volte from France, the volta from Italy, and perhaps most of all the landler from Austria. The current name finds its roots in the German word *waltzen*, which means to slide or glide.

The popularity of the waltz in Europe reached its peak with the great classical composers, such as Mozart, Bach, and Johann Strauss. Numerous other composers likewise contributed greatly to the body of music to which the waltz is performed. Strauss, in fact, increased the waltz tempo considerably, which ultimately led to the creation of a variation of the dance called the Viennese waltz. This dance is characterized by increased tempos, turning, and spinning. It is danced to this day.

The graceful flowing aspects of the new waltz developed in Europe, and a major change was made in the footwork from the step-close-step pattern to the step-side-close pattern we often see today. This was done to try to prevent peasants from dancing the waltz. It didn't work, and the new waltz made its way to the United States with the first settlers. The new waltz was danced from the East Coast to the West Coast as the settlers moved across the country, with different groups putting their special styling and music to the dancing. The waltz has been enjoyed in the United States from elegant ballrooms to Broadway to the western saloons. And the basic waltz step can be found in the dances of almost every nation.

When teaching waltz steps, teach strong heel and toe leads and the down-up-down flow typical to this dance. Starting the waltz requires some special effort, since it is danced in 3/4 time. Have your students perform walking drills or move in and through open spaces on the dance floor as you continuously count 1, 2, 3, 1, 2, 3. Eventually begin to emphasize the first count and the change in the lead for every three counts (since 3/4 has only 3 beats per measure, the first beat is done with one foot in one measure on count 1 then the other foot on count 1 of the second measure). Emphasize gliding with the feet in the heel–toe, toe–heel progression: the dancers roll their feet as they dance, making a slight push from one foot to the other. Another good way to introduce the movements is to teach them as you would aerobics, repeating the moves and changing directions and the lead foot regularly. Only after they master the moves should they dance in the closed position.

Basic Box Waltz

▷ Description

This step starts the dance. It is a box formation that takes six counts to complete. Each half of the box requires three steps.

▷ Steps

Boys start on their right foot and girls on their left foot. The girls' part will be the opposite of the boys' and appear in parentheses following the description of the boys' movements.

1. The boy steps forward on the left foot (the girl steps backward on the right foot).
2. The boy brings the right foot beside his left foot, brushing the ankle and stepping to the right side (the girl brings the left foot beside her right foot, brushing the ankle and stepping to the left side).
3. The boy closes with the left foot beside the right foot (the girl closes with the right foot beside the left).

Now begin the second half of the box step.

4. The boy steps backward with the right foot (the girl steps forward with the left foot).
5. The boy brings the left foot beside the right, brushing the ankle, and steps to the left side (the girl brings the right foot beside left foot, brushing the ankle, and steps to the right side).
6. The boy closes with the right foot beside the left (the girl closes with the left foot beside the right).

Waltzing Underarm Turn

▷ Description

There are many ways to execute underarm turns. This one will be initiated after the first half of the box has been completed.

▷ Steps

The cue for the two dancers is for the boy to raise his left arm, holding the girl's right hand. This is a signal to execute the underarm turn. The girl should take her time, walking in a nice smooth circle for six to nine counts as the boy continues to dance the basic step until both partners are facing again and can get back into the basic or go on to another waltz step.

Waltz Hesitations

▷ Description

These steps are used for avoiding other dancers or for variation in the dance. It is often referred to as a balancé and can be executed in four directions: forward, backward, and to either side.

▷ Steps

The step is simple, proceeding in the preferred direction, holding for the last two counts, and then going back to the starting place on the opposite foot and holding the last two counts. It is sometimes referred to as a swinging pendulum type of a movement.

Waltzing Left Box Turn

▷ Description

This move is a way for the couple to turn by simply making eighth-, quarter-, or half-turns with the basic steps. It requires that the basic step be modified so that the first half of the basic moves forward with the preferred turn and the second half moves backward with the same sort of turn. Have students initially practice it without a partner, turning and facing different walls, and then have them join with a partner.

▷ Steps

The boy initiates the movements. Starting with his left foot, he turns in a curved pathway to his left as the girl curves with her right foot in the same direction. The boy then starts on his right foot (with the girl on her left foot) and goes backward (the girl goes forward), curving the foot path so that another quarter-turn has been executed. This can be done one to four times before moving on to a different waltz step.

Running Waltz

▷ Description

This step provides the dancers with a very nice alternative to the basic box pattern and is often seen in Texas waltz, Cajun waltz, and Viennese waltz dances. It is lots of fun to do and adds a very nice aesthetic look to the dancers.

▷ Steps

Partners can be in the closed position, side by side, or holding hands. Actually, there are as many variations as can be imagined. This dance move is a bit of an oxymoron as a descriptor. Dancers still use the 3/4-time sequence as they move around the room in a running-like pattern, which is really a walk to the tempo of the music (see figure 9.1).

Figure 9.1 The running waltz step.

Foxtrot

One of the all-time great American dances, popularized during the roaring twenties, is definitely the foxtrot. Its roots go all the way back to 1913 or 1914. At this time a new form of music called ragtime had appeared on the music and dance scenes. This marked a major change from the fast waltz tempos and marching tempos that were the predominant music and dance forms at this time. It marked the development of a syncopated rhythm. Harry Fox, a bandleader and dancer with the Ziegfeld Follies vaudevillian show, introduced a new "trotting" dance. This dance, aptly names the foxtrot, fit quite well with the lively music that typified the era and gradually has evolved into the smooth and graceful ballroom dance of today.

Harry Fox played music mainly at the old Amsterdam Roof Garden in New York City. He put together some music that had a little less bounce and more smoothness to go with the new dance. The foxtrot, which is a combination of the one-step and two-step, has endured and evolved throughout the decades. It is danced around the world and is probably one of the most frequently danced ballroom dances currently being performed. While it does not resemble our modern form, the initial movements for the foxtrot were a combination of slow steps and quick steps, just as it is today. It was and is danced to slow and fast foxtrot rhythms (120 to 140 BPM) around the world and is always a favorite of the dancers on the dance floor on any given night. Since Harry Fox operated mostly out of New York City, this is where much of the stylizing of the dance occurred. Along with the swing, it is a dance with a truly American origin.

Foxtrot music is counted in either 2/4 or 4/4 time with a large variety of dance steps being done to the music. However, there always seems to be the characteristic combination of slow and quick steps done in the figures of the dance. Arthur Murray, the great dancer and dance-school founder, named the basic combination of slow, slow, quick, quick the Murray Magic Step. He was quite instrumental in increasing the popularity of this dance form. Once the basic foxtrot rhythm is learned, it is much easier to move on to many of the other ballroom and Latin dance forms.

When teaching foxtrot steps, teach strong heel and toe leads. It is a smoothly flowing, fairly level dance form and can have either a 6-count or 4-count basic step, depending on the particular step that is chosen. It has the same heel–toe rolling of the feet technique as the waltz. In the opening warm-ups practice walking and turning with strong heel and toe leads and roll the feet. Remind the dancers about their body alignment and posture. As was mentioned earlier, stress that the students must have the ankles, knees, and thighs brush to keep the legs from spreading out too much. Also have them keep their weight under the body for good posture while practicing and dancing. The head and shoulders should remain level.

After the line drills have been completed, do the same drills around the room in a counterclockwise circle to simulate the dance flow and get the dancers accustomed to dancing in the normal line of direction for the dance. Use these drills as reviews and lead-up progressions for new steps. Remember the teaching sequence: first working with no accompaniment or partner, then adding percussion or music and then partners and no accompaniment, to finally putting it all together. As the dancers are working, the term *frame* is a great word to use to remind them of their posture while dancing. The dancers dance in the closed position for much of this dance.

Forward Basic Foxtrot

▷ Description

Just as the name implies, this step starts the dance off in a forward, counterclockwise direction. It requires six counts to complete.

▷ Steps

Boys start on the right foot and girls on the left foot. The girls' part will be the opposite of the boys' and is provided in parentheses. This step is usually directed with the cues slow (2 counts), slow (2 counts), quick (1 count), quick (1 count).

1-2 The boy steps forward on the left foot (the girl steps backward on right foot).

3-4 The boy steps forward on right foot (the girl steps backward on left foot).

5-6 The boy steps to the left side (the girl steps to the right) and then closes the right beside the left (the left beside the right).

Foxtrot Promenade

▷ Description

Heads turn slightly as the body opens to view the line of direction and see where the dancers are going. This is a variation of the forward basic used to go down the line with a crossover step; dancers end up facing their partner once again (see figure 9.2).

▷ Steps

1-2 Both dancers do a slow step, the boy with his left foot and the girl with her right, in the line of direction.

3-4 The boy crosses the right foot in front of the left foot (the girl crosses the left in front of the right) with another slow step.

5 The boy steps with the left foot in the line of direction (the girl steps with the right), doing a quick step.

6 The boy closes the right foot beside the left foot (the girl closes the left beside the right), doing a quick step.

Figure 9.2 The Foxtrot Promenade allows for direction changes as the dancers move around the dance floor and some very nice contra-body motion with the crossover steps.

Foxtrot Promenade With an Underarm Turn

▷ **Description**

This is a nice variation added to the promenade on the quick-quick steps.

▷ **Steps**

The boy does the same step while raising his left arm up (the girl's right arm) as the girl does a full turn under the raised arm on the quick-quick steps.

Foxtrot Ad Lib, Pivot Turn, or Left Rock Turn

▷ **Description**

This step goes by several names. It helps dancers change directions and avoid other dancers. During this rock-step, which incorporates two slow steps, the dancers rotate slightly counterclockwise so that when they execute the quick-quick sequence to the side, both dancers will have rotated about a quarter-turn. This can be repeated if the dancers need to rotate more to keep on dancing or to avoid other dancers.

▷ Steps

1-2 The boy steps forward in the line of direction on his left foot, slow (the girl steps backward in the line of direction on her right foot).

3-4 The boy then steps backward on his right foot, slow (the girl step forward on her left).

5 The boy steps forward on his left foot, quick, while the girl steps backward on her right foot.

6 The boy closes his right foot beside his left, quick, while the girl closes her left foot next to her right.

Foxtrot Swing Step

▷ Description

This step is used to allow other dancers to move by or out of the way of others. It is similar in its use to the hesitation step in the waltz. This step can be used more than once if there is still not room for the dancers to proceed after the first swing step.

▷ Steps

1-2 The boy steps to his left side with his left foot and closes his right foot beside the left but does not put weight on his right foot (the girl steps to the right side with her right foot and closes her left foot beside her right but does not put weight on her left foot); this is a slow step.

3-4 The next slow step is done opposite the last one toward the outside of the room.

5-6 The final two quick-quick steps are executed back toward the center of the room; just as always, the boy does a side-step to the left and closes with the right, and the girl does the opposite.

Foxtrot Quarter-Turns

▷ Description

This move is a way to turn the couple by using a four-count rhythm to make eighth-, quarter-, or half-turns with a slow, quick, quick pattern. It is similar to the waltz left box turns, but the timing is very different. This is a change from the six-count foxtrot rhythms discussed in previous steps to a four-count rhythm. This can be executed one to four times before moving on to some other steps.

▷ Steps

This step requires that the basic be modified. The first half of the basic moves forward, with the turn coming on a slow step. This is followed by a step–close to the side for the quick-quick portion of the step. The second half of the basic moves backward with the same sort of turn. Practice alone, first turning and facing different walls, and then with a partner who does the opposite footwork.

1-2 The boy initiates the movements by turning his left foot in a curved pathway to his left for the desired effect, and the girl curves her right foot in the same direction; the boy then steps to the side with his right foot (the girl steps to the side with her left foot); the step finishes with the boy closing his left foot beside his right foot in the quick-quick sequence (the girl closes the right foot beside the left).

3-4 The boy then starts on his right foot (the girl on her left) and moves backward with the left foot (forward with the right), curving the foot path so that another quarter-turn has been executed; the step finishes with the quick-quick sequence again.

Tango

Undoubtedly, the title for most dramatic of the ballroom dances goes to the tango. The tango as we know it today has undergone considerable evolution since it was first done. It is believed to have originated in dances from Spain, France, and Argentina.

The Spanish version was a solo dance performance with the dancer marking sharp accents in the music with the heels of their boots, snaps of their fingers, and flowing arm movements. These arm movements, in all likelihood, are rooted in gypsy Iberian dance and the classical dance of the period—the late 1800s and early 1900s. The dance attire for the dance reminds us of its early roots, with western attire for the boys and thick ruffled skirts for the girls.

The Parisian (French) version from the early part of the twentieth century traces its roots to dances done by refugees from Buenos Aires, Argentina. It is the Argentinean version that has had the most influence on the current version of the tango.

This version is heavily influenced by the gauchos, the cowboys of the pampas region in central Argentina. These cowboys used the dance to try to catch the interest of the local barmaids when the cowboys came into a village. Today, thank goodness, the tango is taken for what it actually is: a very smooth, graceful, rhythmic form of dance that all can enjoy.

The dance characterized by the gauchos included heavy, staccato movements with the body and boots that accented the music. The dance today is known for its smooth, gliding style accented by sharp movements and pauses. Since the dance grew out of the saloons and taverns, its seductive nature grew and grew. Until just before World War I, the dance was banned in Argentina. It had obviously lost its earlier simplicity and moved into being too uninhibited.

Today, the tango is danced to both 2/4- and 4/4-meter music, and its basic step has evolved into a slow, slow, quick, quick, slow pattern. While this is quite similar to the cha-cha, the music and styling for each are very different. It is a dance that all can learn and enjoy. The tango is sometimes described as the sneaker dance, as the dancers can practice steps alone and finish them by looking around as if they are sneaking around. The posture of the dancers is rather stiff, but the dance flows very smoothly. The dancers don't look at each other much during the dance, which comes from its early heritage. When teaching tango steps, teach strong heel and toe leads.

Basic Tango

▷ Description

This is the step that most often starts with the dancers in closed position. It is an eight-count rhythm that is counted slow (two counts), slow (two counts), quick (one count), quick (one count), slow (two counts).

▷ Steps

In American-style tango this first move goes straight ahead in the line of direction; the final quick, quick, slow—also known as "tan, go, close"—is executed at a right angle toward the outside of the room.

1-2   The boy steps forward with the left foot, slow (the girl steps backward with the right foot).

3-4   The boy steps forward with the right foot, slow (the girl steps backward with the left).

5   The boy steps forward with the left foot, quick (the girl steps backward with the right).

6   The boy steps with the right foot at a right angle toward the outside wall, quick (girl steps with the left foot in the same direction).

7-8   The boy closes with the left foot beside right, slow (the girl closes with the right beside the left); this ends the basic step.

Promenade Basic Tango

▷ Description

This is done in the promenade position, which is a position in which dancers are slightly open; the dancers will move in the line of direction for this step.

▷ Steps

1-2   The boy steps with the left foot to the side in the promenade position, slow (the girl steps with the right foot to the side in the promenade position).

3-4   The boy steps forward with the right foot and across in the promenade position as if executing a vine step, slow (the girl steps forward with the left foot and across in the promenade position).

The last three steps—the "tan, go, close" or "quick, quick, close" portion of the movement—will give the dancers time to rotate counterclockwise about a quarter-turn to get back to the beginning dance position; the boy is facing the line of direction and dancers are in closed position.

5   The boy steps with the left foot forward, beginning to rotate to his left, quick (the girl steps with the right foot, turning with her partner).

6   The boy steps with the right foot to the side as he continues turning, quick (the girl steps with the left foot).

7- and-8 The boy closes the left foot beside the right without putting his weight on his right foot, slow (the girl closes the right foot beside the left).

Tango Corte

▷ Description

The corte steps are performed in the tango in many variations. This description is for one of the very basic cortes.

▷ Steps

1-2   The boy steps backward and slightly to his left with the left foot, slow (the girl steps forward and slightly to her right with the right foot).

3-4   The boy steps forward with the right foot, slow (the girl steps backward with the left foot).

5-8   Both dancers execute the quick, quick, slow sequence described in the directions for the promenade basic tango.

Tango Promenade to Fan 66

▷ Description

The fan is one of the movements that is quite often used in the tango (see figure 9.3). While more complex, this step is really a lot of fun for the dancers. It will take 16 counts to execute.

▷ Steps

With dancers in the promenade position, this step begins almost like the promenade basic tango.

1-2 The boy steps to the side in the promenade position with the left foot, slow (the girl steps to the side in the promenade position with the right foot).

3-4 The boy steps forward and across in the promenade position with the right foot as if executing a vine step, slow (the girl steps forward and across in the promenade position with the left foot).

5 The boy steps back with the left foot, quick, and releases the girl with his right hand to allow her to begin a rotation to the left that will allow her to end up beside him, facing the wall, and holding the boy's left hand with her right after the tan-go-close steps; with this preparatory step, the girl simply steps back with the right foot to begin her rotation.

6 The boy steps to the side with the right foot, quick (the girl steps to the side with the left foot, quick).

7-8 Both dancers close with a slow step, the boy's left to right and the girl's right to left. This completes the first half of the step.

Now starts the second half with the fans for an additional eight counts.

1-2 The boy steps forward with the left foot, slow, and closes with the right foot with a slight rotation toward his partner to begin to get into the promenade position (the girl steps forward with the right foot, slow, and closes with the right foot with a slight rotation toward her partner for the promenade position).

Figure 9.3   The tango fan step is a very smooth and attractive step that adds some nice variety to the dance.

3-4 The boy steps forward with the right foot into the promenade position, slow (the girl steps forward with the left foot into the promenade position, slow).

5-8 Both dancers close the step with the tan-go-close sequence, ready to begin all over again.

LATIN-STYLE DANCES

The styles selected for inclusion in this category are the merengue, salsa or mambo, rumba, and swing. The ball–flat technique is the dominant characteristic of these styles.

Merengue

Merengue is a Dominican folkloric dance that is currently danced around the world. It is considered by many to be the Dominican Republic's national dance and to some extent holds the same status with its neighbor, Haiti. The exact origins of the merengue are not clear. One theory is that its musical roots are actually Cuban in origin and that it came to Santo Domingo in the mid-1800s. Even though the merengue was originally quite popular among the masses, the upper class did not accept the merengue for some time because it had a strong connection to the rhythms of African music and its lyrics at the time were quite distasteful and vulgar. Over time, however, the lively spirit of the dance literally invaded the culture.

Some early accounts of the dance's beginnings indicate that it came from a combination of two sources in the late 1700s or early 1800s. The Black slaves from Africa observed the French minuets danced by the French slaveholders and mimicked them. As the European dance was not very much fun, the slaves added more upbeat rhythms. This became the merengue. Another theory regarding the origins of the merengue credit it to the slaves dancing in a circle dance much like the cake-walk dance of the American South, with partners holding hands in a double circle. Partners held hands at an arm's length and the original movements involved only the shaking of the shoulders and the swift movement of the feet.

It took the passage of many years for the merengue to gain national acceptance in the Dominican Republic, particularly among the upper class. The first evidence that acceptance was imminent by all parts of the society came in 1930 when a presidential candidate used the highly spirited music and dance of the merengue in his campaign.

However, it was not until an aristocratic family asked Luis Alberti to write a merengue song with decent lyrics for their daughter's 15th birthday celebration that high society came to accept the dance. The song was not only accepted, but became a hit as well. It is now considered as a sort of theme song or anthem for the merengue. The widespread acceptance of the merengue also was greatly enhanced during that period by the introduction of radio.

Merengue is also one of the most popular Latin American dances in the United States. It is believed that the dance made its way to the United States in the mid-1950s. The tempo for the merengue is quite variable, but it tends to run on the medium to very fast side. The dance uses a step-close, or one-step pattern, and is certainly the easiest of the Latin dances to learn. It is also a great deal of fun to perform.

When teaching merengue steps, teach the ball–flat technique and stress that students must bend and straighten the knees to develop the hip movement known as the Cuban motion.

Merengue Chassé to Left and Right 67

▷ Description

This is the step with which dances most often begin. They can be in closed position, open, or semi-open position or not even touching at all.

▷ Steps

One step is taken for every beat of the music and movements are done in multiples of 4, 8, and 16 counts.

1 The boy steps to the side with the left foot (the girl steps to the side with the right foot).

2 The boy closes the right foot to the left (the girl closes the left to the right).

3 The boy steps to the side with the left foot (the girl steps to the side with the right foot).

4 The boy closes the right foot to the left (the girl closes the left to the right).

5 They repeat this four-step pattern to make a total of eight counts.

6 They do the same thing in reverse, moving to the boy's right.

7-and-8 Repeat side stepping.

Merengue Forward and Backward Walk

▷ Description

This is very similar to the last series of steps, except that it is done forward and backward.

▷ Steps

1 The boy steps forward on the left foot (the girl steps backward on the right foot).

2 The boy closes the right foot to the left (the girl closes the left to the right).

3 The boy steps forward on the left foot (the girl steps backward on the right).

4 The boy closes the right foot to the left (the girl closes the left to the right).

5-8 They repeat this four-step pattern for a total of eight counts.

1-8 They do the same thing in reverse; the boy backs up and the girl goes forward.

Merengue Back-Breaks

▷ Description

This move is simply a step behind the heel of the opposite foot into fifth position, or even slightly further behind the heel of the opposite foot into what is sometimes called fall-away position.

▷ Steps

When the boy executes a step behind, or back-break with his left foot behind the right foot, the girl is doing the same with her right behind the left. This can then be reversed and executed to the other side, with the boy putting his right foot behind his left foot and the girl putting her left foot behind her right (see figure 9.4).

Figure 9.4 Merengue back-breaks, or the fall-away position, provide variation for both partners.

Merengue Underarm Turns   67

▷ Description

These are executed from numerous positions in the dance and can be done in two or four counts.

▷ Steps

Usually, the girl is given a cue when the boy raises his left hand in a closed dance position; this allows the girl to turn to her right in a full turn under the boy's arm. From the open position, the boy is holding the girl's right hand with his left hand, and the same arm raise is given as a signal for the girl to turn to her left with a full turn toward her partner. If the boy wishes, he may step under the raised arms, turning to his left just after his partner gets past him so that they both get a turn under. The girl may do multiple turns.

Salsa or Mambo

Mambo is king of the Latin dances, and it has taken on a new persona with the advent of salsa. Mambo is a combination of primarily American jazz and swing and Cuban rumba music. It developed in the mid- to late 1940s in the nightclubs and casinos of Havana, Cuba. Havana had become a major holiday port for Americans at this time. This is how American jazz and swing music was imported, mixed, and finally combined with Cuban rumba music. The result was mambo music and a dance for everyone. A mambo craze was ignited, and many of the popular bandleaders of the time—Perez Prado, Tito Rodriquez, Pupi Campo, Tito Puente, Xavier Cugat, and so on—developed their own styles of the mambo. The rush was on to dance the newest and most exciting dance of the period.

Of course, the dance and music of the mambo came to the United States, first appearing primarily in New York City's Park Plaza Ballroom. The mambo rush gained in popularity in the late 1940s in New York's Palladium, the China Doll, Havana Madrid, and Birdland nightclubs. Much of the early dancing included extreme acrobatics, which were toned down quite a bit as the dance was introduced into the nightclubs, resorts, and dance studios of New York and Miami.

The name of the dance is attributed to the name of an African voodoo priestess. It is believed that it came to Cuba from the Haitians living there at the time. The voodoo priestess with Haitian roots was believed to help villagers as a spiritual advisor, exorcist, healer, counselor, and organizer of public entertainment. Only the name from this priestess was applied to this new dance. There are no folk dance roots for the mambo.

The mambo craze was short-lived, and those who dance the mambo today are usually considered more advanced dancers. However, salsa is changing that quite rapidly. The greatest contribution of the mambo was the evolution of the cha-cha out of it. The cha-cha added three steps to the dance, cha-cha-cha, which gave the dance its name. It has received increasing attention of late as cultures from around the world mix. Newer versions of the mambo are known primarily as salsa. The influences of today's mambo are seen in African and Cuban dance, jazz dance, hip-hop, and (as some suggest) even certain aspects of ballet. This is a great dance to have in one's repertoire, particularly when visiting equatorial countries.

Mambo is characterized by accenting the second beat of the rather intricate Cuban and African music. Salsa tends to emphasize the first beat of the music. The total count for the steps is the same for both dances; they overlap considerably.

When teaching mambo or salsa steps, teach the ball–flat technique. Stress that students must bend and straighten the knees to develop the hip movement known as Cuban motion.

Salsa or Mambo Basic 68

▷ Description

The basic rhythm is a quick, quick, slow, pattern, which takes four counts; it is repeated again for a total of eight counts to complete the pattern. The quick steps each get one count and the slow step gets two counts. The basic is usually executed in a forward and backward motion.

▷ Steps

1   The boy steps forward with the left foot, quick (the girl step backward with the right foot).

2-4   The boy changes his weight to the right foot, quick, and steps with the left foot beside the right, slow (the girl changes her weight to the left foot, slow, and steps with the right foot beside the left).

5   The boy steps backward with his right foot (the girl steps forward with the left).

6-8   The boy changes his weight to the left foot and steps with the right foot beside the left, slow (the girl changes her weight to the right foot and steps with the left foot beside the right).

Salsa or Mambo Side Basic

▷ Description

This has the same timing as the basic. This step is executed to the side with the boy stepping first to his left (the girl first to her right) and then reversing to the other side. It is often repeated.

▷ Steps

1 The boy steps to the side with the left foot, quick (the girl steps to the side with the right foot).

2 The boy closes the right foot beside his left (the girl close the left foot beside her right).

3-4 The boy steps to the side with the left foot, slow (the girl steps to the side with the right foot).

1 The boy steps to the side with the right foot, quick (the girl steps to the side with the left foot).

2 The boy closes the left foot beside his right (the girl closes the right foot beside her left).

3-4 The boy steps to the side with the right foot, slow (the girl steps to the side with the left foot).

Salsa or Mambo Back- and Front-Breaks

▷ Description

These are begun on the first quick step with either a fifth position step or a fall-away step by both dancers.

▷ Steps

In order for this break to become a front-break, the first quick steps are executed in front of the other foot instead of behind.

1 The boy steps with the left foot behind his right foot, quick (the girl steps with her right foot behind her left).

2 The boy places the weight on his right foot (the girl places the weight on her left).

3-4 The boy steps with the left foot beside his right (the girl steps with the right foot beside her left).

1 The boy steps with the right foot behind his left foot (the girl steps with her left foot behind her right).

2 The boy places the weight on his left foot (the girl places the weight on her right).

3-4 The boy steps with his right foot beside his left (the girl steps with the left foot beside her right).

Salsa or Mambo Underarm Turns

▷ Description

Turns can be done from numerous positions. A simple underarm turn from the basic occurs during the second half of the basic.

▷ Steps

The boy continues with the second quick, quick, slow sequence of the basic. As the girl comes forward, the boy releases his right hand and raises his left hand, signaling her to begin the underarm turn (figure 9.5). The girl goes under the boy's left arm, turning to her right and executing the quick, quick, slow pattern back to her starting position to be ready to go on with other dance steps.

Figure 9.5 The salsa or mambo underarm turn adds a bit of flair to the basic mambo or salsa step.

Rumba

Certainly, the rumba ranks as one of the most popular of the Latin dances in the United States and around the world. This popular Cuban dance, which is probably considered Cuba's national dance, came to the United States in the early 1930s. In the early 1920s, Xavier Cugat formed an orchestra in the United States that specialized in Latin American music. He opened nightclubs at the Coconut Grove in Los Angeles and later moved to the Waldorf-Astoria in New York. It was partially through his efforts, and certainly the efforts of many others, that Latin music and dance began to develop in popularity on both the West and East Coasts. It has continued to grow steadily in popularity since these early efforts.

The original rumba forms, which developed primarily in Cuba, were also being done on other Caribbean islands and in Latin America in general. These roots go back to the 16th century when African slaves were brought to the New World. In fact, at this time there were two main sources contributing to the development of this dance form. Already mentioned was the African influence; the other influence came from dance in Spain. The dance forms that influenced the current rumba include the slow-tempo, native Cuban danzon; the bolero of

Spain, the medium-tempo son, the fast-tempo guaracha, and a rural dance imitating barnyard animals. The rhythms of the music are often accented by the rhythmic sounds of bongos or other drums, claves, maracas, or timbales; the melody carries much of the Spanish flavors. However and wherever the rumba originated and evolved, today the rumba is danced by all ages in ballrooms around the world.

The appeal of the rumba comes from its smooth, flowing, and relaxed manner of movement that forms a romantic style. The characteristic of the dance that has contributed so much to its popularity is probably Cuban motion, which refers to the swaying of the hips as the dance steps are taken. The rumba is danced to slow, medium, and fast tempos. It is characterized by the playful interaction of an aggressive male suitor and the defensive but flirtatious female. It is a spot dance that moves somewhat in a circular pattern.

The rumba is to Latin dance what the waltz is to ballroom. They are two wonderful dances and are both favorites of social dancers. The rumba lends itself to the walking drill extremely well, and the steps can be taught the same way as aerobic steps. The basic rhythmic pattern is slow, quick, quick, with the slow step receiving two counts and each quick step one count. These four counts complete the basic box step and make up the heart of many of the other steps. Some steps require more counts, all in multiple of fours.

As with the other Latin dances, the ball–flat technique for movement is typical of this dance. Dancers should move with a strong, heavy, and forceful push into the floor on the inside edge of the foot. The slow steps should take the entire two counts to give the dance a fully Latin flavor. It thereby can be held for the full two counts—and maybe even a little longer. Weight is on the balls of the feet, the chest is forward, and the dancers move on the inside of the foot as they bend and straighten their legs. Stress that students must bend and straighten the knees to correctly perform the Cuban motion.

Rumba Basic Box 69

▷ Description

This step starts the dance. It is a box formation that takes eight counts to complete. Both halves of the box require three steps.

▷ Steps

Boys start on the left foot and girls on the right. The girl's part will be the opposite of the boy's and is in parentheses following the boy's movements.

1-2 The boy steps forward on the left foot, slow (the girl steps backward on the right).

  3 The boy brings the right foot beside the left, brushing the ankle, and steps to the right side, quick (the girl brings the left foot beside the right, brushing the ankle, and steps to the left side).

  4 The boy closes with the left foot beside the right, quick (the girl closes with the right foot beside the left).

Now begin the second half of the box.

5-6 The boy steps backward with the right foot, slow (the girl steps forward with the left foot).

  7 The boy brings the left foot beside the right, brushing the ankle, and steps to the left side, quick (the girl brings the right foot beside the left, brushing the ankle, and steps to the right side).

  8 The boy closes with the right foot beside the left, quick (the girl closes with the left foot beside the right).

Rumba Underarm Turns

▷ Description

There are many ways to execute the underarm turns. This one will be initiated after the first half of the box has been completed.

▷ Steps

The cue for the two dancers is for the boy to raise his left arm while holding the girl's right hand. This is a signal to execute the underarm turn. The girl should take her time, walking in a smooth circle for four to eight counts as the boy continues to dance the basic step until both partners are facing again and they can get back into the basic or go to another rumba step.

Rumba Back-Breaks

▷ Description

These are begun after half of a basic box has been executed.

▷ Steps

1-2 The boy steps to the side with the right foot, slow (the girl steps to the side with the left foot).

3 The boy steps back into a fall-away with the left foot, quick (the girl steps back into a fall-away with the right foot).

4 The boy places his weight on his right foot and faces his partner, quick (the girl places her weight on her left foot and faces her partner).

This movement is now danced to the left side and then back to the right side, usually before going on to another rumba step. Both dancers reverse the previous steps.

5-6 The boy steps to the side with the left foot, slow (the girl steps to the side with the right foot).

7 The boy steps back into a fall-away with the right foot, quick (the girl steps back into a fall-away with the left foot).

8 The boy places weight on his left foot and faces his partner, quick (the girl places weight on her right foot and faces her partner).

This is then reversed again, using the same steps and directions as described in the first part.

Rumba Walk

▷ Description

This is an easy step that is just as it says: a walking step done in the basic rhythmic pattern of slow, quick, quick. It is done both forward and backward.

▷ Steps

Often, the dancers will do two or three of the basics, walking either straight ahead or going backward, and then move on to another step. When the opportunity presents itself, the boy gets out of this by stepping to the side after one of the slow steps and gets back into another step.

Rumba Rocks 69

▷ Description

A very nice addition to the rumba steps is this movement. Rumba rocks are executed in a straight line forward or backward in the same slow, quick, quick rhythmic pattern of the other steps (see figure 9.6).

▷ Steps

1-2 The boy steps forward with the left foot, slow (the girl steps backward with the right).

3 The boy steps forward with the right foot, quick (the girl steps backward with the left).

4 The boy places his weight on the left foot, quick (the girl places her weight on the right).

1-2 The boy steps forward with the right foot, slow (the girl steps backward with the left).

3 The boy steps forward with the left foot, quick (the girl steps backward with the right).

4 The boy places his weight on the right foot, quick (the girl places her weight on the left).

Figure 9.6   A rock-step adds variety to the rumba.

▷ SWING

Swing dance as we know it today takes many of its characteristics from the foxtrot, which preceded the development of the swing by several years. The music of the late 1920s and early 1930s went through some distinctive changes. The foxtrot, with its slower and perhaps more romantic flavor, was joined by a much livelier, faster, and bouncier type of music. This became the swing. Benny Goodman is often credited with developing the rhythms of swing. His "new" music took its roots from that performed by many of the Black musicians in New York's Harlem and the rural areas of the Deep South. This style was known as jazz.

Despite the hard times of the 1930s in the United States, this new music and the accompanying dance forms spread all over the country. Big bands, with thirty to forty musicians, traveled all across the country and played in every town—both small and large. The attachment of the term *swing* to this form of dance is attributable to two things. Goodman, along with many of the innovators of the time, began accenting the second beat of the measure and the upbeat of the measures to create a swinging mood with the music itself. The dance that accompanied this music began a new movement of breaking away from a partner to dance in an open position, as opposed to the closed positions of the familiar waltz and foxtrot. The new swing dance became characterized by all sorts of turns, or what were called swings, to go with the music.

In 1927, a novelty dance, the Lindy hop, commemorated Charles Lindbergh's solo flight across the Atlantic. It was designed to fit with swing music and employed many exaggerated swings, turns, and lifts over the ensuing years. Contests were held across the United States in which couples would try to outdo other dancers. In fact, when a reporter went to New York City during these early years, he commented that the dancers appeared to be jumping around like a bunch of "jitter bugs"; thus a new term was attached to the swing dance—the jitterbug. Many variations of this new dance appeared over the next several years. A large number of dances influenced the swing style we see today. These included the Lindy jitterbug, Charleston, big apple, black bottom, jive, boogie woogie, shag, rock 'n' roll, and numerous others.

In the 1940s, during World War II, American GIs carried swing music and dances to the battlefronts around the world. Locals around the world picked up the dance form. It is undoubtedly one of the most popular dances today and is danced by people of all ages. It is a must in one's repertoire of dances.

Swing dancing is composed of a 6-count basic step, but has many variations. The descriptions that follow are for a basic 6-count step that is executed as quick, quick, quick-a-quick, quick-a-quick and is counted as 1, 2, 3-and-4, 5-and-6. This is often known as a triple Lindy swing step, which lends itself to 120-BPM music.

When teaching swing steps, teach the ball–flat technique. Stress that students must bend and straighten their knees to develop the Cuban motion.

Basic Swing

▷ Description

This can be danced in an closed or open position. It is like homeplate—when the two dancers get out of sync, they go back to the basic to regroup.

▷ Steps

1 The boy steps back with the left foot to a fall-away or fifth position, quick (the girl steps back with the right foot to a fall-away or fifth position).

2 The boy places his weight forward to the right foot (the girl places her weight forward to the left foot).

3-and-4   The boy steps to the side with the left foot, closes with the right foot, and steps to the side with the left foot again, quick-a-quick (the girl steps to the side with the right foot, closes with the left, and steps to the side with the right again).

5-and-6   The boy steps to the side with the right foot, closes with the left, and steps to the side with the right foot again, quick-a-quick (the girl steps to the side with the left foot, closes with the right, and steps to the side with the left again).

Swing Underarm Turns 70

▷ Description

These can be executed turning to the left and the right from closed and open positions. Dancers can go on to improvise all kinds of turns from these basic ones; there seem to be an infinite number of possibilities with turns! A logical turn to try is the one described here: to join hands and "wring the dishrag," as it is called in some locations. Many turns take on local terms and may only be danced in certain geographic areas.

▷ Steps

After the opening back steps and step forward, the boy raises his left arm and the girl's right arm to initiate a turn to the left or to the right. The turn is done on the quick-a-quick, or chassé, portions of the basic dance step as the boy continues with the basic step in response to his partner and the girl does a full turn in or out with her chassé steps (see figure 9.7).

Figure 9.7   "Wring the dishrag" is one name for a swing double-arm turn.

▷ SUMMARY

These basic steps for the social dances listed in this chapter hit only the tip of the iceberg for the moves that can be done. As always, the dancers will improvise and develop numerous modifications of these basics. So, go forth and enjoy the world of social dancing!

▷ Create Your Own Social Dances ◁

Having given the students the tools they need to learn the basic steps of social dances, the next step is to have them create their own social dances. This phase of the requirements can give students self-confidence and produce immense self-esteem. It also allows them to develop critical thinking and socialization skills.

Checklist for Creating Your Own Social Dance

- Instruct students to create their own routines or steps for a social dance, based on the skills and steps that they have learned.
- Ask students to come up with a routine that includes four variations of steps blended with the basic step. Strong leading and following should be evident between the dancers. The dance routine should display a variety of movements and be executed well to the music.
- Have the students try this alone and with partners or small groups to change the social dynamics and increase the development of social skills.
- Require students to write up their descriptions to emphasize the language aspects of dance.

Rubric

Now that you have your students creating their own social dance routines, here is an example of a rubric that could work for this particular activity or for others with modifications. Just by changing a few words, this rubric could work with other aspects of your warm-ups.

4 Points—Exemplary	The student creates four variations of steps blended with the basic step. Strong leading and following between the dancers is evident. The dance routine displays a variety of movements and is executed well to the music.
3 Points—Acceptable	The student creates three or four variations of steps blended with the basic step. Good leading and following between the dancers is evident. The dance routine displays a variety of movements and sometimes is executed in time to the music.
2 Points—Needs improvement	The student creates some variations of steps blended with the basic step and some evidence of following and leading between the dancers. There is very little variety, and the dance is rarely executed in time to the music.
1 Point—Unacceptable	There is little if any evidence of variations blended with the basic step, little if any evidence of following and leading between the dancers, and virtually no variety. The dance is not executed in time to the music.

Review Questions

Have students submit questions for the class to answer or have students answer questions similar to these suggested in the following list. In addition, these could be used as a homework assignment, as an in-class assignment, or for class discussion.

1. Make a list of the benefits of social dancing.
2. Trace the history of a social dance in a particular continent or country.
3. When creating social dances, what is the main number that is critical to developing such dances?
4. Collect and write up social dances from other sources.
5. Describe the physiological benefits received from social dancing.
6. When creating social dances, what are some of the important things that you should be sure to include?
7. What is the great appeal of doing social dances at a party?

 Observation Questions

1. List the different locomotor movements that you observed in social dance.
2. List the combination movements that you observed in social dance.
3. What formations were used in social dance?
4. What was the tempo of the dances?
5. Did the actions of the participants reflect the theme and attitude of the social dance? Please describe your observations.
6. Did the participants raise their heart rates to the target work zones for aerobic benefits?
7. Was there an opportunity for the dancers to develop movements in all directions?
8. Was there an opportunity for leading with different feet? Please describe the level at which this occurred.
9. Was the dance developed in multiples of 3, 6, 9, 12 or 4, 8, 16, 32, and 64 counts (depending on which dance was performed)?
10. Was the music selection appropriate for your social dance class?

GLOSSARY

▷ BASIC MOVEMENTS

These include both nonlocomotor and locomotor movements. Nonlocomotor movements are usually done in place and do not move the whole body in and through space, as locomotor movements do.

Nonlocomotor Movements
- Swinging
- Twisting
- Stretching
- Turning
- Bending
- Shaking
- Pushing
- Bouncing
- Pulling

Locomotor Movements
- Walking
- Running
- Jumping
- Hopping
- Leaping

▷ COMBINATION MOVEMENTS

These are locomotor movements combined to form a new movement. The following combination movements represent those most often found in this book:

gallop (walk-leap)—An uneven rhythmic pattern, moving forward and backward using a step-close.

polka—An uneven rhythmic pattern (gallop and skip or slide and skip), moving forward, backward, sideways, and diagonally.

schottische—An even rhythmic pattern (walk, walk, walk, hop), moving forward, backward, sideways, and diagonally.

skip (walk-hop)—An uneven rhythmic pattern, moving forward, backward, sideways, and diagonally.

slide (walk-leap)—An uneven rhythmic pattern, moving sideways using a step-close.

two-step—An uneven rhythmic pattern (step-close-step; left-right-left or right-left-right; triple step; or step-ball-change) that requires two counts of the music (1-and-2) to complete, moving forward, backward, sideways, and diagonally.

▷ FORMATIONS AND POSITIONS

butterfly—Partners facing each other join opposite hands and hold them out to the sides.

closed—The closed position is facing your partner, boy's left hand holding girl's right hand, boy's right hand on scapula of girl and girl's left hand on boy's right shoulder.

corner—One's corner is the girl on the boy's left or the boy on the girl's right in circles and squares.

head(s)—Depending on the formation or call of the dance, the head will be the lead group or couple, or the pair that makes the starting move.

open—A floor formation that involves spreading the students or dancers out evenly throughout the room.

partner—When dancing in circles and squares, partners are the girl on the boy's right or the boy on the girl's left or as indicated in the dance.

side(s)—Depending on the formation or call of the dance, the side partners will follow the head couple.

varsouvienne—Standing side by side, the partners are holding left to left hands in front and right to right hands behind the girl's right shoulder. Also known as the "over the shoulder" or "sweetheart" position.

▷ RHYTHMIC ELEMENTS

accent—Ranges from weak to strong, soft to heavy; the emphasis placed on a movement.

basic pulse—Even, steady, and constant; the underlying beat in music.

even rhythmic patterns—Sounds or movements that are performed with an equal amount of time between each.

rhythmic pattern—The duration of sounds, or movements and their relationship to silence, or the lack of movement; often emphasized by accent(s).

uneven rhythmic patterns—Sounds or movements that are not performed with an equal amount of time between each.

▷ SELECTED DANCE STEPS

The cues given in these descriptions have been found to be the most beneficial to students. They are encountered with the greatest frequency when teaching dance at the K-12 level.

balancé—Can be a step and touch performed twice over four counts or a step-ball-change for three steps counted 1-and-2.

bleking—Feet together, then hopping on the right foot, extending the left foot diagonally with the heel touching the floor on count 1, and hopping on the left foot diagonally with the heel touching the floor on count 2; repeated and held, alternating feet.

buzz swing—Partners are in a closed position, with both right feet parallel and touching. Each person shifts weight right to left and continues as in pushing a skateboard and performing the swing.

cha-cha rhythm—Slow, slow, quick, quick, slow; counted 1, 2, 3-and-4; the basic is forward and backward, cha, cha, cha in place, and then backward and forward, cha, cha, cha in place.

Charleston—Forward on the left foot, kick or touch the right foot forward; backward on the right foot and touch the left foot back.

chassé (rock-step)—A slide to the right, stepping right, left, right, and placing the left foot behind the right foot; rock backward on the left foot, and lift the right foot up then put it down, ending on the right foot; a slide to the left stepping left, right, left, and place the right foot behind the left foot; rock backward on the right foot, and lift the left foot up and then put it down, ending on the left foot; counted 1-and-2, 3, 4.

chug (foot chugs)—Scooting forward and backward on both feet without losing contact with the floor; doing the same on either the right or left foot alone.

do-si-do—Partners face and walk around each other, first right shoulder to right shoulder, back to back, left shoulder to left shoulder, end up back where they started; usually takes eight counts.

double Lindy (basic jitterbug)—Left toe, step left, right toe, step right, step left back for a rock-step, using an even rhythm; often cued "toe–heel, toe–heel, rock step"; one beat to each movement, counted 1, 2, 3, 4, 5, 6; girl does the opposite; a rock-step is a step backward, then a step forward in two counts with the girl doing opposite footwork.

elbow turns—Can be either right or left elbow turns when partners lock elbows and walk around in a circle back to where they started.

foxtrot (or magic step)—Slow, slow, quick, quick (slow, two beats, slow, two beats, quick, one beat, quick, one beat); step the left foot forward, step the right foot forward, step the left sideways a short step, close right to left and take weight on the right; the girl does opposite footwork.

grapevine (carioca)—Step to right side on the right foot, step the left foot behind the right foot, step the right foot to side, touch the left in front of the right, repeat in multiples of four or eights on both sides.

heel shuffles—Alternate touching the right and left heels forward.

hustle—Step to right side with the right foot, step behind the right foot with the left foot, step to right side with the right foot, kick with the left foot and clap; repeat to the other side; each of the steps gets a full beat of the music.

jazz square—Walk forward on the right foot, step across with the left foot, walk backward on the right foot, backward on the left foot; alternate sides by changing the lead foot.

Lindy—See *single Lindy*, *double Lindy*, and *triple Lindy*.

pivot step—Touch the left foot forward, keep the right foot in place, make a half turn (shifting weight from the left to the right foot); repeat to face front again.

plié—A ballet movement in which the feet are turned out and the knees bend while the back is held straight.

promenade—Individuals or couples move around the floor counterclockwise unless told otherwise told to do so; a step that utilizes the step-ball-change forward and backward and at other times from side to side; counted 1-and-2, 3-and-4.

right- and left-hand star—Executed by everyone in the figure joining either right hands or left hands in the middle of their group, depending on the call, and continuing to walk around in a circle either clockwise for a right-hand star or counterclockwise for a left-hand star.

rock (rocking step or rocking horse)—Put weight forward on the right foot, then step backward on the left foot, alternating sides and directions.

shag—Almost the same as a triple Lindy except that styling and direction for the basic step is forward and backward instead of to the side; there are a number of variations from the basic, which is forward three, backward three, and rock-step; six counts total, counted 1-and-2, 3-and-4, 5, 6.

shuffle—In square dancing, the shuffle is an easy, light walk in time to the music with the weight kept on the balls of the feet. In modern tap, it is a flat-footed brush of the foot on the floor.

side touch—Touch the foot to the side, bring the foot back to the closed position, and step on it; alternate sides and forward and backward movement as well.

single Lindy—Step, step, rock; backward step, using an even rhythm.

step-ball-change—Weight is put on one foot, transferred to the ball of the opposite foot, and then transferred back to the other foot; often counted 1-and-2 for the entire movement.

step-kick—Step on the right foot, kick the left foot across; alternate sides.

step-touch—Step right to the side and touch the left foot next to the right foot; alternate sides and forward and backward movement as well; the touch can be modified to be a kick.

swing—Can be one of many forms, closed dance position, buzz swing, two-hand turn and swing, elbow turn and swing, and so forth; perhaps the most common is the closed position, partners facing, holding boy's left hand to the girl's right hand, boy's right hand on the girl's scapula, and girl's left hand on the boy's upper right arm or shoulder; the couple rotate, walk, or dance around clockwise for as long as is needed in a particular dance.

two-step—Quick, quick, slow, slow, uneven rhythm; counted 1 (quick), 2 (quick), 3, 4 (slow), 5, 6 (slow).

triple Lindy—Left, step-close-step, right, step-close-step, left, rock-step, uneven rhythm; counted 1-and-2, 3-and-4, 5, 6; styling is side to side with a drop-step backward; the girl does opposite footwork.

two-handed skipping swing—Each person holding hands, left to right and right to left, while skipping in a circle.

waltz—Three smooth walking steps on each beat of the music; counted 1, 2, 3.

SUGGESTED RESOURCES

The resources in this section are organized into two categories: professional organizations, and books and other written materials. Virtually every need that you could possibly identify when perusing this text can be found here.

▷ PROFESSIONAL ORGANIZATIONS

American College of Sports Medicine (ACSM)

401 W. Michigan St.
Indianapolis, IN 46202-3233
Mailing address: PO Box 1440, Indianapolis, IN 46206-1440
National Center: 317-637-9200,
Regional Chapter Resource Center: 317-637-9200, ext. 138
www.acsm.org

The ACSM is the consummate resource for fitness programming and the parameters of exercise. It is an excellent resource for all you ever wanted to know about primarily the technical side of exercise.

Aerobics & Fitness Association of America

15250 Ventura Blvd., Ste. 200
Sherman Oaks, CA 91403
877-YOURBODY, or 877-968-7263
www.afaa.com

This professional association is one of the leaders in the fitness industry and carries a plethora of information for its users regarding the whole fitness industry. It is an excellent resource for just about any issue on the practical side of exercise.

American Alliance for Health, Physical Education, Recreation and Dance (AAHPERD)

1900 Association Dr.
Reston, VA 22091-9527
800-213-7193, ext. 490
www.aahperd.org

AAHPERD is one of the largest professional associations in the United States for health, physical education, recreation, and dance professionals. It can assist in all areas of fitness and is capable of providing an abundance of information and assistance for anyone involved in these areas of fitness.

Country Dance and Song Society (CDSS)

132 Main St., PO Box 338
Haydenville, MA 01039-0338
www.cdss.org

The CDSS is an established organization that focuses on traditional dance forms. It actually is found all around the world. It has a huge list of resources that are available to participants of this form of dance.

International Dance Exercise Association, Inc. (IDEA)

10455 Pacific Center Ct.
San Diego, CA 92121-4339
800-999-4332, ext. 7
www.ideafit.com

IDEA has had great success primarily in the aerobics end of dance. This organization has everything that one would need to learn about this part of the industry.

Cooper Institute

12330 Preston Rd.
Dallas, TX 75230
972-341-3200; fax 972-341-3227
www.cooperinst.org

The Cooper Institute is the place where a multitude of high-level research related to fitness is conducted. It can provide individuals with lots of information about training and personal fitness. The Cooper Institute is very focused on aerobics and dance as major components of the fitness model.

Lloyd Shaw Foundation Preserving America's Dance Heritage

PO Box 11
Macks Creek, MO 65786
573-363-5868; fax 573-363-5820
E-mail: sales@lloydshaw.org
www.lloydshaw.org

The Lloyd Shaw Foundation is the "keeper and preserver" of American folk dance forms. It can provide you with a multitude of music resources related to American dance. In addition, it carries information on international folk dance.

Dance Vision

9081 West Sahara Ave., Ste. 100
Las Vegas, NV 89117-4803
800-851-2813
www.dancevision.com

Dance Vision is an excellent resource for information and materials on ballroom and Latin dance.

Educational Activities

PO Box 87
Baldwin, NY 11510
800-645-3739; fax 516-623-9282
E-mail: learn@edact.com
www.edact.com

Educational Activities carries a wonderful selection of music and materials primarily for school-aged groups.

Human Kinetics Publishers, Inc.

PO Box 5076
Champaign, IL 61820
217-351-5076; 800-747-4457
www.humankinetics.com

Human Kinetics is a great resource for information and materials related to the health, physical education, recreation, and dance professions.

Ken Alan Associates

Aero Beat Music and Video
7985 Santa Monica Blvd. #2
Los Angeles, CA 90046-5112
800-536-6060
www.kenfitness.com

This resource is included because it can provide all that you would ever need for your aerobics programs.

Kimbo Education

PO Box 477
Long Branch, NJ 07740
800-631-2187; fax 732-870-3340
E-mail: info@kimboed.com
www.kimboed.com/about.htm

Kimbo is an established provider of music and information for rhythmic activities. It has been around for a very long time. Their focus has been primarily on school-aged groups.

Putumayo World Music

324 Lafayette St., 7th Floor
New York, NY 10012
888-788-8629
E-mail: info@putumayo.com
www.putumayo.com

Putumayo is the byword when it comes to being *the* international resource for music and related materials. Putumayo goes all over the world to bring the best that there is of music and dance from other lands.

Supreme Audio, Inc.
PO Box 550
Marlborough, NH 03455
800-445-7398; fax 800-346-4867
E-mail: Supreme@SupremeAudio.com
www.supremeaudio.com

Supreme Audio is the definitive resource for electronic sound equipment. The company's employees are extremely knowledgeable about this end of the industry and will do all that they can to assist with whatever need you may have.

World Wide Games, Inc.
7790 Marysville Rd.
Ostrander, OH 43061

This is an excellent location for games and activities from around the world. It can serve to provide excellent ideas to promote dance and fitness.

▷ BOOKS AND OTHER WRITTEN MATERIALS

Casey, B. (1985). *Dance across Texas.* Austin: University of Texas Press.

While this book was written two decades ago, it still holds a place on the market as one of the best resources in print on country western dance.

Fleming, G.A. (1976). *Creative rhythmic movement: Boys and girls dancing.* Englewood Cliffs, NJ: Prentice-Hall.

This is another classic on dance for your library. It ranks as one of the all-time best books on children's creative dance.

Howley, E., and B. Franks. (2003). *Health fitness instructor's handbook.* 4th ed. Champaign, IL: Human Kinetics.

This is the most comprehensive and up-to-date book available for health and fitness professionals who want to learn about the latest advances in physical fitness. It provides the latest information on the fundamentals of fitness, exercise physiology, and biomechanics. It has been used in the ACSM Health Fitness Instructor Workshops since 1986; it will help you develop meaningful and safe fitness programs, including exercise for special populations.

Kassing, G., and D.D. Jay (2003). *Dance teaching methods and curriculum design.* Champaign, IL: Human Kinetics.

This text explains, with sample unit plans, how to teach the basics of 10 popular dance forms for K-12 settings. It further explains how to apply educational theories to dance and presents dance education in the context of the national standards for dance. In addition, it helps readers build portfolios that demonstrate their ability to create lesson plans, a unit plan, and a dance curriculum.

LIKHA Pilipino Folk Ensemble. (2005). www.likha.org/galleries/tinikling.asp (accessed 8/17/05).

This Web site provides the site visitor with all there is to know about tinikling. The site has links to photos, videos, and audio. A brief history is provided with an excellent and thorough description of how to execute the dance.

Marcus, B., and L.A. Forsyth. (2003). *Motivating people to be physically active.* Champaign, IL: Human Kinetics.

This is a comprehensive reference describing proven methods for helping people change from inactive to active living. The behavior change methods are useful not only for healthy adults but also for individuals with chronic physical and psychological conditions. The renowned authors describe intervention programs for individuals and groups in workplace and community settings.

Sachs, C. (1937). *World history of the dance*. New York: W.W. Norton.

This book is a wonderful resource for the history of dance prior to 1937. It contains one of the most complete and comprehensive histories of the subject.

Sharkey, B. (2002). *Fitness and health*. 5th ed. Champaign, IL: Human Kinetics.

Here is your guide to both a deeper understanding of the activity–health relationship and a map for meeting your needs and goals. More than 140,000 copies of this classic have been sold. It explains how your body responds to physical activity, why physical activity is so beneficial to health, and the way in which physical activity affects your life.

Wright, J. (2003). *Social dance: Steps to success*. 2nd ed. Champaign, IL: Human Kinetics.

Social Dance: Steps to Success will teach you all the moves for eight popular dance styles: swing, cha-cha, foxtrot, polka, waltz, rumba, tango, and mambo or salsa. This is an excellent resource for your dance library and teaching.

ABOUT THE AUTHORS

**John Bennett
and daughter Rebecca**

John Price Bennett, EdD, has been teaching dance to people of all ages, from preschool to older adults, since 1969. He is a professor in the health and applied human sciences department at the University of North Carolina Wilmington, where he has taught dance since 1992. His primary teaching areas in dance are pre-K-12 children's creative dance, folk, square, ballroom, and Latin dance. His major focus in his teaching and research is on the preservation of our intangible cultural heritage through the medium of dance and bringing people together through dance.

John has written more than 100 publications and given more than 350 presentations throughout his career, and he stays in high demand to teach dance and provide staff development across the United States and abroad. He has been bestowed with many honors, including the *American Alliance for Health, Physical Education, Recreation and Dance* (AAHPERD) Honor Award for 2004 for meritorious service. He has served in many capacities on AAHPERD committees and is a member of the National Association for Sport and Physical Education and the National Dance Association (NDA). He has received numerous state and national teaching awards.

Pamela Coughenour Riemer, MA, has been teaching physical education since 1969 and has had recreational dance as a major component of her curriculum. Currently she is a teacher in the Scotland County School System in Laurinburg, North Carolina. Her teaching integrates the North Carolina Standard Course of Study across the entire curriculum. Her physical education program was a North Carolina President's Council on Physical Fitness Demonstration Center for 14 years.

Pamela was named North Carolina Secondary Physical Education Teacher of the Year in 1990-1991. She was the creator and choreographer for the Sycamore Lane Dance Company that has performed at 10 state AAHPERD conventions and 3

**Pam Riemer, grandson Bailey,
and daughter Carri**

national AAHPERD conventions along with more than 200 presentations and staff developments on a state, national, and international level. She was one of the authors for the current North Carolina Standard Course of Study dance component. Pamela has served on the board of directors for the North Carolina Dance Association and is a member of AAHPERD, the NDA, and the North Carolina Dance Association. She was hired as a consultant for the U.S. Department of Defense to teach and demonstrate her techniques for teaching recreational dance in Wiesbaden, Germany.